D1315043

Today I Am a Woman

Today I Am a Woman

STORIES OF BAT MITZVAH AROUND THE WORLD

EDITED BY

Barbara Vinick & Shulamit Reinharz

INDIANA UNIVERSITY PRESS

Bloomington & Indianapolis

This book is a publication of

Indiana University Press
Office of Scholarly Publishing
Herman B Wells Library 350
1320 East 10th Street
Bloomington, Indiana 47405 USA

iupress.indiana.edu

⊗ The paper used in this publication
meets the minimum requirements of the
American National Standard for
Information Sciences—Permanence
of Paper for Printed Library Materials,
ANSI Z39.48-1992.

Manufactured in the United States of America

Library of Congress Cataloging-in-Publication
Data
Today I am a woman : stories of bat mitzvah
around the world / edited by Barbara Vinick
and Shulamit Reinharz.
 p. cm.
 ISBN 978-0-253-35693-2 (cl : alk. paper)
 ISBN 978-0-253-00517-5 (eb)
1. Bat mitzvah. 2. Bat mitzvah—History.
3. Judaism—History. 4. Jews—History. 5. Jews—
Social life and customs. I. Vinick, Barbara H. II.
Reinharz, Shulamit.
 BM707.T63 2011
 296.4′43409—dc23   2011020214

2 3 4 5 16 15

For

Emily and Julia Vinick,
Rachel and Abigail Garrity,
Yael and Naomi Reinharz

CONTENTS

PREFACE

Shulamit Reinharz

In 1997, an interesting and unusual partnership was formed between Brandeis University and Hadassah, the Women's Zionist Organization of America. That partnership began with a national study of what American Jewish women were thinking, leading to publication of *Voices for Change: Future Directions for American Jewish Women.*[1] Following up on the work we had done together, the Hadassah-Brandeis Institute (HBI) was established on the Brandeis campus to continue studies on Jewish women.

From the start, the focus of the HBI has been different from the original research, however. Rather than looking only at the attitudes and experiences of Jewish women in the United States, the HBI examines those of Jews worldwide, including women, girls, men, and boys. After all, Jews are an international community, or as anthropologists say, a "diasporic" society, with a core and many branches. We might even call Jews a double-diasporic society, in that there currently are two centers of Jewish life: the United States, where approximately 40 percent of world Jewry lives, and Israel, where another 40 percent lives. While recognizing the numerical strength of these two core communities, it is also important to note that the remaining 20 percent of Jews lives neither in the United States nor in Israel. This 20 percent is scattered around the world in groups that may be large (e.g., the former Soviet Union), medium-sized (e.g., England, France), small (e.g., Cuba, Greece), or tiny (e.g., Peru). Many Jewish communities are difficult to identify by geographic boundary, since they are in transition from one place to another (e.g., Ethiopians and Russians in Israel).

In some communities, such as those of North Africa, Jewish life has disappeared altogether. For those communities, what we have is the living memories of community members who have moved elsewhere. Some of these people try to recreate the customs of their former homes when they resettle. In other areas, like the United States and Israel, Jewish life is growing.

A Jewish person is expected to feel connected to and responsible for all other Jews throughout the world. How can we do this if we don't know how Jews live their lives elsewhere? And while we should feel responsible for one another, this does not mean that Jews in one country should tell Jews in another area how to live their lives Jewishly. It may be the case that the existence of a diaspora with multiple Jewish groups and the adaptive variety in Jewish life have contributed to the unusual record of survival of the Jewish people. Certainly, we cannot attribute survival to Jews being treated well throughout the centuries.

Nevertheless, if there is one thing we would like to see happen in Jewish communities around the world, it is increased Jewish learning for girls and, consequently, more opportunities for bat mitzvah, the rite by which a girl becomes a Jewish adult. Without bat mitzvah, a girl never has the opportunity to declare her Jewishness in front of her community. The marriage ceremony does not fulfill that purpose, and, of course, we cannot assume that all Jewish girls will eventually marry. A Jewish boy typically has both a brit milah (circumcision) and a bar mitzvah. A Jewish girl should at least have a bat mitzvah!

This book opens the door to many Jewish communities—core, large, medium, small, and tiny—by focusing on one point of entry, the bat mitzvah ceremony. In a previous book, *Esther's Legacy: Celebrating Purim around the World*, we chose a different focus.[2] Queen Esther of Persia obviously is a heroine in Jewish legend, and her story has become the basis of a holiday. But how important is Purim in actuality? Is the holiday practiced worldwide? With what kind of variations? How is this ancient Jewish woman's life interpreted in various global contexts? The research for *Esther's Legacy* led to some surprising results. First was the way in which local culture affects the meaning of the holiday. An example is the story of Marina Fromer:

Stalin died on Purim, in 1953, in March. I was only five and lived in Leningrad. I did not understand why everyone around me was crying: neighbors, pupils, teachers.

That was in the morning.

In the evening of that same day, my uncle stormed into our room and shouted: "Der gazlen geshtorbn"—The villain is dead! He then turned to me and told me the story of Purim. He explained that it was symbolic, that it was fitting. For the Jews, this was Purim, and Stalin, Haman of our present days in Russia, was dead. From that day on, I knew and remembered the story of Purim, and of Russia.

Pleased with the work we did on Purim, we decided to open another female-centered door into worldwide Jewish life—the bat mitzvah. Do Jewish girls around the world celebrate a bat mitzvah? Who does and who doesn't, and why? And how do the celebrations vary?

This book is organized into nine regions: Africa; Asia; Australia and New Zealand; the Caribbean; Europe; the former Soviet Union, former Yugoslavia, and Eastern Europe; Latin America; the Middle East and North Africa; and North America. It may be surprising to learn that Jews live in some of these areas and that their community is organized enough and their members identified enough to initiate girls into Jewish adulthood via a bat mitzvah ceremony. Although some of the communities exist only in memory at this point, those memories have an impact on how people live today, and so these stories need to be retained. In addition, many countries have changed their borders or their names, or disappeared altogether. For example, the Soviet Union, Yugoslavia, and East Germany do not exist anymore but have divided into many smaller countries (in the case of the former two) or been absorbed by another (in the latter case). Boundaries, people, and customs are constantly shifting. And in some cases, there are isolated Jewish communities where the people seem disconnected from shifting governmental boundaries while closely mirroring the non-Jewish local environment in which they live.

Just as each story in this collection is different, the introductions we have written also vary a great deal. Some will tell you about the history of the Jewish community. Some will focus on the community's relationships to the Holocaust or to the state of Israel, while others will explain the local customs about girls in general and how these affect Jewish girls. We tend to give more information about Jewish communities that are relatively unknown than about those that are familiar. Finally, we encourage everyone who reads this book to explore these Jewish communities further. The list for further reading at the end of this book is a good place to start.

A word about language: *bat* means "daughter" in Hebrew, and *mitzvah* means "commandment" or "Jewish responsibility." A girl who has accepted her responsibilities as a Jewish adult is called a bat mitzvah. The occasion on which this occurs is also called the bat mitzvah, or the bat mitzvah ceremony, although according to Jewish law, a girl becomes a bat mitzvah regardless of whether or not there is any ceremony marking the occasion. The plural is b'not mitzvah, meaning "daughters of the commandment." In some cases in this book, the authors of the bat mitzvah accounts use the English plural "bat mitzvahs." We have not changed their usage. In a similar vein, we have not standardized the transliteration of Hebrew words, which varies from region to region. For example, in Spanish-speaking Latin America, the guttural sound that is most often written as *ch* in English is usually written as *j*. Translations of frequently used Hebrew and Yiddish words are in the glossary at the end of the book.

NOTES

1. Amy Sales, ed., *Voices for Change* (Waltham, Mass.: Brandeis University Center for Modern Judaic Studies, and Hadassah, 1995).

2. Barbara Vinick, ed., *Esther's Legacy: Celebrating Purim around the World* (Waltham, Mass.: Hadassah-Brandeis Institute, 2002).

ACKNOWLEDGMENTS

Our sincere thanks go to Rabbi Edgar Weinsberg, Myrna Tichenor, Kulanu: All of Us, Harriet Bograd, Karen Primack, Benjamin Phillips, Professor Jonathan Sarna, Esty Frimerman, Rebbitzen Layah Lipsker, James Gwinn, Irina Wulf, Catarina Cameira Sheldrick, Andrew Eschelbacher, the late Louis Fox, Linda Saris, Martin Ozoria, and Cantor Emil Berkovitz, whose assistance in gathering and examining these materials was invaluable.

We are grateful to Sarah Twichell, the coordinator of the Hadassah-Brandeis Institute, for first-rate copyediting and manuscript preparation, and to Dan Carlinsky, our persistent agent, for his forbearance. Janet Rabinowitch, our editor at Indiana University Press, is among this project's most steadfast supporters.

Our deepest appreciation goes to the hundreds of people who directed us to potential contributors and especially to the authors, who revealed themselves and their communities so generously. We very much regret that we could not include all of the wonderful articles and photographs we received from around the world. Although extremely interesting, those contributions not directly related to bat mitzvah could not be part of this volume. We hope that a future publication can highlight past and present Jewish communities in countries not represented here.

Barbara Vinick
Shulamit Reinharz

Today I Am a Woman

Introduction

Barbara Vinick

PERSONAL MEMORY

*W*hen I was thirteen, in 1956, the boys in my Hebrew school class at our Conservative temple in Massachusetts were the stars of bar mitzvah ceremonies. They met with the cantor, who prepared them to read their haftara and give a speech. The bright ones read from the Torah as well, and led the service. Girls in the class did not do these things. There were no b'not mitzvah. To tell the truth, shy and self-conscious, I felt relieved that I didn't have to "perform" and be the center of attention. Although I can't recall discussing it, I'm sure that not everyone shared my relief. Other girls must have felt left out and overlooked, having to wait for confirmation, a graduation ceremony the next year that took the place of b'not mitzvah for girls.

At our temple, bat mitzvah celebrations did not start until the late 1960s. The cantor from my childhood years, now deceased, recalled a struggle with the ritual committee, which finally acquiesced when its members were reminded that the other Conservative temple in town had already given girls the opportunity to participate in b'not mitzvah.

One of the first bat mitzvah girls was Cindy Frisch. Her mother, Shirley, remembers that the ceremony was strictly circumscribed: only on Friday night; only a prayer service followed by an added-on haftara reading; only pastries (no feast); and no separate invitations. So the entire congregation was invited through the temple bulletin, the social hall was decorated with greenery stapled to bulletin boards, and the sanctuary was full for this pioneering effort. Since then, girls in the congregation have been allowed to adopt the same ceremony as boys, and in recent years, more and more are wearing tallitot.

COMING-OF-AGE: RITES OF PASSAGE

Societies always have formally marked the passage of young people, both boys and girls, into adult responsibilities. A favorite area of anthropological study, such *rites de passage* have been documented everywhere. For Jewish girls, the rite of passage is the bat mitzvah, a public ceremony that gained public acceptance in the twentieth century.

My temple's history parallels the story of bat mitzvah in the United States. The first U.S. bat mitzvah took place in 1922, when Judith Kaplan, the eldest daughter of Lena Kaplan and Mordecai M. Kaplan, the father of the Reconstructionist movement, read a portion from the Chumash and said a blessing from the dais at a Saturday service in the living room of a New York brownstone that served as the first sanctuary of the Society for the Advancement of Judaism. Judith had prepared for less than a week, as her sisters recall in the testimonies I was privileged to obtain for this book. Many people think that Judith's was the first bat mitzvah in the world. This is not the case.

HISTORY OF B'NOT MITZVAH

Selma Kaplan Goldman, one of Judith's sisters, pointed out an entry in her father's diary[1] written on a trip to Italy in 1922. He briefly describes attending a synagogue in Rome, where a young girl and her father ascended the bimah (platform from which the Torah is read) for recognition of her "entering minyan" at age twelve. She recited the *Shehechiyanu* prayer and received a blessing from the rabbi. (Kaplan notes his own daughter's ceremony a few months later in a few lines in the same journal.)[2]

While the origin of bat mitzvah in the United States is well known, the beginnings of formal recognition of Jewish girls' coming-of-age elsewhere are not so clear. The third-century codification of law, the Mishna, specifies that a boy automatically reaches maturity at age thirteen and one day, when he becomes responsible for mitzvot. A girl reaches maturity at age twelve and a day, when she must fast on Yom Kippur. Public religious bar mitzvah ceremonies evolved for boys after the fifteenth century, but it took a long time for girls' coming-of-age to be recognized in any way.

Brandeis scholar Jonathan Sarna, in an address at his daughter Leah's bat mitzvah,[3] noted that the first indisputable mention of girls' public coming-of-age appears in the writings of the nineteenth-century sage Joseph Hay-yim ben Elijah al-Hakam of Baghdad. His *Ben Ish Chai* advised a simcha (celebration) when girls assumed their womanly obligations at age twelve. In Germany, according to quotes in Erica Brown's chapter in *Jewish Legal Writings by Women*,[4] b'not mitzvah were advanced in the nineteenth century to counter the inroads of the Reform movement, which sanctioned neither bar nor bat mitzvah.

Early ceremonies, such as the one described by Rabbi Kaplan in Italy and his daughter Judith's in New York, were hardly comparable to bar mitzvah ceremonies for boys. After all, Torah reading is a mitzvah not incumbent upon females. Largely educated by their mothers in the domestic realm of Jewish life, girls usually participated in the service only minimally.

JEWISH DENOMINATIONS AND B'NOT MITZVAH

But times change. In the United States and elsewhere, as Jews became part of the secular culture, domestic education could no longer be counted on as the sole source of Jewish knowledge for girls. Formal Jewish education came to be seen as necessary for children of both genders. As women obtained higher secular educations and began to assume leadership roles in synagogues, and as the women's movement burgeoned, so did acceptance that Jewish girls' coming-of-age should be recognized publicly by the community.

But for several decades, there was reticence about b'not mitzvah from more traditional leaders, personified by the learned Rabbi Moshe Feinstein who, in the 1940s, forbade any bat mitzvah celebrations in the synagogue and repudiated even home celebrations. As Norma Baumel Joseph delineates in a 2002 article in *Modern Judaism*,[5] however, even Rabbi Feinstein, known as a great opponent of bat mitzvah observances in the United States, came to accept them within certain limits. Conservative congregations took the lead, and in them the bat mitzvah ceremony, beginning after World War II, became "a regular feature of American Jewish life," according to an article by Paula Hyman in the *YIVO Annual* of 1990.[6] The Reform movement, which originally allowed but did not embrace such ceremonies, followed, and by the 1970s, most Orthodox congregations were permitting some kinds of bat mitzvah ceremonies in synagogues.

Extrapolating from statistics of the National Jewish Population Survey of the United States[7] (which, unfortunately, did not collect specific information about b'nai mitzvah of young family members), I estimate that in the years 1998–2003, more than 80,000 girls participated in bat mitzvah ceremonies nationally. According to the Synagogue Council of Massachusetts, virtually every congregation in my state, regardless of denomination, hosts bat mitzvah ceremonies of some kind. The Chabad (observant Chasidic group) in my town, for example, hosts all-women prayer services on Friday night, led by the bat mitzvah girl. The girls meet weekly for eight months with the rabbi's wife, who has designed a service strictly in accordance with Jewish law. She seeks to instill pride, knowledge, and spirituality among her students. The girls pledge to continue their studies for a year after their bat mitzvah.

BAT MITZVAH AROUND THE WORLD

When I began to think about collecting coming-of-age testimonies from around the world, I suspected that bat mitzvah ceremonies would be confined mainly to the United States. As the collection grew, I learned that b'not mitzvah have been fostered by Jewish communities the world over. Just as bat mitzvah ceremonies are regular events on the calendars of Jewish congregations in the United States, so are they in Latin America, in the Caribbean, in Europe, in Africa, and even in the Far East. Tzivos Hashem, the children's organization founded in 1980 by the Lubavitcher rebbe Menachem Schneerson (the late leader of the Orthodox Chasidic movement) and based in Brooklyn, sponsors Bat Mitzvah Clubs International, which has provided materials to more than 200 clubs for non-

Orthodox girls in the United States and around the world. The Hadassah-Brandeis Institute (a research institute focusing on Jews and gender that is directed by Shula Reinharz), in collaboration with the Reconstructionist Rabbinical College's Kolot Rosh Hodesh: It's a Girl Thing! program, initiated the Bat Mitzvah Project for sixth-grade girls in the United States and Canada. The monthly sessions focus on the relevance of mitzvot in the daily lives of girls of bat mitzvah age. Even in Israel, where secular families have traditionally celebrated with a nonreligious birthday party and Orthodox families were not able to mark the event in the synagogue, bat mitzvah ceremonies are becoming more common, if not universally accepted.

The bat mitzvah was welcomed first in Sephardic communities (made up of Jews whose ancestors were expelled from Spain and Portugal more then 500 years ago) and continues to be endorsed in Sephardic circles. But the Ashkenazim (Jews whose ancestors came from France, Germany, and Eastern Europe) of Europe and the United States have gone further in granting young women the same ritual status as young men. The World Union for Progressive Judaism (an organization of Reform, Reconstructionist, and Liberal congregations founded in 1926 in London) now has a presence in forty countries. The greatest inroads have been made in Israel and in the countries of the former Soviet Union. There are no statistics, but girls and boys are equally likely to celebrate b'nai mitzvah in the typically small, egalitarian congregations that belong to the WUPJ, according to a spokesperson.

With a dizzying array of forms—a group or single ceremony, the bat mitzvah girl reading Torah on the bimah or saying a prayer from behind the mehitza, an elaborate choreographed performance using the latest technology or a simple recitation of the Sh'ma—bat mitzvah ceremonies worldwide are not easy to categorize. Some are more like the confirmation ceremony in which I participated in the 1950s, while others are identical to bar mitzvah ceremonies for boys. Unlike bar mitzvah ceremonies, however, they are not enshrined in tradition. Some observers applaud this as an opportunity to make the ceremony more personal and meaningful. Families have used the bat mitzvah to showcase the talents of their daughters and to celebrate cultural elements from their family's history. Other observers, such as Erica Brown in the article mentioned above, decry the lack of uniformity. She calls upon the Orthodox rabbinic establishment to adopt a standard ceremony.

Especially in the United States, some people have condemned the excesses of bat mitzvah parties and the absence of spirituality. In January 2004, an article in the *Wall Street Journal* about parties for twelve- and thirteen-year-old non-Jews spurred a flurry of letters to the editor from Jews offended by this mimicry of the nonreligious aspects of the event. Yet celebrations that involve a festive community get-together are an integral part of Jewish culture and tradition, and there are precedents in Jewish legal writings that encourage bat mitzvah parties, albeit not on the lavish scale they have reached in some places. The *Ben Ish Chai*, cited by Erica Brown and Jonathan Sarna, declares that a girl should wear a new dress for the occasion, and Rabbi Yitzchak Nissim, the former Sephardic chief rabbi of Israel from 1955 to 1973, wrote in favor of a se'udat mitzvah, a festive meal to celebrate a bat mitzvah.

ABOUT THIS COLLECTION

In 2000, it would have been very difficult to collect the testimonies found in this volume. Now, thanks to the internet, I was able to communicate with people everywhere in the world relatively quickly and easily. Beginning with a list of contacts from a previous project of the Hadassah-Brandeis Institute (*Esther's Legacy: Celebrating Purim around the World*),[8] this collection reflects a web of connections: some writers were found through personal contacts (relatives of friends, friends of relatives, and so on), others by suggestions from colleagues, by searching websites, or via leads from people who could not themselves contribute. Although it is said that there are no more than six degrees of separation between any two people in the world, I had never seen the principle in action more clearly than while working on this project.

This is not a systematic collection: it is neither a scientific survey nor a complete inventory of bat mitzvah practices. That remains for the future. This compilation is about variety. One of the goals was to include as many countries as possible, to show that Jews live now or have lived in the past in virtually every corner of the world. Authors include young women who recently celebrated b'not mitzvah, parents of bat mitzvah girls, women who recall their own b'not mitzvah years ago, women who participated in adult b'not mitzvah, and community leaders.

Authors also include women who did not participate in formal bat mitzvah ceremonies. Some, including the descendants of Anousim—literally, "forced ones," Crypto-Jews who were forced to convert, yet maintained remnants of Jewish practice—have written about recognizing their Judaism and other personal coming-of-age experiences. Others come from communities where bat mitzvah was unheard-of. Authors from the Indian subcontinent, where concepts of purity and cleanliness are prominent in women's traditional roles, have written about their family's recognition of the arrival of puberty, an event usually overlooked in Western society. (In *Jewish and Female*, published in 1984,[9] Susan Weidman Schneider notes an unusual private celebration in which a mother gives a specially designed moontree necklace to her daughter.) Others have written about adult b'not mitzvah. In the United States, Hadassah has sponsored the Eishet Mitzvah program with the Frankel Center for Jewish Family Education in Jerusalem to prepare women for bat mitzvah as part of a joint curriculum of study.

One of the major themes shared by b'not mitzvah around the world is the involvement of the whole family. Many Jewish communities, decimated by world events and struggling to rise from the ashes, are using b'not mitzvah as a way to educate the family as well as the bat mitzvah girl herself. Psychologist Judy Davis, in a 1994 issue of *Lilith* magazine devoted to contemporary bat mitzvah practices, describes b'not mitzvah as a milestone for mothers and fathers.[10] It may be the first time they present themselves publicly as religious adults. Parents who help the bat mitzvah girl prepare for the ceremony often further their own Jewish learning and strengthen their ties to the Jewish community. As parents shop for and plan the celebration, their bonds with their daughters can be strengthened and everyone's self-images can be enhanced by the successful completion of tasks.

It is difficult to generalize about personal responses to bat mitzvah and coming-of-age practices. Working on *Esther's Legacy* taught me that everyone has a story to tell. Potential authors were given few guidelines; they were told only to write about coming-of-age in a personal way and they were encouraged to share something about their communities. Some of the stories may be troubling to readers looking for inspiration, but we felt it was important to represent a range of experiences. As these testimonies show, some young women feel pride in traditional roles, while others have felt discrimination keenly because of their gender. You will discover anger, frustration, indifference, and embarrassment in these brief pieces, as well as satisfaction, delight, self-esteem, and sweet nostalgia. A collection of testimonies from only the satisfied and spiritually advanced might have been uniformly uplifting, but it would not have represented the full range of Jewish experiences.

Feel free to open this volume to a page at random to see what you find. Like me, you will probably be surprised to find Jewish communities in places you never thought of.[11] You may identify with the feelings and experiences of people very far from where you live, a connection that Jewish life engenders. You may grieve the loss of communities that no longer exist. But finally, I hope you will feel that this is a heartening collection. We can be proud of our variety, of our tenacity to endure in the face of challenges and forced journeys from country to country, of our ability to adopt elements from the cultures in which we live while retaining our essential identity, of our facility to change with the changing conditions of our lives while maintaining our core values. Our names and rituals may be different depending on our countries of origin, but the principles that join us together are more powerful than the variations that keep us apart.

NOTES

1. Mel Scult, ed., *Communings of the Spirit: The Journals of Mordecai M. Kaplan*, vol. 1: *1913–1934* (Detroit, Mich.: Wayne State University Press, 2001), 163.

2. Ibid., 159.

3. Personal communication to Shula Reinharz, 2006.

4. M. D. Halpern and C. Safrai, eds., *Jewish Legal Writings by Women* (Jerusalem: Urim, 1998), 233–258.

5. Norma Baumel Joseph, "Ritual, Law, and Praxis: An American Response to Bat Mitsva Celebrations," *Modern Judaism* 22 (2002): 234–260.

6. Paula Hyman, "The Introduction of Bat Mitzvah in Conservative Judaism in Postwar America," *YIVO Annual* 19 (1990): 134.

7. C. Kadushin, L. Saxe, and B. Phillips, eds., "National Jewish Population Survey 2000–2001: A Guide for the Perplexed," *Contemporary Jewry* 25 (2005): 1–35.

8. Vinick, ed., *Esther's Legacy.*

9. Susan Weidman Schneider, *Jewish and Female* (New York: Simon and Shuster, 1984), 131–133.

10. Judy Davis, "Bat Mitzvah/Bar Mitzvah: Every Family's Rite of Passage," *Lilith* (Fall 1994): 30–32.

11. *Jews in Places You Never Thought Of* is the title of a book edited by Karen Primack, in association with Kulanu. Kulanu, an organization that helps remnants of the Jewish people worldwide, helped me to find many of the authors in this volume.

Africa

*T*his section includes entries from six sub-Saharan African nations—Democratic Republic of the Congo, Nigeria, South Africa, Uganda, Zambia, and Zimbabwe. There are Jews in many other African countries as well. Besides long-term residents, Jews are Peace Corps volunteers, doctors helping with the AIDS crisis, and businesspeople. There are also communities of indigenous peoples (in Ghana and Cameroon, for example) who have adopted Jewish identities and practices.

Seeing itself as a partner with other young countries after World War II, the Israeli government sent water technicians and other specialists to assist the newly created African states, and many Africans came to Israeli universities to study. Since the 1980s, Israel has maintained on-again, off-again relationships with many of these African nations because of shifting political circumstances.

Researchers of Jewish demography usually divide the continent into three sections: North Africa (which is included with the Middle East in this volume), South Africa, and the rest of sub-Saharan Africa. The Jews who live in Africa arrived via diverse routes and have diverse histories. Many African countries, including South Africa, received Jews as immigrants or refugees from Europe after the Holocaust. Ugandan Jews, on the other hand, are relatively recent converts. Today, there are approximately 80,000 Jews in South Africa and about 15,000 in the rest of Africa.

DEMOCRATIC REPUBLIC OF THE CONGO

Selma Lipsky tells us that her family emigrated from the island of Rhodes to the Belgian Congo (now the Democratic Republic of the Congo). She calls Rhodes, formerly a part of Italy but now a part of Greece, by its Greek name, Rodos. Selma's extended family, the Israels, was among the first families to settle in the Belgian Congo, her father arriving in 1929 and her mother ten years later. Selma and her family left the Congo in 1959 so that she could attend school in Belgium. In 1960, after independence was declared and violence erupted, her entire extended family, about thirty people, left the Congo to join her family in Belgium. Today, there are no Jews in what was formerly called Zaire and is now the Democratic Republic of the Congo.

Although there was no bat mitzvah ceremony in the Belgian Congo, a Jewish girl was celebrated in a females-only party after she got her period. Nowadays, the issue of whether or not a girl has begun to menstruate is unrelated to her bat mitzvah. Instead, she becomes a bat mitzvah when she reaches a certain age and has mastered certain material.

Selma Lipsky

There were no bat mitzvahs in the Congo when I was growing up. We had a small community, and bar mitzvahs were for the boys. But there was a custom when a girl became a young woman.

After she got her period, maybe the next week, there would be a tea party. The girl would be given presents, especially jewelry. Women in the family would come—grandmothers, aunts, cousins. It would be only for the family, and only for women.

Your grandmother would look at you and say, "Oh, you are now a woman." The mother would be happy that her daughter could have children in the future. As for the girl, she would be red and green with embarrassment.

I never had to endure this, because my family had already left the Congo, and the relatives weren't around at that time. But I remember my older cousins' parties. My family came from Rodos originally, where the tradition probably came from, maybe related to an Arab custom. I know that it is no longer done.

NIGERIA

In this amazing story, Remy Ilona tells not only about the coming-of-age rite for girls in his area, but also suggests that an entire tribe—the Igbo (or Ibo)—has Jewish origins. In 2006, Remy, a lawyer and author of *The Igbo: Jews in Africa?* (self-published, 2002), accompanied anthropologist Daniel Lis (formerly Swiss, now Israeli) on a tour around southeastern Nigeria. Their goal was to meet various groups of Igbos, some of whom are sincere in their desire to learn more about Judaism and convinced that they originally came from Israel. "It is true that we have over 40 million Igbos, all stating . . . that they are 'Jews,' but only a tiny fraction of this 40 million, perhaps only a few thousands, have started *teshuvah* [repentance]," he has stated.[1] According to Brent Rosen, an Illinois rabbi who spent a month with the Igbos in 2005, "I have no doubt that their feelings of connection to the Jewish people are real and heartfelt—and that they have been kept alive and nurtured by the Igbo people for centuries."[2]

Remy Ilona

The Ibos occupy a major area of the southern part of Nigeria. The tribal name, Ibo or Igbo, is probably a derivative of Ivri. Historians can only guess that the Israelites who begat the Ibo people left their kith and kin during the movement from Egypt to the Promised Land. It is probable that the Ibos are a part of the Hebrew stream that settled in Ethiopia. Their religion is purely the Judaism of the law and prophets. They saw the Bible for the first time in the fifteenth century, yet from immemorial times they have been in strict obedience to the law of God.

My father told me that in 1945, as he was about to leave for the Second World War, when Ibos fought in the British colonial forces, his father, Ezeofido Ilona, summoned him and laid down a set of do's and don'ts. My father said that he realized in later life that illiterate Ezeofido, who never saw, held, or beheld a Torah, actually repeated the Ten Commandments to him in that talk.

The life of the Ibo can be described as culturally Hebraic. Male children are circumcised on the eighth day after birth. Ibos value traditional Hebrew marriage more than Christian marriage, which the colonialists introduced. Burial of Ibos is unmistakably Hebraic in form and content.

Perhaps 20,000 Ibos have returned fully to rabbinical Judaism. A strong minority have stuck to their own religion—Hebrewism. Others have developed a syncretistic Judaic-Christian religion that normally goes by the name Sabbath Church, and a tiny minority are developing a very crude version of rabbinical Judaism, which they have dubbed Traditional Church.

In Ozubulu, in Anambra state, Judaic passage to adulthood is called *isi mgba*. (The celebration is known by other names in other parts of Iboland.) Young girls are dressed up in *jigida* (beads). *Uri* (camwood) and *nzu* (white chalk) are used to make beautiful patterns on their bodies. On the appointed day, after decorating their bodies, they move singly or in groups, with music and dancing, to the marketplace. When they are gathered there, older women move in and begin to instruct them on the responsibilities of womanhood and motherhood. When the instructions are over, merriment starts. Feasting, music, and dancing take over. The whole clan turns out. People give gifts to the maidens. Afterward, suitors can start moving in.

My niece Uchenna Ezimmadu, who is twenty-one, was orphaned early and grew up in the home of her maternal grandparents. A young woman with great academic promise, she is presently studying English at the Abia State University, one of the Ibo universities in Nigeria. At the time of her entry into puberty, *isi mgba* had practically died out. Only daughters of Ozubulu whose parents had never left Judaism participated. For those like Uche, whose parents and grandparents were converted by European Christian missionaries, this important Judaic rite was ignored. Now, many Ibos have started to reject cultural colonialism and to free themselves. Uchenna has decided to become an Ibo-Benei Yisrael activist to educate others in the universities about the Ibo relationship with Israel and about the importance of going back to our roots of Torah, the only way pre-

Remy Ilona's niece Uchenna Ezimmadu encourages Judaism
among her Ibo university peers in Nigeria, 2001.

scribed by God, the same God the whole world acknowledges to be the only true God.

SOUTH AFRICA

Given the relatively large size of the South African Jewish community (80,000 people), we have included two bat mitzvah stories. Eighty percent of South African Jews belong to Orthodox congregations, and both stories take place in them. The Cape Town Hebrew Congregation introduced bat mitzvah ceremonies in 1940. Veronica Belling, the Jewish studies librarian at the University of Cape Town, explains the ups and downs of the ritual and the concern she feels that it has become trivialized.

In photographer Anne Lapedus Brest's account, girls experience the bat mitzvah as a group and the ceremony is not considered to be religious. She, too, is ambivalent about how b'not mitzvah celebrations have evolved to become ostentatious displays. In both South African cases, there are major differences between bar mitzvah and bat mitzvah ceremonies, as is true for Orthodox congregations worldwide.

Veronica Belling

I became a bat mitzvah in 1960 at the Cape Town Hebrew Congregation, also known as the Gardens Synagogue, the oldest Orthodox Jewish congregation in South Africa. Established in Cape Town in 1841, the synagogue had introduced bat mitzvahs twenty years before mine. My grandfather had joined the shul when he arrived from Lithuania via London at the turn of the century. My parents were staunch supporters, and my mother ran the children's services for many years. Thus, there was never any doubt that my sister and I would be celebrating our bat mitzvahs there.

The idea of a bat mitzvah, or "girls consecration service," as it was referred to in those days, was first discussed in 1939. It is possible that the advent of Reform Judaism in South Africa in the 1930s could have influenced the decision in favor of its introduction. In 1940, the first four girls completed their "dedication course" and were presented with bat mitzvah certificates during a Sabbath service. By 1945, the girls consecration service had become an annual event associated with the festival of

Shavuot, when, according to tradition, Moses received the tablets of the law on Mount Sinai. Both my sister and I celebrated our bat mitzvahs on Shavuot.

Over the years, the ceremony became more and more elaborate. From a simple dedication prayer recited in unison, the ceremony gradually grew into a pageant incorporating the cantor and the choir. The dedication prayer developed into a speech dedicated to a theme, such as "women in the Bible" or "women in Israel."

Originally, the girls bat mitzvah course, covering the Jewish festivals, kashrut, and the maintenance of a Jewish home, was conducted outside regular school hours by the Cape Town Board of Jewish Education, and culminated in a final examination. Both my sister and I prepared for our bat mitzvahs in this way.

However, as the Jewish community prospered, the majority of the school-age population began to attend the Jewish day school. The material required for bat mitzvah was incorporated into the Jewish studies syllabus, and a special examination was no longer required. As the number of girls having bat mitzvahs became larger, they were often held twice a year, in the autumn and in the spring, and no longer on Shavuot, but on a Sunday afternoon, and not necessarily in the synagogue, but in a hall. This was the case in my daughters' time.

The pageant, the parties, and the gifts grew more ostentatious. The Hertz siddur presented by the synagogue to my sister and me became a Soncino Humash and a small pair of silver candlesticks. The customary book or pen presented by family and friends was transformed into a check. On occasion, communal bat mitzvahs even gave way to solo bat mitzvahs.

I have the impression from my daughters and their friends, who remember little of their bat mitzvahs, that when the syllabus was incorporated into the Jewish day school curriculum the content of the bat mitzvah was downplayed at the expense of the ceremony itself. As the ceremony became more elaborate, it became less meaningful.

Because it has no basis in Jewish ritual, the bat mitzvah has become more of a social than a religious event and thus lends itself to abuse. Negative elements, such as competition relating to dresses, parties, and gifts,

Veronica Belling's sister on her bat mitzvah
day, Cape Town, South Africa, 1963.

unavoidably creep in. A young girl from a poor family might have to bear the stigma of not being able to afford a bat mitzvah at all.

Thus, I must confess to being ambivalent on the subject of bat mitzvahs. As a feminist, I believe that girls deserve greater recognition in Orthodox Judaism. On the other hand, I believe that the bat mitzvah should be made more meaningful religiously to the girls who participate.

Anne Lapedus Brest

I came to South Africa in 1961 from Dublin, Ireland. It was common practice for South African girls, Orthodox and Reform, to have a bat mitzvah. My daughter, Angela Shannon Brest, had one at our Orthodox shul in 1987. The shul is known as the Sandton shul, but the correct name is the Beth Hamedrash Hagadol, Sandton. There are 1,200 members. My information about bat mitzvahs applies to Orthodox shuls. I imagine Reform bat mitzvahs are similar, except that Reform women sing in the choir, and Orthodox women do not.

As long as the girl is of a Jewish mother, she is entitled to have a bat mitzvah in the Orthodox shul. At Jewish day schools, classes do the bat mitzvah together, although the very religious kids do it on their own. If they go to a non-Jewish school, Jewish girls are taught at cheder, usually before school starts in the morning, and they get together for the bat mitzvah, from about a dozen to almost thirty of them. It varies.

Mothers form a committee (I'd hate to be part of it) to choose material for the girls' dresses. They are usually white with a contrasting color. My daughter's was white with turquoise. Mothers can have the outfit made by their own dressmaker to suit their child. The dresses are supposed to be tzneeus (modest), and not a mini or sleeveless. Some of the girls push it a bit, and the dress is on the short side! But it is supposed to be on the knee, not higher. If the girl wants a strapless dress, then she wears a bolero or a shawl in chiffon or any material of her choice, as long as her shoulders are well covered.

Orthodox bat mitzvahs are not officially religious ceremonies. The word God is pronounced Hashem, and not the normal way we pronounce God's name when reading from the Torah. The ceremony is on Sunday, not Shab-

Angela Shannon Brest (*front, second from left*) and her bat mitzvah group, King David Jewish school, Sandton, South Africa, 1987.

bos. The girls are *not* on the bima like bar mitzvah boys. They stand with their backs to the Aron Hakodesh and face the front. Families are allocated seats in the shul downstairs. Men and women can sit together, like at a wedding—not like at a shul service, where they can't.

The girls take turns reading in English and then in Hebrew, both collectively and separately. They have learned to project their voices, so it sounds very good. They read from a booklet, but they usually know the readings by heart. (Sometimes, in the excitement of it all, a kid can faint. It has happened.) The pieces relate to the theme of the bat mitzvah— something meaningful about a character in Jewish history, or something from the prophets, or they elaborate on something from the Torah.

The choir's songs depend on the readings. They always start with *Boroch Haboh* as the girls walk in, the same as when a bride enters. (The mothers are usually crying at this point.) If the theme is "Israel," the choir sings songs like *Yerushalayim Shel Zahav* (Jerusalem of Gold) and other Israeli songs, old or modern. If the theme is "women," they include in their repertoire songs like *Ayshes Chayil* (Woman of Valor). After the girls have finished, the rabbi blesses them and makes a speech. There is more singing from the choir, and the ceremony ends with *Hatikvah*.

After that, the girls have their own parties. We had a catered tea and savories in the garden. Some have it in a hall with a band. Some take the child to Israel instead. Bat mitzvahs are getting more and more over the top.

UGANDA

Rachel Namudosi Keki was born and raised in the Abayudaya community of eastern Uganda. (*Abayudaya* means "people of Judah" in the Luganda language.) A member of a family singing group that has made award-winning recordings of Abayudaya Jewish music, Rachel, who graduated from Makerere University in Kampala, has returned to the community and teaches in the high school. In 2003, she made a successful lecture tour of the United States, telling audiences about her community.

Semei Kakungulu, a Ugandan governor and military leader, founded the Abayudaya community in 1919. He declared himself a Jew and attracted 3,000 followers, who formed the original community. During the 1970s, there was heavy religious persecution by dictator Idi Amin, who outlawed the practice of Judaism. Many Jews were lost to other religions during this period. The community has also struggled with problems common to Africa, including poverty, limited educational opportunities, and lack of access to health care.

With increased contact and support from world Jewry, the community is currently growing in numbers and strength. There are now close to 1,500 community members and six modest synagogues. Spiritual leader Rabbi Gershom Sizomu, who studied in Los Angeles, was ordained as the first black sub-Saharan rabbi in 2008. The Abayudaya observe Shabbat, festivals, and fast days; study Torah; and follow the mitzvot, including the laws of kashrut. The community has established a high school and a primary school that serve students of all religions, as well as a successful interfaith coffee-farming cooperative. In 2002, half of the members

Rachel Namudosi Keki at her rabbi's home, Nabugoye Hill, in the Abayudaya community of eastern Uganda, 2003. Photo by Rabbi Howard Gorin.

underwent a conversion ceremony through a Conservative Beit Din in order to affirm their status in the eyes of world Jewry. Other conversions have followed.

Rachel Namudosi Keki

I will always remember my bat mitzvah celebration at the age of twelve. It was one of the most interesting times of my life and still rings in my mind. Our community rabbi, who had previously taught me the Hebrew alphabet, trained me for about a month to read a few lines from the Torah. I was very happy to learn to read from the Torah in our sacred language.

A few days before my bat mitzvah, I received many fine gifts and letters from my parents, relatives, and friends. They included religious items such as siddurim, as well as flowers, pens, and clothes. Of all the gifts, I cared most about the blue *kitenge* dress from my father. This dress is part of my African heritage, and I felt proud wearing it to synagogue for prayers. Together with a white hat, I wore the colors of the flag of Israel.

On my bat mitzvah day, I finally had a chance to read from the Torah before the entire congregation. After reading, I received my parents' blessing. Everybody was happy, and I was showered with sweets! The whole synagogue was strewn with them, and the younger children ran up excitedly to collect them. We had a lot of wine and bread for kiddush and motzi. Afterward, we ate a festive meal of matooke (mashed bananas), rice, fish, and beans. Many songs were sung, and I was asked to lead some of them, including our Abayudaya community motto, "We Shan't Give Up." I felt very special.

After my bat mitzvah, I was given a chance to lead prayers, including the Prayer for Eretz Yisrael and the Prayer for the Congregation. I was now a full adult member of the Jewish people, and I was happy to contribute to the life of our Abayudaya community.

ZAMBIA

Zambia is a land-locked country in southern Africa. Formerly Northern Rhodesia, the country is named after the Zambezi River. The Jewish population peaked at 1,200 in the mid-1950s, but in the 1960s, when Zambia became independent, many of the Jews emigrated abroad. As is true with many Jewish communities, those of Zambia are urban and live in the country's capital.

In 1978, the Council for Zambia Jewry, to which Vera Galaun refers below, was founded in Lusaka to oversee Jewish communal activities there. This includes devotion to tikkun olam, as the council provides assistance to political refugees and the poverty-stricken with medical and financial aid. In Zambia's shrinking Jewish community, we can see the role that memory plays in retaining traditions. The community has published its own history, so that when memory fades, information will still be available. Not only is the community shrinking, it is also aging, a phenomenon it shares with many other Jewish groups. Shrinking and aging occur when people have few children, or when children move away, leaving older people behind. The community can grow once again when new members join, but in order to have continuity with the past, they must know their history.

Vera Galaun

Before independence from Great Britain in 1964, there were about 300 Jews in Zambia, formerly Northern Rhodesia. Today, the Jewish population numbers 50 adults and 15 children and is made up of a small core of early settlers, plus some expatriates on short-term contracts. The affairs of the community are managed by the Council for Zambia Jewry under the chairmanship of my son, Michael C. Galaun, and three other trustees.

There is one synagogue in Lusaka, the capital, at the corner of Cha Cha Cha and Katunjila roads. The community practices southern African Orthodox Judaism. Religious services are held on the High Holy Days and Passover, and are conducted by members of the community. Other festivals are celebrated in private homes. Our size does not warrant the engagement of a rabbi.

No bat mitzvahs have been celebrated in Zambia in recent years. The daughters of the early settlers are well past the age of bat mitzvah, and the daughters of the current expatriates celebrate in the home countries of their parents.

Casting my memory back to the years prior to 1964, I can recall several bat mitzvah ceremonies held in Lusaka. A rabbi based in Lusaka taught both boys and girls the history of the Jewish religion as well as Hebrew reading and writing. He conducted Sabbath services and other yom tovim services. Following the Sabbath morning service in the synagogue, all the worshippers who were present would be invited by the parents of the bat mitzvah to a brocha in the adjoining communal hall. Additionally, families celebrated with a dinner or luncheon and/or a party for peers and friends in honor of the bat mitzvah girl.

ZIMBABWE

Elsie Alhadeff's family came to Zimbabwe from Rhodes, an island in the Aegean Sea that now belongs to Greece and is called Rodos. As Sephardic Jews (descended from the Jews of Spain and Portugal), they spoke Ladino, a Judeo-Spanish language that is in danger of extinction. The transition of Jewish customs from generation to generation is clearly visible in her story.

From its establishment in the late 1800s, Zimbabwe, formerly Rhodesia, has had a contentious and tumultuous history, changing names, fortunes, incorporated territories, and ruling elites. Before and during World War II, many Jewish refugees arrived in Zimbabwe, mostly from Rhodes and Lithuania, and the Jewish population reached its high of 7,000. Since then, the community has shrunk to just 260 because of civil war in the 1970s and the poor economy of the country, which now has the lowest life expectancy in the world.

In spite of the poverty and political chaos of the country, the Jewish community of Zimbabwe has survived. In Harare, the Sephardic and Ashkenazi congregations had to join forces in the early 2000s to ensure a minyan, but there are two Jewish schools (including Sharon Jewish Day School, which Elsie's daughter Doreen attended), a home for the aged, Zionist youth groups, and communal organizations led by the Jewish Board of Deputies.

Elsie Alhadeff

My husband and I are Sephardim, born in Zimbabwe, then Southern Rhodesia. Our parents' mother tongue is Ladino-Spanish, very similar to the Spanish spoken in Mexico and parts of California. Our main language is English, but we can speak Ladino, and our children completely understand it and can speak a little.

Our parents were born in Rhodes, which at the time was under Italian occupation. When we visited there in 1986, we saw where our parents lived in the Old Jewish Quarter, surrounded by high stone walls built centuries ago, probably by the Knights of St. John. My mother's house was still intact, adjacent to the rubble of the big synagogue destroyed in the Second World War. My mother-in-law's house was also still standing, funnily enough across the road from Synagogue Sha'are Shalom, which has the same name as ours in Harare.

My mother, now ninety and living with us, tells me that in Rhodes island, b'not mitzvah ceremonies were not held to mark girls' passage into the adult Jewish community. The community was close and religious, and the limelight fell on boys and their bar mitzvahs. Not much consideration was given to girls for celebration of their coming-of-age.

In Zimbabwe, bat mitzvah ceremonies were at first held mainly by the Ashkenazi community, followed later by the Sephardi. Both congregations have now been practicing this beautiful custom for about twenty years. I never had a bat mitzvah ceremony, but my daughter Doreen was fortunate to celebrate her bat mitzvah in 1984. She and three other girls who attended the Sharon Jewish Day School in Harare celebrated a most wonderful and memorable occasion.

The ceremony was held in shul on Shabbat, and the girls looked beautiful in their white dresses, like young brides, angelic, their hair so attractively done, and all looking immaculate. They stood by the ark and each took a turn to read, in Hebrew, the Ten Commandments. Oh, it was a moving and emotional experience for all who attended. We can still hear our daughter's lovely, clear voice resounding in shul, reciting her commandments. Appropriate prayers were recited by our minister, which concluded the service.

This was followed by a scrumptious tea for the families and invited guests in our adjacent hall. Here, the girls each made a speech of thanks. It was touching to hear what each one had to say. The only regret is that, as it was held on Shabbat, we were not permitted to take photographs or a video.

That evening, a party was held at the home of one of the bat mitzvah girls, and in true Jewish style, there was a beautiful spread of food, lovely music, and dancing. The party ran late into the night. On Sunday, each family celebrated in their own way. We held a luncheon at home and invited our family and good friends. We will always have fond memories of the occasion, and are thankful to our close-knit community for allowing our daughter to experience a bat mitzvah at that stage in her life.

NOTES

1. *Kulanu Newsletter* 12:2 (Summer 2005): 1.
2. *Kulanu Newsletter* 12:3 (Autumn 2005): 10.

Asia

The first Jews who came to Asia were traders from Iraq and neighboring countries, successful entrepreneurs who created prosperous lifestyles for their descendants. Among the most prominent families were the Sassoons, who built a huge business empire in the Far East in the 1800s and, through their philanthropy, established Jewish institutions that remain to this day. Forced out of Russia by revolution, war, and pogroms, large numbers of Jews emigrated in the 1920s to Asia, notably to the Manchurian city of Harbin (which already had a substantial Jewish population). More arrived from Middle Eastern countries such as Syria and Iran. World War II brought another large wave of immigrants fleeing the Holocaust. The majority of those people later left for Israel and the West when they could.

For the most part, the Jewish communities of Asia have not been the target of governmental repression or violence. With the notable exceptions of those in Pakistan and Burma, the small Jewish communities that remain are generally secure and are expected to survive. But there have been changes. As the younger generations whose parents and grandparents settled in the Far East have moved to Israel, the United States, and Britain, their places have been taken by often-temporary new immigrants seeking economic opportunity.

CHINA

In 2004, the First International Symposium on Judaism in China was held at Nanjing University, where Professor Xu Xin, who has traveled and lectured widely throughout the United States, heads the Judaic Studies Department. It may come as a surprise that there are several academic centers devoted to Jewish studies in China, a country with no indigenous Jewish communities that exist today. The city of Kaifeng in northeastern China was home to a Jewish community beginning as early as the ninth century. But through the generations, as their descendants encountered few barriers to acceptance into Chinese society, the Jewish population assimilated, intermarried, and largely forgot the traditions. (Recently, some have renewed an interest in Judaism.)

Economic opportunity is the primary motive for Western Jews who move today from their countries of origin to China. The 250-member Jewish community of Shanghai, which has been growing by 30 percent annually through a third great wave of Jewish immigration, is composed of people from the United States, Israel, France, Argentina, Venezuela, Russia, Canada, Australia, and Britain, augmented by Jewish businesspeople and tourists passing through. The community experienced earlier periods of growth in the 1920s, when Russian Jews escaping revolution and pogroms arrived, and in the 1940s, when a great wave of Europeans seeking refuge from World War II flocked to one of the few countries that did not require an entrance visa.

Founded in the 1800s by Sephardic Jews from Baghdad and Bombay, Shanghai's Jewish community's most notable families were the Sassoons and Hardoons, who established great business empires. These were the people who built the magnificent Ohel Rachel Synagogue, which now belongs to the Chinese government. Unfortunately, the synagogue is rarely allowed to open, a situation that had personal consequences for young Andrea Feuer, who now lives in Georgia in the United States. Nevertheless, her bat mitzvah experience was positive thanks to the Chabad-

Lubavitch rabbi and his wife, who nurtured Andrea's enthusiasm for Jewish learning.

Established in the 1940s and based on the principles and teachings of Jewish sages of the eighteenth century, the Chabad movement is dedicated to the preservation and revitalization of traditional Jewish practices and values worldwide. Today, there are more than 4,000 emissaries like Rabbi Shalom and Dina Greenberg, originally from New York, who live and work in far-flung communities, including six in China: Beijing, Guangzhou, Hong Kong, Kowloon, Pudong, Shanghai, and Shenzhen.

Andrea Feuer

I am fourteen years old. My mother, Raya, a chemical engineer, is Venezuelan, and my American father, Bruce, is a lawyer. My younger sister, Annika, is five. I was born in Venezuela, and at the age of four I moved with my family to Puerto Rico, where I lived for three years. Then we moved to Atlanta, Georgia, where we lived for six months before my father was transferred to Shanghai, China, where we lived for five and a half years.

While we were there, I attended the Shanghai Changning International School and the Shanghai American School. My father was the general manager of Shanghai Centre. When we moved there in 1996, Shanghai was an isolated city. The Jewish community was just forming and had less than a hundred members. Both my parents played important roles in the foundation and growth of the Jewish community. My mother was the treasurer, and my father was the president.

While living in China, my family saw the Jewish community grow in quality as well as quantity—"quality" referring to the arrival of a Chabad-Lubavitch rabbi, Shalom Greenberg, and his wife, Dina. Their arrival meant that the community could come together as one and pray together. But use of the synagogue was considered a privilege that was rarely allowed. Thus, because we were not allowed to use the synagogue for Sabbath, we used the tenant activity room in Shanghai Centre, where the rabbi led the services. Here in the States, people take a synagogue for granted, so living in China taught me to be respectful and thankful for whatever I have.

I had my bat mitzvah in 2000, when I was twelve. As preparation for this event, I attended weekly classes with the rabbi's wife. With Dina, I learned to read Hebrew and studied the Bible. Many people came to my bat mitzvah, some from the United States. It was a huge event because it was the first bat mitzvah ever in China.

A few days before the big day, a representative from the Chinese government called my father to tell him that my services could not be held in the synagogue. It is important to remember that the synagogue is the property of the Chinese government. Imagine, all the invitations were already printed and all the arrangements were set, and my mother had to make new arrangements in just a few days. Even with such short notice, the event turned out to be great. The services were held in one of the rooms in the Portman Ritz-Carlton Hotel. I will never forget it.

HONG KONG

Like other Jewish communities in Asia, Hong Kong's most prominent families were originally from Baghdad. In 1901, the Khadooris and the Sassoons built Ohel Leah Synagogue, a counterpart to the Ohel Rachel Synagogue of Shanghai, where, as he describes, Michael Durbin nervously conferred with Rabbi Kermaier about his daughter, Zagny's, upcoming unorthodox Orthodox bat mitzvah. Still standing in its prime location near Hong Kong's central business district, Ohel Leah is surrounded by two luxurious apartment towers and the Jewish Community Center, which houses two kosher restaurants, a kosher market, a swimming pool, sports facilities, and a library. The Hong Kong community of about 2,500 prosperous Jews from a variety of countries supports four additional synagogues and the Carmel School, East Asia's only Jewish day school, founded in 1991. Zagny found warm support there from her teacher Dov Locker, whom she calls Moreh Dovi. With tolerant Chinese neighbors (such as the chefs and managers who prepared Zagny's bat mitzvah feast of kosher Chinese delicacies at the Peninsula Hotel), a cohesive community, beautiful surroundings, and an upscale lifestyle before and after the Chinese takeover from Britain in 1991, one Jewish resident claimed, "For us, Hong Kong is paradise."

Andrea Feuer accepts her gift prayer book from
Rabbi Shalom Greenberg, Shanghai, China, 2000.

Michael Durbin and
Zagny Ormut-Durbin

MICHAEL DURBIN

Sometimes, not as often as we might like, but perhaps more often than
we realize, things just have a way of working out. And on a few occasions,
things work out in ways that exceed one's every expectation and hope,
even when the route is a circuitous one.

When we started to ponder Zagny's bat mitzvah service and celebration, we had several simple goals in mind, all having the delightful advantage of offering up seemingly insurmountable challenges:

· We wanted as traditional a service as possible, but also one where the
differences from a bar mitzvah boy's experience would be minimal.

- We wanted the experience to be consistent with Zagny's wonderful Jewish education at Carmel School, including the involvement of her teacher Dov Locker. But at the same time, we realized that our format might cause him great difficulty in being present.
- In the back of our minds, we also were aware that there was some possibility that this might be Zagny's last year at Carmel School. So we were searching for a way to mark that important transition in a meaningful way.

At the outset, we viewed this in technical terms—a challenge to determine what would be in and out of the service. My first meeting with Rabbi Kermaier was very stiff; both of us were wary. I recall attending with a checklist—bracha, kaddish, aliyot, Torah reading—all the while wondering how I was going to explain to my wife, Lori, any "concessions" I made.

I think that it is fair to say that Rabbi Kermaier, not knowing us very well, had every reason to be cautious. What was being discussed, after all, was something that had not really been presented previously in Hong Kong or, as things turned out, anywhere else in the world.

In the end, the rabbi and I made a connection over something that many might not consider really important to the issues at hand: we saw eye to eye on the recitation of the kaddish and the reading of the names of our relatives who could not be there to see Zagny, the granddaughter of survivors and immigrants, honor her family and ancestors in her bat mitzvah ritual. While we anticipated with great pleasure Zagny's chanting of her parasha, in many respects this was of greater importance to us than all of the other parts of the service.

Somehow, from the moment it became obvious just how sensitive Rabbi Kermaier was to our needs in that regard, the focus ceased to be checking items off a list, and instead became one of searching together for the best possible way for Zagny to mark this important step in her life. The individual components did not become less critical and, candidly, the fact that certain items would differ from a bar mitzvah service gave us considerable pause. But there emerged a shared sense that something very spe-

Zagny Ormut-Durbin with Rabbi Yaakov Kermaier, Hong Kong, 2000.

cial had to be created for our very special girl. Without comment or fanfare, the only thing that became important was the creation of something special for Zagny.

This focus on the one thing that truly mattered led to a day of rich celebration of our Jewish life for our whole family. The remarkable, at times painful, emotion of the day included the beauty of the ritual, Rabbi Kermaier's special thoughts, Dov Locker's involvement, and the participation of family, friends, teachers, and fellow Carmel students.

And then there was kashrut . . .

From the outset, Rabbi Kermaier was candid that he would be unable to attend our evening celebration if the dinner were not kosher. We had no difficulty respecting that, all the more as the rabbi never made it a matter of pressure or conflict. Truth be told, kosher food was not something that was on our radar screen in the months leading up to the bat mitzvah. But about the time we were tasting dishes at the Peninsula, we began to ponder what a tremendous and sincere effort the rabbi was extending, and how the evening celebration would not be complete without his and Elana's attendance.

I must admit that this kind of project—kosher food presentation in a traditional Chinese venue that had never previously attempted it—somehow appealed to my perverse love of logistical challenges. The minutiae of seating plans, with the mechitza placed lengthwise, was not enough to occupy that portion of my brain for the duration. Here was something we could really sink our teeth into! After all, we were not dealing with meat and potatoes. We were dealing with twelve courses of dishes that had not been prepared in this manner ever before in this restaurant. All the more fun with only fourteen days to go!

Try finding acceptable ingredients for "preserved taro paste" when no one even has a recipe, and you will get the general drift. It is more difficult than getting a recipe out of Bubbe. We've done both now and can vouch for it.

We are not shomer shabbat and the laws of kashrut do not hold sway in the Ormut-Durbin household. But for this occasion, everything that should be involved in a bat mitzvah celebration was going to be involved. In the end, we had a sense that this was one more way to teach our children, in a very practical and clear way, the absolute importance of respect, of commitment, and of mitzvot.

And so, in the end, things just worked out, in ways far exceeding our fondest expectations.

As they sometimes will.

ZAGNY ORMUT-DURBIN

When I first heard and saw the parasha which I was meant to learn for my bat mitzvah, I was afraid. Afraid that, in the six months I had, I wouldn't be able to learn the whole of Shelach in Bamidbar. But when I began to study it, Moreh Dovi, my teacher, told me that I didn't have to do the whole thing, "just most of it," which made me worry a little less.

As I continued to learn, I began to enjoy the learning. Not only did Moreh Dovi help me to learn how to sing the parasha, he also helped me to understand it, so that I could interpret it from my own point of view. Starting in January, I met with him twice a week. Even when he was in Israel at Pesach, we carried on with our lessons over the phone.

Toward the summer, I also met with Rabbi Kermaier once a week. We had all sorts of interesting discussions about my parasha and its meaning. During my last session with him, we talked about what had to be done in order to make the Chinese kitchen at the Peninsula Hotel kosher. We had a good laugh about it; it wasn't the easiest thing to do.

Sunday, June 25, 2000, was a very special day for me. I proved to myself that I could study and understand this very long parasha from the Torah, and that I *can* sing in front of an audience. But most of all, I learned how important and wonderful it is to be with family and friends when we celebrate important events in our Jewish life.

INDIA

Several Jewish women living in the United States, such as author Jael Silliman and artist Siona Benjamin, have offered outsiders a glimpse into Jewish culture within India. But almost no one has written about bat mitzvah. Shalva Weil, the author of one of the stories from India included here, is an anthropologist at Hebrew University in Jerusalem. Born in the United Kingdom, Shalva has specialized in the Jews of India since writing her doctoral thesis at Sussex University. In 2002 she edited a volume entitled *India's Jewish Heritage: Ritual, Art, and Life-Cycle* (Mumbai: Marg), which is the culmination of her photographic and literary work over the years. "I still remain fascinated by Indian Jews, and continue to research new areas of their rich culture," she says.

Two of the authors included here, Noreen Solomon Daniel and Ruth Solomon, are sisters-in-law descended from prominent Bene Israel families. The largest community of Indian Jews, numbering about 5,000, the Bene Israel claim that they came to India after a shipwreck in 175 BCE. Noreen and her husband, Romiel, have been active members of the Rego Park

Jewish Center in Queens, New York, where they have lived for more than a decade since leaving Mumbai. Their lectures and demonstrations concerning the history and customs of the Jews of India have informed and fascinated audiences on the East Coast. Ruth and her husband, Jonathan, remain in Mumbai where they are members of the Jewish Religious Union, founded in 1935, the only Progressive (Reform) synagogue of the more than twenty that formerly existed in India, most of which are not active now.

Galia Hacco is a Cochini Jew from an ancient Indian Jewish community whose history and customs are different from those of the Bene Israel. Born in Kerala in the south of India and now living in Israel (where most of the Cochini Jews have emigrated), she started the Nirit Singers, a group of women interested in learning and singing traditional songs in Malayalam, the language of her native region. Both the language and the songs are unfamiliar to most of the younger generation. Galia's discussion of coming-of-age with members of her group, along with the testimonies of Ruth and Noreen, demonstrate the cultural emphasis on women's cleanliness and purity among Indian Jews. Their essays also testify to the tradition of celebrating the fruitfulness of the natural world.

Shalva Weil

I carried out my doctoral fieldwork as an anthropologist among the Bene Israel in Israel, where the majority of Indian Jews lived in the 1970s. I focused on the community residing in the town of Lod, near the airport, where we made our home, living the lives of Indian Jews and coming to understand their culture. The community accepted me generously, inviting me to every communal event and occasion. Basically, the women adopted me, and I became a member of the Stree Mandel, the women's organization of Lod.

When I became pregnant with my first child, the women fed me special sweetmeats so that I would give birth to a boy. Despite their efforts, I gave birth to a girl. Soon after, the community held a naming ceremony for her. The women dressed me in a beautiful sari and tucked a coconut and fruits near my belly, over which they recited the traditional blessings, and wished me better luck next time: "May you have five sons in the future." (After that, I gave birth only to sons.) They named my daughter Ilana Tamar, *Ilana* signifying a tree and *Tamar* a date, since she was born on Tu b'Shvat, the festival of the trees.

After three years of fieldwork, we left Lod and went to live in Jerusalem. We celebrated Ilana's bat mitzvah in our new community in the Katamon quarter of Jerusalem, where she made a drasha (speech) in synagogue on her parasha—Beshalach in the book of Shmot (Exodus). Some people in our Orthodox community thought it was too revolutionary for a woman to speak inside the synagogue, and one man walked out and left the community. (Today, in the same synagogue, it is a matter of course for women to give drashot in the Saturday morning services. However, it is still considered inappropriate for a woman to read from the Torah.)

We held Ilana's bat mitzvah party in a small hall in Jerusalem. I invited many of my new Israeli friends, Ilana's school friends, our relatives, and some of my closest Indian friends from Lod. They and their husbands came up to the party in a bus. Upon their arrival, they enacted the Eliahoo Hannabi ceremony that they celebrate on every auspicious occasion, such as weddings, pregnancies, and childbirths. This was the same ritual that they had enacted for Ilana at her naming ceremony.

The women prepared five different kinds of fruits and nuts—coconuts, dates, almonds, apples, and bananas—which they placed in a dish on top of a melida, a composition of rice flour and sugar. The mixture was piled up and covered by the fruit, and a rose and a myrtle leaf were placed in the center. Frankincense was burned by the side. One of the husbands, who was also a hazan, opened with the *Shema*. Then came recitation of the words *Eliahoo Hannabi* [Elijah the Prophet] about a dozen times, the prayer *Veyitenlekha* ("May He Give You," a blessing associated with Elijah), and other hymns, like Psalm 121, *Esa Enay* ("I Will Lift Up My Eyes").

The hazan made a blessing over a cup of wine, picked up the contents of the melida, and made a blessing over each fruit in a set order: for example, the blessing for the fruit of the trees, in the case of the apples, and the blessing of the fruit of the earth, in the case of the bananas. Each fruit was distributed in turn, first to Ilana and our family, and then to all the participants in the hall. The melida mixture was blessed and distributed in similar fashion. Even the petals of the roses and the myrtle were passed around after they were blessed for their incense. Then, the party partook of the festive meal.

Ilana came of age in the Indian Jewish community and has since qualified as an architect in Tel Aviv. In January 2003, she accompanied me to the Taj Mahal Hotel in Mumbai for the launch of my new volume, *India's Jewish Heritage*, to which she contributed a chapter on Indian synagogue architecture.

Noreen Solomon Daniel

There has been a Liberal synagogue in Bombay for fifty years. Reform rabbis go there from the U.S. and England. My husband's parents were among the 150 members, as are my brother and his family. There are some bat mitzvahs there, as these are the most Westernized people in India. But the rest of Jewry in India, who are Orthodox, look down on this. I never had a bat mitzvah and really don't miss it. There are so many other things that a Jewish woman can do.

I lived in Pune, 300 miles from Bombay, when I was growing up. We are Bene Israel, a people who have lived in India for 2,000 years. I remember a coming-of-age ritual that very few people know about. Nobody has brought this to light. When I've spoken to people doing research, I've never been asked, so I've never talked about it.

At age fourteen, on the evening when I started to menstruate, my mother sent my brothers out of the house. She sat me down and put something in my lap. It was a handkerchief and wrapped in it were a variety of dried fruits and nuts—walnuts, almonds, dates, figs, raisins, and coconut. Coconut is especially symbolic; all parts are useful. (The Bene Israel use a lot of coconut, as it is plentiful on the coast, where we come from. When a bride goes to her new home, they give her a coconut.) There was also a flower garland of jasmine. These are symbols that a woman has flowered and now can bear fruit. I strung the flowers in my plait, and ate the fruits and nuts.

My mother is a doctor, so I knew about menstruation. But I had never heard of this custom. It is very private, just within the family. My mother didn't call her friends. I think that if there were a grandmother or aunt nearby, then maybe they would have been there. In truth, I was a little embarrassed. When I confided in my girlfriend, who was Hindu, she told me that her mother had done something similar.

There are other customs that have to do with menstruation. If a woman has her period, she shouldn't light the candles on Shabbat. Her husband will do the ceremony. Also, we used to make our own crisp flat bread, like chapatti, for Shabbat. And in India, we used to make our own grape juice (not wine) for Shabbat. (I used to do it early in my marriage.) But you don't make them if menstruating.

Ruth Solomon

I am a member of the Jewish Religious Union, affiliated with the World Union for Progressive Judaism. Student rabbis are sent to Mumbai (formerly Bombay) by the American Joint Distribution Committee (JDC). We were lucky to have Rabbi Leon Morris, then a student, in our midst when our daughter Michelle started Hebrew classes leading up to her bat mitzvah. Leon was very popular with our congregation, and the children loved studying Torah with him. I would drive Michelle to the JDC hall, where the classes were held. (Our synagogue was burned down during the intercommunal riots in Mumbai in 1992, although Jews were not the arsonists' targets.)

Bat mitzvah traditionally is not considered a milestone in a girl's life in India. Here, Jewish society places all the emphasis on a boy's bar mitzvah, after which he can be counted in the minyan for important prayers and rituals. A girl is not counted in the minyan, so Jews in India have thought of a bat mitzvah as mostly superficial. Our older daughter, Sharon, is not a bat mitzvah. But our son was taught Hebrew and the Torah long before age thirteen, when he was called up to read before a large congregation at his bar mitzvah.

When Leon came to our community, he spoke to us of the importance of a girl's bat mitzvah. He told us that women were counted in the minyan in the West, and that there were women rabbis. We thought it would be wonderful if Michelle, our youngest, could be a bat mitzvah.

One day, after driving Michelle to her Hebrew class, I was passing the time reading a magazine. Leon came up to me and asked if I was a bat mitzvah. When he suggested that I study Hebrew and have a bat mitzvah

Ruth Solomon and her daughter Michelle, Mumbai, 2003.

with Michelle in 1995, you could have knocked me down with a feather. I had always imagined one had to become a bat mitzvah at age twelve, before the age of menstruation. Here I was, a mother of three with a son of twenty-four. How could I be a bat mitzvah? Leon assured me that I most definitely could.

So, instead of reading magazines, I started learning to read the Torah. Slowly but surely, the alphabet became familiar and my confidence grew. Michelle was learning very quickly, of course, and I had to do extra homework to keep up with her! We tried to coax Sharon to study with us, but as all the students were twelve and she was twenty, she did not relish the idea.

On the day of our bat mitzvah I stood beside my daughter as Leon spoke of the wonderful gift of Torah. I had tears in my eyes as he handed the Torah to Michelle's grandfather, who passed it to my husband, who then passed it to Michelle, symbolizing the handing down of the Torah from generation to generation. As she read her Torah portion, Michelle's voice sounded so beautiful to us. We reveled in the moment and thanked God for his precious gift of our lovely daughter.

Then, it was my turn. With a sense of pride and achievement, I went up to read my portion. Bat mitzvah means "daughter of the commandment." Reading the Hebrew words from the holy scroll created in me a new awareness and sensitivity toward my obligations and privileges as a Jewish woman. It strengthened my loyalty to Judaism and made me aware of my duty to preserve this holy heritage which I am fortunate to have as my birthright.

Galia Hacco

I came to Israel in 1954 with my sister and eight other teenagers in a youth aliyah group. I was thirteen and my sister was fifteen. Our parents came two years later. We were from Kerala state, on the southwest coast of India, where tradition and research both say that Jews have lived for more than 2,000 years. Today, there are fewer than a hundred Jews in Kerala. Among the six synagogues that remain is the beautiful Paradesi Synagogue in Cochin, a cultural remnant of the old Jewish communities of Kerala whose members made aliyah in the 1950s.

In 1974, I attended my cousin's wedding in a moshav in the Negev. It was there that, for the first time, I heard the special wedding songs sung by Cochini Jewish women in my mother tongue, Malayalam, the vernacular of Kerala. I was impressed with the songs, and I wanted to learn them.

I began to relearn Malayalam, which was not spoken at home, and to learn the songs of my ancestors. Several years ago, I began to teach them to a Cochini Jewish women's group of forty-seven members in the Indian Jews' synagogue in Rishon-le-Zion. We meet once a month for three to four hours to study and sing in Hebrew and in Malayalam.

At one of the meetings of our women's group, I asked the members to describe how their lives had changed at age twelve, when Jewish girls now have bat mitzvah celebrations, and the role of traditional songs at that age. This pushed a button, and for the first time we had a lively discussion about menstruation and about linking the songs with coming-of-age.

The women realized that they had been taught to be ashamed of their bodies. Simcha, a retired midwife, age sixty-eight, expressed some common themes:

At home we didn't talk about adolescence at all. When I began to menstruate, my aunt explained everything and taught me how to prepare a pad out of cloth. Now I was a "big daughter," given good food—almonds, eggs, fresh milk, and soup made from young chickens. When we were in the "woman's way," we couldn't touch a holy book or sit at the same table with the boys and men. We couldn't enter the synagogue, even on holidays, and had to stand in the courtyard.

Rivka, a nurse, age sixty, was more analytical and critical of her experience:

Among Cochini Jews, the period is looked upon as impure. When a girl comes of age, there is no preparation, mental or physical, for what is to come. There is no discussion. Strict limitations are put on her: not to sit at the table eating with everyone, not to touch a prayer book, not to sit with everyone in the women's section of the synagogue, not to play outside. All these rules make the girl feel ashamed.

Others, such as Tsipporah, a substitute teacher, had more positive memories:

In the Cochini community, parents don't talk about sex and men. They're afraid their kids are too young. This is too bad, but from the first day I got the "woman's way," my mother took good care of me. I didn't know anything. She explained what to do. Every month, I got good tasty food. I remember her saying, "I want you to have a strong back." After my first period, I felt more mature. I stopped playing outside. "Now, you are a big girl. You have to be serious, not make noise," my mother said.

It was at about this time that many of the women began to participate in singing the Malayalam songs. As Simcha recalled: "At home, we had a notebook of songs my mother kept. It had been given to her mother by her grandmother. I was eleven at my aunt's wedding. I was singing with my mother and some friends in Hebrew and Malayalam. This was the first

Cochini women sing a Malayalam song at the Indian
Jews' synagogue in Rishon-le-Zion, Israel, 2003.

time I sang." And Tsipporah remembered: "From age five, I learned Hebrew at home with a private teacher. We didn't learn much of the meaning, but enough to read the prayer book. After I got my period, I stopped
studying Hebrew. At thirteen or fourteen, I started to study the Malayalam Jewish songs to sing at weddings in the community."

Coming-of-age and learning the songs were not formally linked. But
at the age of twelve or thirteen, girls usually became aware of the songs
and began to participate, feeling more like the young women they would
become and less like the little girls they were leaving behind.

INDONESIA

Barry Halpern is a businessman now living in Colorado whose work took him to the island nation of Indonesia. There, his daughter, Lisa, probably had the first, and possibly the last, bat mitzvah in that overwhelmingly Islamic country. Settled first by Dutch Jews in the spice trade in the 1920s and 1930s, Java, the island where the capital, Jakarta, is located, at one time was home to 2,000 Jews. Following the Japanese invasion and internment of Jews during World War II and the rise of nationalism in the 1960s, most Jews left.

Today, as Barry documents, the only Jewish life in Indonesia is led by Jews from other countries who live there for business, educational, or service reasons. A handful of the Jews who formerly made homes there remain in Surabaya. They are descendants of Iraqi traders, most of them elderly, with limited knowledge of Jewish practices and limited resources. One has to admire the fortitude of these little-known few who are determined to hold on to their Jewish identity and their modest synagogue, the only one in Indonesia.

Barry Halpern

Surabaya, an hour's flight east of Jakarta, is the second-largest city in Indonesia, with a population of about 5 million people. Indonesia has the fourth-largest population in the world, 90 percent of which is Muslim, and only one synagogue, the one in Surabaya. Acquired from the Japanese in 1945, the synagogue was built originally by Dutch colonialists. It is set up as an Orthodox synagogue, but there has not been a rabbi there for who knows how many years (a hundred?). There are no prayer books, and there is no Torah in the ark.

In total, there are some twenty-five Indonesian Jews. They are descended from Iranian and Iraqi immigrants. All but two of them live in Surabaya (the other two live in Jakarta). The Indonesian government does not bother them, probably because there are so few. Some have mixed marriages; some were born or have lived overseas. Almost all of them are very poor.

The Surabayan Jews are ignorant of many Jewish practices. They hold a Passover seder, but are unaware of the traditions to observe. A couple of the men put on tefillin every day, yet they no longer know or understand the true meaning. Services are never held in the synagogue because they do not have enough men for a minyan; they do not count women or any man who has not had a formal bar mitzvah. (After discussions with us, we believe they will use a more modern interpretation of "Jewish adult.") They do, however, know that they are Jewish and are fiercely protective of their Judaism and aware of their heritage and their biblical ancestors.

We did not know any of this until our daughter, Lisa's, bat mitzvah took place there in October 1997. How did that happen?

In Jakarta, where our family lives, the Jewish community has no official membership. But it's there, and it's growing. Our list of 75 individuals and families represents every continent on earth with the exception of Antarctica. We hold monthly Friday evening services (conducted by laypeople, mostly me) and Sunday brunches. There were 112 people, including about a dozen Israelis in town on business and two Lubavitch rabbis, who brought kosher chickens and matzah, at our community seder. We had 80 people at our Rosh Hashanah services. And, for the first time, a rabbi officiated when Michael Robinson, a retired Reform rabbi from California, and his wife, Ruth, came to visit.

Before his arrival, Rabbi Robinson had asked us if there were any young people in Jakarta who would like to become a bar or bat mitzvah. After some discussion and debate, there were two: Adam Goldstein, fourteen, who had lived in Indonesia almost all of his life and had never seen a bar mitzvah or been to a synagogue, and our daughter, Lisa, fifteen, who had seen only one bar mitzvah, that of her two brothers.

Both Lisa and Adam worked hard over a four-week period of study. More important, we felt they were committed to taking on the responsibilities of a bar and bat mitzvah.

As part of Rabbi Robinson's visit, we planned to fly with him to Surabaya so that he could conduct Shabbat *shuvah* services in the synagogue, which we knew would be appreciated by the Surabayan Jewish community. We planned to arrive Friday afternoon, conduct Friday evening services, and then have the bar and bat mitzvah ceremony on Saturday morning.

We invited everyone to attend—the entire Jewish community from Jakarta and all of the Surabayan Jewish community. Fifteen of us came from Jakarta, including a young man from New York who was touring Indonesia, happened to find us, and wanted to come to witness the events and see the synagogue. Of course, the celebration included members of the Goldstein and Halpern families and a few friends of Adam and of Lisa. But it did not include Lisa's grandparents, cousins, aunts, and uncles nor most of her friends. Such is the disadvantage of living in a land so far away.

In Surabaya, as we drove up to the synagogue, none of us really knew what to expect. I had met only one Surabayan Jew: Rivka, married to an Indonesian Jew, was born in Bombay, lived in Israel for a short time, and had made her home in Indonesia for thirty years.

As we got out of the car and looked in the synagogue's window, we couldn't believe our eyes. Most of the chairs were full. Surabaya had come out to meet us! There were elderly people, young adults, and children, all of them Jewish or with some Jewish blood. And they were all so thrilled to see us. We greeted all of them, many with hugs and kisses. They had never seen so many Jews! Also greeting us were three Americans. One, a backpacker from Philadelphia, was "just passing through"; the other two were exchange students in Malang, a town ninety minutes by car outside of Surabaya. The three of them had heard there was a synagogue and wondered if it held services. They had not seen it before that Friday night.

And so, we held a service, though not a long one. The temperature outside was probably ninety; inside, probably eighty-eight. As the building is located on a main road, you could hardly hear what was being said due to the traffic rolling by. But there we were, in the only synagogue in Indonesia, with Rabbi Robinson leading us in prayer, for probably the first such service in how long? Fifty years at least.

While Friday night was emotional, Saturday morning continued and intensified the feeling. Lisa and Adam were exceptional in their roles. Lisa's chanting of the blessings in Hebrew was exquisite. Both delivered speeches about the meaning of this event to them. If anyone has ever doubted the commitment of a child who becomes a bar or bat mitzvah, seeing and hearing Lisa and Adam on this day would have left no doubt whatsoever of the impact and meaning of this event on their lives.

Lisa Halpern and Adam Goldstein are welcomed
to the synagogue in Surabaya, Indonesia, 1997.

In her comments, Lisa added an ending, hastily written after the Friday
night service. She said that though most of her "blood family" wasn't with
her, she knew that she had found another family in Surabaya, and that her
new family made her proud to be there, proud to be Jewish, and proud to
be a part of history.

Adam delivered an emotional address in which he talked about being
from a mixed marriage, never living in the U.S. or in the home country
of his Malaysian mother, and never knowing until then what it meant to
be a Jew.

At the conclusion of Lisa's and Adam's ceremony, there was not a dry
eye in the synagogue. We had only a very, very small Mishnaic Torah (a
scroll containing writings on the law and traditions). So, when we would
normally have passed around a Torah, Rabbi Robinson asked if anyone
wanted to make a comment to Lisa and Adam. My wife, Ellen, asked me
to speak for both of us, as I am the more practiced speaker. Well, I got up,

opened my mouth, and nothing came out! I was too choked up to speak. I managed to blurt out something about how the proudest moments in a parent's life come when their children mark a special milestone. I also played a recorded message from our other children, Peter, Fara, and Phil.

Several others in the congregation also spoke, most of them people whom we had met only the evening before. But they spoke as family. Several of them told us that this Friday and Saturday were the happiest two days of their lives.

After the service, we all enjoyed a lunch catered by the local Hyatt Hotel. Then, all too quickly, we had to leave for the airport and the return to Jakarta. Since then, we have found it difficult to tell people about these events in a way that delivers the emotional and spiritual impact we felt. I hope that my words give at least a small idea of what happened in Surabaya.

PAKISTAN

Zvia Epstein, the author of the following story, now lives in Israel where she teaches English. In *Esther's Legacy* (2002), Zvia wrote:

> My father was chief engineer of the port of Karachi. We lived in Manora, an island, in a compound near the dry dock. My father claimed that we originally came from Spain to Kutch in India, and from there to Pakistan. We had a nice life; it was normal to have servants. Every day a launch would take us to the mainland where we went to school, and pick us up. I had Muslim and Parsee friends, and we went to each other's houses. My family was very Zionistic. I got married in England, and eventually made aliyah to Israel in 1971 after my sister and brother. (72)

Temperament and disposition have a lot to do with attitudes about opportunity for bat mitzvah. Some in this volume accept traditional roles, while others wish for the same status as men in religious practice. High-spirited Zvia and her sisters were among the first to wear sleeveless dresses and were called the "crew-cut Benjamins" because they had cut their long hair. Little wonder that Zvia resented not having a bat mitzvah and reveled years later at her granddaughter's bat mitzvah celebration.

At the beginning of the twentieth century, about 2,500 Jews lived in Pakistan, most in Karachi, the capital. After violent incidents against Jews following the establishment of the state of Israel in 1948 and again in the

1950s and '60s, most Jews left for India, Israel, and the United Kingdom. Today, amid the virulent anti-Zionism promoted by the government, few Jews remain in Pakistan.

Zvia Benjamin Epstein

Bat mitzvah for girls! In Karachi, whoever had heard of such a thing? We girls never had. In fact, we were not allowed to step inside the synagogue when we were "unclean." On High Holy Days, there was a special marquee added onto the synagogue where we girls sat with our friends, usually other "unclean" girls, or close friends who sat with us in solidarity. It was also a place away from the prying eyes of aunts and mothers, and it was where the boys came out to flirt a little before going back in. This was where we held court, for a little while at least—until the mothers came out to check.

My family was four sisters and one brother. My brother had a fancy bar mitzvah: a dinner, a party, the whole works, like a wedding. Pictures were taken of him posed with his tallis on his head and around his shoulders. We looked on. I hated it. It meant that, according to our religion, my younger brother was considered superior to me.

When my daughter was bat mitzvah age, we were living in Israel. I was a member of the Conservative synagogue in Rehovot. I tried hard to get her to attend religious instruction classes, and have the bat mitzvah I never had. She refused and skipped classes. So, she did not have a formal ceremony.

This year, I finally got my wish. My eldest granddaughter, Shelley, became a bat mitzvah at the age of thirteen at Temple Bene Israel in Tustin, California. She sang from the bima and read her haftorah wearing a tallis.

Sweet revenge!

THAILAND

The Jewish community of Thailand was not established formally until 1964, but Jews have been living in Thailand, then Siam, at least since the seventeenth century, when Spanish missionaries first reported the presence of Jewish merchants from Iraq. In the 1920s, an influx of Jews arrived from

Zvia Benjamin Epstein with granddaughters Shelley and
her sisters on the occasion of Shelley's bat mitzvah at
Temple Bene Israel, Tustin, California, 2003.

Harbin in China. During World War II, another group arrived from Syria and Lebanon. Currently, there are about 300 Jews, most living in Bangkok and making their living in the production and trade of precious gems and jewelry. There are three synagogues in Bangkok—an Ashkenazic, a Sephardic, and a Chabad house that caters to a large contingent of travelers from the United States, Israel, and around the world.

Beverly Frankel, who now lives in California, teaches in a middle school, where she uses her experience living in Thailand to the advantage of her students. Among many interesting themes, Beverly's story illustrates how Jews have adapted the resources and cultures of their host countries to Jewish practices and customs.

Beverly Frankel

My daughter Karen had a bas mitzvah on a Friday evening in Bangkok in 1984. She had taken Hebrew lessons from Ruth Gerson, whose husband, Mike, grew up in Thailand and was president of our Jewish community for many years. Ruth, a natural teacher who headed the Sunday school, taught Hebrew to most of our kids in preparation for bar and bas mitzvahs, and bonded with every one of them.

Karen's bas mitzvah was in the rainy season. We were planning an outdoor garden reception at our home. To propitiate the weather gods, we decided to perform traditional Thai rituals to ensure good weather: giving incense and flowers, and lighting candles at the Erawan shrine to protect against rain. After all, hedging their bets worked for my friend Sonja's family. They had no rain at her son Frank's bar mitzvah, so why not continue a good thing when it works? We were all deeply involved in the Bangkok National Museum, learning about Buddhism, the spirit nature of the Hindu gods, and other aspects of Thai culture, so this made perfect sense to me and my children. Buddhism is a very accepting religion, so asking for a little protection for a Jewish cause is right up there with the best of prayers. And it didn't rain. So there!

Salim Eubanni, the Jewish lay leader of our small community, who had attended a yeshiva in Syria, conducted the service, as he conducted all our services. Although she was very nervous, Karen did wonderfully. She has a beautiful voice, clear and lilting. And she looked beautiful in a blue silk dress and jacket of her own design, sewn by a dressmaker, the way things are done in Thailand. Her two brothers, having traveled the same route, were impressed that their little sister could master Hebrew, the new language, so well. Actually, she outdid both of them, being a natural linguist and claiming both Thai and English as her native languages.

Karen was born in Bangkok and had lived in Thailand ever since. The congregation was composed of people who had known her as a little girl, some as a baby. It was a wonderful mix of our Thai friends (every bit as proud of her as we were), Christian friends, multinational friends, and Jewish friends. My husband and Salim added a special part to the usual service to explain to our non-Jewish guests what was going on and its significance.

It was the tradition to invite the whole Jewish community, whether we knew them or not. There weren't many of us, and it was always enlightening to see who showed up. Karen's grandparents had flown out from San Francisco and Philadelphia for the occasion. She was thrilled; it made the family complete to have them there.

I was the seventh-grade life sciences teacher at the International School in Bangkok, which most of the international community attended. Seventh-grade students are twelve, turning thirteen, so I was the teacher of every friend Karen invited to her bas mitzvah and to the party afterward. There was a very warm, supportive, family feeling.

We had a small reception at the temple after the service, and then everyone was invited to come to a lawn party on the grounds of our tropical-style house. There was a catered dinner buffet, a live band, and dancing, with tables set up all over the lawn to accommodate the guests. Karen made a speech, I made a speech, her dad made a speech, others made speeches. It was a long, lovely evening.

Australia and New Zealand

*O*ceania is a somewhat imprecise geographic region that usually refers to Australia and New Zealand as well as New Guinea and the islands of the Malay Archipelago (e.g., the Philippines and Singapore), where Jews constitute a tiny minority far from other Jews. Nevertheless, Jews have attained influence in many spheres of life in these countries and have experienced little anti-Semitism throughout their history of settlement.

Australia may be the only country in the world where Jews first immigrated as convicts. Sixteen men arrived in 1788, when Australia was a prison colony for Britain. The Jews of New Zealand arrived in a more conventional manner, as traders in the 1830s. When gold was discovered in Australia in the 1850s and in New Zealand in the 1860s, both countries experienced an increase in the number of Jews. Jews fleeing the Nazis augmented Jewish populations prior to World War II. But New Zealand admitted relatively few refugees or displaced persons during and after the war, in contrast to Australia. Immigrants from the former Soviet Union and South Africa increased both countries' Jewish communities significantly at the end of the twentieth century.

AUSTRALIA

The Jewish community of Australia is small (about 100,000 people, less than half of 1 percent of the total population) but vibrant. Intermarriage tends to be low compared to other countries in the diaspora, hovering at about 22 percent. The community continued to grow through the 1990s, primarily through immigration from the former Soviet Union and more recently from South Africa, whose Jews now represent the largest group in the Australian Jewish population.

The majority of Australian Jews live in Sydney, where there are twenty Orthodox and Progressive (Reform) congregations, and in Melbourne, where there are close to forty large and small congregations. There are Jewish congregations in Adelaide, Perth, Brisbane, Canberra, and Tasmania and on the Gold Coast, which has seen the largest gain in Jewish population. Progressive synagogues support women rabbis and women presidents; among the Orthodox, women have not been accepted into these roles, but have been welcomed as members of governing boards.

As in the United States, since the late twentieth century almost all congregations, both Orthodox and Progressive, have made a practice of hosting some kind of bat mitzvah celebration. In line with this change, most of the girls have participated in a bat mitzvah preparation program in their Jewish day schools, in which some 70 percent of Jewish students in Australia are enrolled. Individual b'not mitzvah, with girls wearing tallitot and reading from the Torah, are the norm in Progressive synagogues. Orthodox b'not mitzvah tend to be group affairs on a Sunday, but individual b'not mitzvah are not unknown within this group, especially among modern Orthodox Jews. According to a journal article published in 1999, the first Orthodox solo bat mitzvah in Australia took place on a Sabbath in 1998 in Melbourne, with the girl leading a service for women during which she read from the Torah.[1]

In the following essay, Peta Pellach tells of her three daughters' modern Orthodox b'not mitzvah in Jerusalem and Sydney based on her family's practices within traditional halacha (Jewish law). Choice in the content of the ceremony is a feature of girls' religious coming-of-age that boys' b'nai mitzvah do not share to the same extent.

Peta is a director and teacher in the Florence Melton Adult Mini-School in Sydney, which is part of an international network of community-based schools for adults to acquire Jewish literacy. A fifth-generation Australian on her father's side, Peta has an M.A. in international affairs from Columbia University in New York. She is a Mandel Jerusalem Fellow, one of a cadre of educational leaders in the diaspora, who told us that she is "committed to empowering women through education."

Peta Pellach

I turned twelve and was aware that then I was a woman under Jewish law. From then on, I would have to fast and to repent on Yom Kippur, and if I ate something *treif* (not kosher), the sin would be mine. It was an awesome responsibility. There was no ceremony and no party, but it was a milestone in my life.

My parents had given me a choice: I could wear the pretty white dress, learn the few lines by rote, and have the party that was associated with bat mitzvah in Sydney in those years, or I could participate in the Montefiore Home Debutante Ball four years later, at age sixteen. The latter was far more prestigious and exciting. It was my choice. For the most part, the girls in our predominantly modern Orthodox community made the same choice. It was deemed unnecessary to make a fuss over bat mitzvah.

For my daughters, it was quite different. A generation later, it seemed ludicrous to ignore such an important event in their lives. We asked the question that was not asked when I was twelve: "Why shouldn't a girl mark her coming-of-age? Boys all do. What about us?"

My eldest, Meirav, turned twelve while we were living in Jerusalem for two years. We spent quite some time debating about what we would do publicly to mark her coming-of-age. Some of the girls at her school read from the Torah in women's tefillah groups. A family conference decided that we did not want to proceed along that path. For us, reading the Torah is an exciting option for women, but it is not a mitzvah, not an obligation. As we were marking Meirav's entry into Jewish adulthood and her new responsibility for fulfilling mitzvot, we decided we should focus on her obligations as a woman.

We realized that we were privileged to have some choice in the matter. For many boys, the routine learning and performance of maftir and haftarah lacks personal meaning. There is no discussion about the process of entering adulthood. There is only one option to mark the occasion. Fortunately, for women there is still choice. That is something we can celebrate.

Ultimately, we designed a beautiful ceremony. After davening shacharit (chanting the morning prayer service) at the Kotel, we returned to a wonderful Jerusalem venue where Meirav delivered an extensive d'var Torah, interspersed with communal singing. Her words, in both Hebrew and English, were based on the learning she acquired in six months of intensive preparation. Together, we had studied her parsha, her family tree, and the meaning and significance of her name. All the guests were presented with song sheets so that they could participate in the singing of appropriately selected songs, which were accompanied on keyboard by her younger sister. Of course, there was food and drink, and family and guests made a significant contribution to tsedakah to mark the occasion.

The bat mitzvah of our middle daughter, Michal, followed two years later in Australia. As her birthday falls on Shavuot, her ceremony, held in the evening, began with Havdalah. The format was similar to Meirav's, and guests participated in the singing and dancing with wonderful ruach (spirit).

When it came to our next daughter, Cygal, we felt that we had mastered the bat mitzvah ceremony. Unfortunately, her paternal grandfather passed away only a few weeks before the event, so we canceled the singing and dancing, as typically occurs for a year following the death of a close relative. Nevertheless, the extent of Cygal's learning and commitment was evident, and the love of family and friends was palpable.

In all three cases, the significant part of the bat mitzvah was not the ceremony itself but the coming-of-age, the change of status. Each of my daughters learned something significant and personal in order to prepare to become a bat mitzvah. Each excelled in her commitment to learning, and each presented to those who were assembled words that were meaningful and appropriate. More important, each of my daughters came to under-

Peta Pellach's daughters Michal, Cygal, and Meirav (*left to right*)
at Meirav's bat mitzvah in Jerusalem, 1990.

stand what bat mitzvah was all about: that they were marking publicly
their acceptance of the responsibilities that come with Jewish adulthood.

NEW ZEALAND

The current Jewish population of New Zealand is fewer than 10,000 (with
some estimates as low as 3,000) individuals, who are centered mainly in
Auckland and Wellington. Intermarriage and the outmigration of youth
to Australia and Israel have been widespread, and immigration recruit-
ment efforts have recently been directed toward South Africa, Argentina,

and Israel. In a country that prides itself on biculturalism, encompassing native Maori and Pakeha (white Anglo-Saxon) groups, Jews constitute an ambiguous subgroup, largely invisible to the general population.[2] In 1999, the author of a newspaper article wrote, "Jews in New Zealand today go unnoticed."[3]

Despite their very small numbers, Jews have played prominent roles in New Zealand history and politics. The first Jews arrived in New Zealand as traders from England in the 1830s. One former premier was Jewish (Julius Vogel in 1873), as were seven mayors of Auckland, the largest city in New Zealand. Jewish women, such as photographer and former Briton Marti Friedlander, have taken leadership roles in understanding Maori culture and promoting Maori status.

Today, the Jewish community of New Zealand supports a number of Jewish institutions. Auckland and Wellington each have two synagogues, one Progressive and one Orthodox. There are small congregations in Christchurch and Dunedin. Wellington and Auckland boast thriving Jewish day schools with Wellington also offering a Jewish kindergarten.

In the following section, Rochel Zajac describes the activities leading up to the bat mitzvah of young girls at the Orthodox Wellington Hebrew Congregation, the oldest in New Zealand (established 1843). In 1977, the congregation moved into the new Jewish Community Centre, which houses the synagogue (Beth El) and other Jewish institutions, including a kosher co-op, a social club, a kindergarten, a day school, and the offices of a monthly newspaper, the *Centre News*. Rochel prepares bat mitzvah students at Auckland Hebrew Congregation.

Progressive congregations encourage girls to read from the Torah when they become b'not mitzvah, as illustrated in the article by Rabbi Patti Kopstein. She and her husband, Rabbi David Kopstein, served separate congregations in the wine country of northern California before their tenures as co-leaders of Progressive congregations in Auckland, New Zealand, which she writes about here, and then at Beit Shalom in Adelaide, the capital of South Australia, where she was the first Jewish chaplain at the University of Adelaide. An accomplished photographer, Rabbi Patti Kopstein's photographs illustrating weekly Torah portions have been featured at the Adelaide Jewish Museum, as have been the dreidels she and her husband have collected for twenty years. In 2006, the Kopsteins moved to Hong Kong, where Rabbi David Kopstein serves the United Jewish Congregation of Hong Kong.

Rochel Zajac

I would like to tell you about a place far away from London and the community where I grew up. I live in Wellington, New Zealand, with my family. As rebbetsin of the Wellington Hebrew Congregation, I have the opportunity to teach the bat mitzvah girls in our community. I generally have six months to a year to prepare them. Lessons are held weekly. Mothers encourage their daughters to attend and are actively involved in all the preparations. (I say "mothers," but sometimes it is also fathers.) I enjoy combining the classes with arts and crafts. Usually when we are concluding our lessons, we make one special craft as a memento.

What do the girls want? What do the parents want? What does the community expect? The girls look forward to dressing up, and some get to wear makeup. Everyone wants something memorable, an event that will have an everlasting impact on the girls, something that they can look back upon and recall with pride. "For my bat mitzvah, we learned how to read the first ten verses of Eshet Chayil and the translation. We applied the verses to biblical women." Or, "We studied a Mishnah in Pirkei Avot [Ethics of the Fathers], and then prepared a project and presentation on the verses we learned."

I am often asked, "When are we going to prepare for the bat mitzvah?" My response is that everything we study is for the bat mitzvah and beyond. In the past, I have arranged mother-daughter evenings when we watch a video about the laws of family purity, discuss the topic, and then visit the mikvah in the community center. It is enlightening and informative for both mothers and daughters.

The formal part of the celebration takes place in the shul, a service with speeches and readings. Afterward, there is a party in the community center or another hall. The families spend a lot of time arranging the details, from the catering of the kosher food to the decorations and the program that follows. Traditionally, families draw up family trees that are

Wellington, New Zealand, bat mitzvah girls, 2002.

displayed in the hall, together with baby and school photos and perhaps some artwork. The party usually includes speeches, thank yous, gifts from the girls to their mothers, and speeches or readings by their fathers.

I try to make some kind of souvenir with the girls to help them remember their b'not mitzvah and what they meant to them. On one occasion, we hand-decorated tambourines with a verse from Eshet Chayil and wrapped them in flowing ribbons. These were displayed on a table and then used as centerpieces for the lunch that followed the service. On another occasion, we sewed velvet siddur bags and had each girl's name and the date of the bat mitzvah professionally embroidered on the front.

At one bat mitzvah celebration, the girls, who had practiced Israeli dances, danced in a circle with their mothers. The circle grew, as many women and girls joined in. As each woman joined and held hands and danced the steps to the music, it was like linking hands with the chain of Jewish women back to Sarah, Rifkah, Rachel, and Leah, back to our Jewish mothers and grandmothers, who may not have known how to read Hebrew or recite a speech about the Torah portion of the week. This was a special women's celebration, a celebration of life, womanhood, maturity, responsibility, and acceptance of participation in the adult Jewish community.

My hope is that a celebration like this is not the culmination of a few years of Hebrew school and bat mitzvah lessons, but a beginning of Jewish knowledge and education. I hope that the girls grow to be young women who are proud of their heritage, and that maybe the small amount of study I have directed will have some effect on their lives ahead.

Patti Kopstein

Life's journey may be an easy one, or a difficult and challenging one. Carole Nathan of Auckland, New Zealand, embarked upon a challenging and difficult journey, and in the end found commitment and community.

As an adult, Carole converted to Judaism. She already was a grandmother—a strong, confident woman alone. It was after her conversion that life put her on a rollercoaster. The rabbi with whom she had studied moved away from New Zealand, leaving her, as a new Jew, spiritually hesitant and lacking in confidence. Then came an even greater challenge: an allergic reaction to an eye medication severely harmed her already-troubled eyes, and she experienced blindness for many months.

This is when I arrived as one of the two rabbis serving Beth Shalom in Auckland. As her eyesight slowly improved, we encouraged Carole to re-enter synagogue life. Always keen on language and music, she resumed her study of Hebrew and then moved on to learning to chant from the Torah. It was a team approach: my husband, Rabbi David Kopstein, taught her to chant, and I helped her to develop confidence enough to co-lead services. As she became more relaxed and confident in her Judaism and in her ability to contribute to the synagogue, Carole stepped wholly into the life of an active, committed Jew.

Not long before her sixtieth birthday, Carole stepped up to the bimah and chanted her own aliyah from the Torah. Wearing special contact lenses and spectacles, she bent low over the Torah scroll so that she could see and chanted strong and clear. This was indeed Carole's coming-of-age in Judaism, her bat mitzvah without the party or the fountain pens. After years of spiritual growth and study, of physical blindness and recovery, she had become a bright star, an honor to Beth Shalom, to Auckland, and to all Judaism.

Carole continues to flourish. She continues to study Torah and to chant on Shabbat. She has been the solo Torah reader for the entire parasha. I am proud to say that she learned her Hebrew and her cantillation skills well, and those skills have been of benefit to everyone around her. And, best of all, she understands every word she chants.

NOTES

1. Sue Beecher, "The Treasure Chest of Diversity: Australian Jewish Women Respond to Feminism," *Australian Feminist Studies* 14:30 (1999): 272.

2. Livia Kathe Wittmann, "'I Live a Fragmented Life': Cultural Identity as Perceived by New Zealand Jewish Women," in *Feminist Thought in Aotearoa/New Zealand: Differences and Connections*, ed. R. DuPlessis and L. Alice (Auckland: Oxford University Press, 1998).

3. Leonard Bloksberg, "Being Jewish Down Under," *Jewish News of Greater Phoenix* (August 13, 1999), 1.

Caribbean

*M*any tourists have marveled at centuries-old synagogues and Jewish headstones in Caribbean cemeteries, which indicate that Jews have a long history in the Caribbean. The first Jews arrived in the 1500s from the Recife area of Brazil, a Portuguese outpost. When Recife was briefly under Dutch rule, the Dutch government allowed Jews to practice their religion freely, in contrast to the Portuguese, who insisted on conversion in accordance with the rules of the Inquisition. When Recife reverted to Portuguese rule, the Jews left for safer locales such as the Netherlands, New Amsterdam (New York), and various Caribbean islands under the flags of Holland (Curaçao), England (Barbados, Jamaica), France (Martinique, Guadeloupe), or Denmark (U.S. Virgin Islands). Typically, the governments of the islands welcomed these original Jewish settlers as skilled traders, often incurring the wrath of the Europeans who had preceded them and resented the competition. Nevertheless, many small communities flourished despite some discriminatory legislation.

Through the years, the Caribbean Jewish communities established synagogues and other Jewish institutions, but then lost members through assimilation and emigration. Jews fleeing the Nazis and settling in the Caribbean islands revitalized some communities for a time. From 1936 to

1939, for example, Trinidad was the most welcoming beacon in the world, as it had no visa requirement and only a £50 landing deposit. At the Evian Conference in 1938, the Dominican Republic offered to accept up to 100,000 Jewish refugees. The Dominican Republic Settlement Association was formed to help settle Jews in Sosua, a small town overlooking the Caribbean Ocean. About 700 European Jews reached the settlement, where they were assigned land and provided with cattle. In 1943, the number of Jews peaked at 1,000. In 1990, a small museum was dedicated to mark the fiftieth anniversary of the founding of Sosua's Jewish community.

Today, most of the Jewish communities that remain in the Caribbean are small, often relying on the annual infusion of winter tourists to maintain their synagogues and augment their services. Some, like Trinidad and Sosua in the Dominican Republic, have lost all but a tiny remnant of their Jewish population. Others, such as Barbados and Jamaica, have hope for the future of their communities. This section contains stories from five of the twenty-four islands and island groups in the Caribbean, as well as the island of Bermuda off the coast of North America.

BARBADOS

Jews have been residents of Barbados, a small island nation 200 miles off the coast of Venezuela, since 1627, when they were expelled from Brazil. These Jews of Portuguese descent built prosperous businesses and in 1654 erected the beautiful Nidhe Israel Synagogue, where Arel Oran celebrated the bat mitzvah that her mother describes in the following story. After damage by a hurricane, the synagogue was rebuilt and reopened in 1833, but by 1925 no Jews were left on the island. The synagogue was closed and the building sold.

In 1931, Moses Altman left Poland and found his way to Barbados, the first of thirty Ashkenazi families who escaped the Nazis and reconstituted the Jewish community. When the old synagogue was slated for demolition in the early 1980s, the Altman family was instrumental in raising the funds for its restoration. In 1987, the synagogue reopened and was commemorated by a postage stamp issued by the government.

The few Jewish families who make Barbados their permanent residence justifiably feel proud of the effort to save not only their historic synagogue, but also the old Jewish cemetery and the new Nidhe Israel Museum next door. Jimmy Altman, a grandson of Moses Altman, was born in Barbados and has remained. "A few of us try to keep the candles burning for Jewish culture on the island," he wrote in 2002.[1] His mother, Rose, who came from New York in 1946, recounted in *Esther's Legacy* an incident typical of island life: "There was an article in the Pittsburgh press about the Jewish community here. The writer had dinner at my house and mentioned it in her article. Later, I got a phone call. A man wanted to make a reservation for twenty people for dinner! On a small island, you're a big fish."[2]

Sharon Oran

The Nidhe Israel Synagogue of Barbados dates back to 1654, making it the second-oldest synagogue in the Western Hemisphere. Until recently, there had *never* been a bat mitzvah conducted within its hallowed walls.

The Barbados Jewish community is a small Conservative congregation with about sixteen families. We have neither a resident rabbi nor any opportunity for structured Jewish education. Most children learn about Judaism during summer camp or at home from their parents. This environment makes learning Hebrew and a haftorah difficult for both girls and boys.

Rabbi Ari in Margate, New Jersey, tutored our daughter, Arel, for her bat mitzvah during the summer of 1998. She then practiced her haftorah every evening for the following months. Prior to her bat mitzvah, she also received weekly instruction from a visitor to the community, and a week before her big day we brought baal tefilah (prayer leader) Offie Schiffman to Barbados for further tutoring. We and Arel made sure she was ready, knowing that this was not only a special day for her, but also for the future of young Jewish women in Barbados.

All of Arel's friends are non-Jewish, but they came to watch her and to experience a Jewish service for the first time. Friends and family flew in from New Jersey, New York, California, and Maryland to celebrate the beginning of 1999 and Arel's bat mitzvah, which took place on January 2.

It was a special moment watching Arel on the bima, which stands toward the back of the synagogue in the center. She sang her haftorah with integrity as her grandparents, brothers, and extended family watched with pride and joy. As a symbol of the meaning of her bat mitzvah, she chose to take an additional name in memory of Granny, her great-grandmother Sarah Oran, who was her special friend.

We celebrated Arel's bat mitzvah with a dinner and dance that evening. In Barbados, there is no such thing as a party coordinator, so we had to make the evening special with the help of members of the family. Arel's Grandma Hilde hand-stitched thirty blue voile tablecloths. As a memento for each guest, Arel and I dried pomegranate seeds from our tree, wrapped them in fine netting, and nestled them in boxes with an inscription explaining the connection between pomegranate seeds and the 613 mitzvot that Jews are obliged to observe.

We had a candle-lighting ceremony during which we used the candle from Arel's Havdala naming service to light the candles of her grandparents, brothers, and godparents and a special candle for her Grandmother Anita, who had died two years previously.

The evening was a celebration of family, the diversity of friends, and the significance of women in sustaining Judaism, no matter how many obstacles appear. We hope that Arel will prove to be the first of many young women who will embrace the tradition of bat mitzvah in Nidhe Israel Synagogue in Bridgetown, Barbados.

BERMUDA

Erica Lipschultz is a 2007 graduate of Brandeis University. A student activist, she represented Bermuda in an international debate competition in Lima, Peru, in 2004. Erica's father is an oceanographer at the Bermuda Biological Station for Research and her mother is a lay leader and spokesperson for the small Jewish community, which holds monthly and holiday services at rented facilities. Erica's bat mitzvah in 1999 must have required a great deal of planning to enable family and friends to enjoy what Bermuda has to offer.

Six hundred miles off the coast of North Carolina, Bermuda is Britain's oldest colony. Reached in the 1500s by Spanish explorer Juan de Bermudez, the island has never had a large Jewish community. In 1694, the Bermuda Colony levied a special tax on Jews doing business there, and

Arel Oran at the bimah of the historic Bridgetown
Synagogue, Barbados, 1998.

although it was repealed in 1760, few Jews returned. In 1943, representatives of the Allies met for a little-known conference in Bermuda to consider methods of rescuing European Jews from the Nazis. Nothing came of it, however. Bermuda now welcomes diverse tourists to its beautiful hotels, golf courses, and marinas, but in the 1950s and '60s, there was some blatant discrimination against minorities, including Jews. Presently, there are fewer than a hundred Jews who make their home in Bermuda; there is no permanent synagogue or rabbi.

Erica Lipschultz

The week before my bat mitzvah had been hectic. We were constantly going to and from the hotel to make sure everything was okay. My mother's best friend had to come to calm my mother down, which was a large job.

My bat mitzvah was a weekend-long event. People arrived on Thursday and Friday nights. On Friday night, we took a cruise from the hotel to our house for Shabbat services and dinner on our lawn. Saturday morning began with Torah study. My Roman Catholic best friend joined in, which made for a very interesting discussion. We then had the service on the top floor of the Marriott Hotel. I was so nervous! But the service went great, my parents cried—the usual. I felt very grown-up.

That night, we held two parties, one for my friends and one for the family. My favorite memory is having Havdalah outside while two of my friends had a pillow fight in the hallway behind us! My party was the social event of the year. People still ask me today to have another bat mitzvah.

The next morning, the extended family had brunch and then we all went on a snorkel trip. My bat mitzvah was an incredible experience. I met new family members and introduced some of my friends to a new side of myself that they had not seen before.

CUBA

Unlike many other places in the world where the Jewish population is shrinking, the Jewish community of Cuba is growing and will probably continue to grow. In the period between Fidel Castro's rise to power and the fall of the Soviet Union, Cuba's major patron, it remained stagnant or diminished. But after 1991, governmental attitudes toward religion softened, and more Jewish foreigners came to visit the Cuban Jewish community, bringing a wide variety of resources. The center of Cuban Jewish life is Havana, which has three synagogues, each serving its own set of Jews: Sephardi, Ashkenazi Conservative, and Ashkenazi Orthodox. In January 2007, twenty couples, some of them seniors, married in a Jewish ceremony at the restored Conservative Beth Shalom Synagogue, the largest of the three in Havana. The large-scale nuptials were preceded by seventy conversions, including whole families and dozens of young Cubans.

José Levy Tur, the president of the Sephardi synagogue of Cuba, wrote the entry for Cuba, and he describes his daughter's experience with enormous pride. As in most of Latin America, Jews arrived in Cuba at the end of the fifteenth century, at the time of the expulsion of the Jews from Spain and Christopher Columbus's voyage to the Americas. Among those who arrived were Jews who had converted to Catholicism in order to escape the Inquisition. Sometimes these people are called Marranos (disparagingly), Crypto-Jews, Conversos, or Anousim ("forced ones" in Hebrew). The roots of the current Jewish community extend to 1906, when some Jews came from the United States and founded the United Jewish Congregation. Shortly thereafter, the first wave of Sephardim arrived from Turkey and Syria. In 1914, they created their own congregation.

José Levy Tur

Danayda Levy Toledo's Hebrew name is Deborah. She chose it herself because it translates in Spanish to "bumblebee," that creature of nature which, with its hard work, gives us the honey that sweetens our life and is so beneficial to our health. Deborah was born on June 15, 1989, in the capital of Cuba. Her parents are José Levy Tur, the president of the Sephardic Hebrew Center of Cuba, and Florinda Toledo Nuñíz, a specialist in the Bureau of Labor and Wages.

Deborah has been raised in the heart of the community and feels proud to be Jewish. Her bat mitzvah took place in August 2001 at eight o'clock in the evening in our temple and coincided with Kabalat Shabbat.

During the months before her bat mitzvah, she studied Judaism and learned the parashá for the week, Ekev. She made her commentary on the fact that the second passage of the Shemá appears in this Torah por-

Danayda Levy Toledo's bat mitzvah invitation, Havana, Cuba, 2001.

tion. It is significant that on that night, together with members of the local community, a delegation of American Jews was present. They were very pleased to see that, with ceremonies like the bat mitzvah of Deborah Levy, the continuation of Judaism in Cuba is guaranteed. As you can see, the invitation to the ceremony symbolizes the union that exists between Israel, the Kotel (the Western Wall), and Jews dispersed around the world.

Among the gifts Deborah received for her bat mitzvah was a Tanaj in two volumes written in Hebrew and in Spanish, which has enabled her to continue her studies.

CURAÇAO

Samuel Coheno, the first Jewish settler, arrived in Curaçao in 1634. The Jewish community of Curaçao is so old that its synagogue, Mikve Israel, is identified as the oldest in continuous use in the Western Hemisphere. Located in the island's capital of Willemstad, Mikve Israel has become the most popular tourist attraction in Curaçao, perhaps because of the sand on its floor. On Yom Kippur, the community reads the story of Jonah and the whale in Papiamento, the local language.

The Jewish community's population peaked at 2,000 in 1800 and is now about a quarter of that size. The community is shrinking because young people go abroad to study and typically do not return. On the other hand, when Jews marry non-Jews, the families typically raise the children as Jews and join one of the two synagogues on the island.

In the bat mitzvah story by Josette Capriles Goldish, a Curaçao-born expert on the history of the island now living in the Boston area, we learn about the struggle of her cousin Erin Blanken to become a bat mitzvah. We can see the changes taking place in the community, many of them initiated by Erin as a consequence of her determination.

Josette Capriles Goldish

In October 1999, my husband and I took a trip from Boston to the Caribbean island of Curaçao. Strapped between us on the plane was a blue duffel bag. It had its own seat and we were fully responsible for its welfare. Not until we arrived in Curaçao did my concerns for its safety fade away, as we cleared customs uneventfully and stepped into the humid, ninety-degree afternoon.

A whole crowd had come to meet us at the airport, but the honor was really for our special passenger. In this duffel bag, packed in bubble wrap and swathed in a large prayer shawl, we had brought a Torah, the holy scroll containing the five books of Moses, which Jews read from beginning to end each year during weekly Sabbath services. Too precious to ship with our luggage, it traveled with its own ticket under the name Torah Goldish: the American Airlines computer had insisted on a last name, a date of birth, and a passport number for this unusual passenger and we had been happy to give it ours.

My cousin Erin Blanken, who received us that day with her family, was becoming a bat mitzvah a few days later at a ceremony to be held at her home. At that time, services at the Sephardic Mikve Israel-Emanuel synagogue, the oldest synagogue in the Western Hemisphere, still followed a traditional pattern of sorts, with very limited participation by women. The congregation had agreed to allow bat mitzvah girls to read the haftorah portion in the synagogue during Saturday morning services, but women had never been given an aliyah and had never been taught to read from the Torah. Erin had, however, persisted in her efforts to have a fully egalitarian bat mitzvah celebration—if not in the beloved synagogue, at least at her own home. Even when she was not sure where she would be able to borrow a Torah for use on her special day, she continued to attend weekly synagogue services and prepare with Rabbi Michael Tayvah for the October date.

As the year progressed, it became unlikely that a Torah would be forthcoming from the communities in her immediate environment and so we arranged to bring her this one, borrowed from a friend in Boston. Our friend's great-grandfather had fled the pogroms of Russia with this holy object, arriving with it in the United States a century ago. And now, here it was, in the hands of the descendants of Sephardic Jews who had fled Spain and many other European countries and settled on this small Caribbean island in the 1650s.

The actual ceremony took place in the family's backyard on a beautiful, cloudless Saturday afternoon. Erin led the mincha (afternoon) service in this improvised setting. A short time into the ceremony, her mother's eldest sister opened the ark—a beautiful wooden cabinet loaned to the family by another cousin—and handed the Torah to Erin's youngest aunt, who marched it solemnly to the bimah, a dining table covered with a priceless tablecloth, embroidered by the bat mitzvah's late great-grandmother Linda Senior. After Erin's little sister had helped with the undressing of the Torah, her mom raised it up against the brilliant sky of that afternoon; over a hundred invited friends and relatives looked on as history was made.

The entire afternoon was a most respectful mix of the old and the new. In my role as gabai (ritual director), I was required to call up three persons to receive their aliyot and to pronounce the *ofertas*—misheberachs—for each of them in Hebrew and Portuguese, as has been done for centuries by this community in Curaçao. Erin faultlessly used the Sephardic chant of her ancestors to read her Torah portion and then proceeded to give a little talk about what she had read. She also told us of the steps she had had to follow to get to this day. She was candid about her disappointment upon hearing that she could not have the ceremony at the synagogue, but she continued in an upbeat tone about the decisions taken thereafter. She ended by telling us that people had asked her what she would do next, after the high of this bat mitzvah celebration had passed. Without hesitation, she told us her response: "Read Torah again!!!" And that, indeed, is what she has done many times since.

During the year that followed, the Mikve Israel-Emanuel congregation voted to have fully egalitarian services in their beautiful synagogue, which has been enhancing the architecture of downtown Willemstad since 1732. Today, Jewish men *and* women receive aliyot and read the Torah from the age-old bimah of what is often called the mother community of the Americas. It is an honor much cherished and not taken for granted.

JAMAICA

Jews have made their way to Jamaica since the sixteenth century. In the eighteenth century, Britain encouraged Jews to migrate to Jamaica, as it sought their expertise in trade. Many came, notably from Amsterdam, and in 1720, 18 percent of Kingston's white population was Jewish. Now,

Erin Blanken reads from the precious Torah flown
from the United States to Curaçao, 1999.

assimilation and emigration have reduced the Jewish community to about 250 people. Although small in number, the community nevertheless supports its Jewish institutions, as Tina Matalon's story demonstrates. Tiffany Matalon's grandfather Eli was a past mayor of Kingston and held the posts of minister of education and minister of justice. Tina Matalon is the marketing manager of Restaurants of Jamaica.

Ainsley Henriques, past chairperson of the Jamaica National Heritage Trust, encapsulates the history of Jamaica's Jews in his family's history on the island. As past president of the elegant, hundred-year-old Sha'are Shalom Synagogue on Duke Street in Kingston, where Tiffany Matalon celebrated her bat mitzvah, Ainsley spearheaded the creation of the Jamaican Jewish Heritage Center, which opened in Kingston in 2006. When asked about the future of Jamaican Jewry, he answered, "This is a pluralistic society that respects everyone's religion, and it will be Jamaican economic opportunity and tolerance that will ensure our survival for at least another generation."[3]

Ainsley Henriques and
Tina Matalon

AINSLEY HENRIQUES

The first Ainsley in my family, born in 1828, left his house on Duke Street in Kingston to two of his ten children, daughters who remained unmarried. My grandfather Ainsley grew up on a sugar plantation, Serge Island Estate, that his father, Ivanhoe Mordecai, purchased in 1897. He brought his bride, Pearl, a native of the Ukraine, to the family estate in eastern Jamaica, where my mother was born. She first married my father, Manny Henriques, and then Zacci Matalon, a Jamaican senator and, later, lay magistrate of the parish. Tiffany Matalon (whose bat mitzvah is described below by her mother) is the grandchild of Zacci's brother, Eli.

Many synagogues have been built in Jamaica over the past 350 years, the first in Port Royal, which was destroyed by the great earthquake of 1692. Kahal Kadosh Neveh Shalom, built in 1704 in Spanish Town, the old capital, lasted until a century ago. Others were built in Montego Bay and at least three more in Kingston. The descendants of many pious Sephardi and Ashkenazi families still worship in Synagogue Sha'are Shalom every Sabbath and on all Jewish holidays.

TINA MATALON

From about age six, our daughter, Tiffany, attended Sabbath school on Saturday mornings before services at Synagogue Sha'are Shalom. There, the children of our community learn Jewish traditions and customs through a variety of activities, including arts and crafts projects and theatrical productions. When she got older, we formed a Star of David Club at our school, Hillel Academy, Kingston's main private preparatory and secondary school, which was founded in 1969. The children meet every Monday afternoon to continue to learn about Jewish traditions. As part of the program, we organize Purim and Hanukah parties and child-oriented Passover dinners.

Tiffany prepared for her bat mitzvah at our beautiful synagogue, which has a sandy floor. As part of her preparation, she attended services every Sabbath for six months.

We have traditions here that I have never seen anywhere else. At the start of the service, we opened the ark and Tiff and her dad went up. She said a special prayer and placed a bouquet of fresh roses on the ark. Then the ark was closed and the service began.

During the service, in keeping with the commandment given by God to Moses that the Torah must be handed down through all generations, my husband's uncle handed the Torah to my husband, who in turn handed it to Tiffany. Unlike other places, where the bat/bar mitzvah participates in only a part of the service, she conducted the entire service, reading the Hebrew fluently.

ST. THOMAS

Built in 1833, the Synagogue of St. Thomas, which today has about eighty members, is the oldest synagogue under the American flag in continuous use. According to a brochure of the Hebrew Congregation of St. Thomas, the sand on the floor is symbolic of the days of the Spanish Inquisition, when secret Jews used sand to muffle the sound of their prayers. The ark, benches, and bima are made of mahogany and are original to the build-

Tiffany Matalon is addressed by her uncle as her mother, father, and sister, Leah, look on at her bat mitzvah in Kingston, Jamaica, 2003.

ing, as are the chandeliers and the eleventh-century Spanish menorah behind the bimah. Originally Orthodox, the synagogue is now affiliated with the Reform movement.

Jews have lived in St. Thomas, one of the three major islands in the U.S. Virgin Islands (along with St. Croix and St. John), since 1655 when St. Thomas was under Danish rule. The Jews of the island were granted freedom of religion in 1685, a long time before the Jews of many European countries. The Jewish community today numbers about 400, roughly the size it was at its earlier peak in the 1850s. One of St. Thomas's most famous Jewish residents was Camille Pissarro, the father of Impressionism, who was born on the island in 1830.

Former freelance art director Jessica Rosenberg has lived in St. Thomas since 1985, when she left New York City. The mother of three children and an avid sailor, Jessica is a photographer and artist whose work is well known in the area.

Jessica Rosenberg

It was never a question of whether or not Dylan would become a bat mitzvah. We wanted her to enjoy this spiritual experience, to feel the pride of having accomplished a task so different from all others, and to realize her sense of place in the world along with the history and heritage that have been passed along to her. We felt that she should be especially aware of her significance in the Jewish community of St. Thomas, as it is a bit scattered.

Dylan studied diligently to learn her haftarah and read from the Torah. She didn't complain as bitterly about this as she does about her regular school studies. She spent many hours with Herb Horwitz, who had also tutored her brother, Nathan, and developed a warm, caring relationship with him. His devotion made an impression that I believe will last a lifetime.

Dylan attends a Jewish camp each summer for a month. She loves the camp and the friends she has made there. She is in touch with many of them on a daily basis. As we had hoped, the people she loves from camp, as well as the Jewish friends she has here, have helped Dylan to form a deep Jewish identity.

I think that the bat mitzvah, as a symbolic marker, seemed more important and poignant to me, her mother, than it did to Dylan. It was a joyful (and yes, tearful) moment when Rabbi Starr placed his hands upon her shoulders in front of the ark and spoke in hushed tones to Dylan about the significance of her achievements that day.

Our daughter had just passed into another stage of her life, and we were overjoyed to be sharing this occasion with many friends and family. Most important, her ninety-four-year-old grandfather was there and had the first aliyah. He had wanted to be with her, and it was a wonderful moment. Dylan would have been heartbroken if he had been unable to attend. Tragically, he passed away four days later. But we feel so privileged to have had him with us for the event.

NOTES

1. "Barbados," in Vinick, *Esther's Legacy*, 13.

2. Ibid., 14.

3. Ben G. Frank, "Jamaica's Tiny Jewish Community Marks 350 Years," *Jerusalem Post* (October 26, 2006), www.jpost.com.

Europe

*J*ews have lived in Europe since the time of the Roman Empire, when they were expelled from Jerusalem. In the Middle Ages, depending on the authorities and the prevailing attitudes of the people in the regions where they resided (usually in segregated areas), Jews either were tolerated because some had useful skills in business or served as money lenders, or they were reviled, persecuted, murdered, forced to convert to Christianity, or expelled. In the 1200s, violence against Ashkenazi Jews drove them from Germany and northern France to Poland and Lithuania. Sephardic Jews were forced to leave Spain in 1492 and then established communities around the world. Many descendants of Sephardim are only now discovering their Jewish roots.

In the twentieth century, 6 million innocent Jewish individuals were killed in the attempted genocide referred to as the Holocaust. The Jewish communities of Western and Eastern Europe were decimated. In most of these countries, Jewish populations have never rebounded because of postwar assimilation, emigration, and intermarriage. The few countries where the Jewish population has increased in size have done so because of immigration, mostly from the former Soviet Union.

But Jews are resilient. Even in the face of renewed and increasing anti-Semitism and unexpected challenges today, communities of committed Jews in nearly every European country refuse to let Jewish life fade away. Often, the international Chabad organization or the Joint Distribution Committee help to energize these communities and care for the basic needs of their members. As a result, virtually every country hosts Jewish day schools and programs of study for bar and bat mitzvah. In nearly all the European countries where Jewish life exists, Jewish women are taking leadership roles.

Public recognition of young women's coming-of-age is now firmly in place in all but the most traditional Orthodox communities of Europe, with ceremonies still evolving in each setting. In Orthodox congregations, girls do not read from the Torah as part of their bat mitzvah celebration, but many have individual bat mitzvah ceremonies rather than the group ceremonies of years past. Thanks to the creativity of parents in consultation with religious leaders, girls can take active parts in ceremonies similar to those of boys, sometimes for congregations of women only. In Progressive (sometimes called Liberal or Reform) congregations, ceremonies for girls are virtually the same as those for boys. Sephardic communities may be more traditional than Ashkenazic, but it is difficult to generalize since bat mitzvah ceremonies reflect still-changing ideologies about women's roles in Jewish practice.

The following stories present snapshots of girls' coming-of-age ceremonies—past and present, public bat mitzvah and private moment—in Western Europe. Like all the stories in this book, they are a suggestive sampling, not meant to be exhaustive of the varieties of experience.

AUSTRIA

Jews have lived in Austria since their arrival in the first century with the Roman legions. Sometimes, Jews were accepted into mainstream society (as in the thirteenth, sixteenth, and early nineteenth centuries), and at other times, they were the objects of enmity and violence (as in the fourteenth, fifteenth, and twentieth centuries). The data about the Jewish population currently living in Austria are interesting. Whereas the number of Austrian Jews who perished in the Holocaust is estimated at 70,000 (there were 300,000 in 1918, mostly in Vienna), today Austria has approximately 15,000 Jews, only about 800 of whom lived in Austria before World War II. The vast majority are immigrants from the former Soviet Union and other Eastern European countries. While the population of Austrian Jews is a fraction of its former number and neo-Nazis remain a problem, the Jewish community is alive and vigorous. The website of the Jewish community of Vienna lists ten schools of Jewish learning, youth and sports organizations, a publication called *Di Gemeinde* (The Community), kosher grocery stores and restaurants, a home for the aged, and an organization to deal with the psychosocial needs of victims of the Holocaust.

Beatrice Kricheli does not tell us in which of the fifteen synagogues in Vienna her bat mitzvah took place. The elaborate Vienna Synagogue (Stadtempel) is the only prewar survivor of all the former structures. Reopened in 1963, the Vienna Synagogue houses the community's offices amid strict security after a 1982 terrorist attack.

Like many recent bat mitzvah girls around the world, Beatrice comes from an international family whose love and support were important to her, even though her relatives could not participate in her ceremony in person.

Esther, who preferred not to use her last name, is a member of Or Chadasch, the Progressive synagogue in Vienna established in 1991. Or Chadasch is a double haven for Esther, whose sense of Jewish continuity was fractured by the Holocaust and whose spouse, like more and more partners of Jews in open societies, is not Jewish. Thanks to nurturing Jewish institutions in formerly inhospitable places like Austria, Esther's daughter has a chance to grow up with more knowledge and a more positive sense of Jewish identity than did her mother or grandmother.

Beatrice Kricheli

My bat mitzvah was on November 24, 1999. My parents wanted to celebrate with a big bat mitzvah party, but I did not want to. Then they wanted to give me a trip to America, so that I could see my relatives there, and I could see what America was like. But that, too, was not it.

We decided to celebrate my bat mitzvah at home in Vienna with some relatives and close friends. As is usual with Sephardim (I am half Sephardit and half Ashkenasit), we drank wine and people gave toasts. My father said things about my becoming a woman that he had never told me before. I started to cry.

My grandmothers called me from Canada and from Israel. I will never forget their words: "Betty, my darling, now you have become a woman. Never forget how important the Jewish woman is in the whole of Jewish history. Never forget who you are, where you come from, and what you will have to do as a wife, as a mother, and as a daughter. But you will be more than this."

My grandfather, too, was very pleased, because I am his only granddaughter. He talked to me about what it is like to be grown-up, and how I have to make my life as good as I possibly can.

My mother was proud of me. I am the only daughter. She told me, "Betty, my sunshine, a Jewish woman has a lot more to do than you think to keep family life stable and to raise her children." My older brothers were also proud of me and celebrated my bat mitzvah like it was their own bar mitzvah.

I think that after my bat mitzvah a lot of things changed for me. Everybody, including my father, started to treat me more like an adult. As for me, I took on more responsibility and started to see life differently. I did go to America, where I met relatives I had not seen for years. They were really nice and did not treat me like a little girl.

Like me, I hope all Jewish girls have a beautiful bat mitzvah and a beautiful time in their lives.

Esther

"Switch on your tape recorder and learn for your bar mitzvah! Whamm!!" That was mother Bette Midler slamming the door in a movie, ending a major discussion with her twelve-year-old son, as the tape recorder intoned, *Baruch atah Adonai . . .*

A scene from a movie. That was all I had as an outline of what bat mitzvah preparations should be. As the daughter of a non-Jewish father and a Jewish mother who survived the Nazi regime in Vienna as a child, I am provided only with broken traditions and nonexistent family advice. Which would not be a big problem, but . . . I have a daughter who is eleven years old.

When I realized that it was time to start bat mitzvah preparations, I was not concerned about my daughter learning to read Hebrew or about the order of the prayers. And, at eleven, she was such a bright philosopher that writing a speech would not be a problem. My main concern was how to encourage this restrained girl, with such a reserved manner, to speak in front of the community. Her strict "No, I won't do that!" gave me a taste of what would happen if I continued to think about the preparations as I had been doing. And, as I am definitely not a Bette Midler–type mother, it became clear that I needed help.

Irit Shillor, the visiting rabbi at our Progressive congregation, Or Chadasch, has been a tremendous help. Since late autumn last year, she has directed the preparations, which are a patchwork of different efforts. My daughter attends the religion course at the Israelitische Kultusgemeinde (Jewish community) of Vienna, where she learns basic Hebrew and, with great joy, about the background of the holidays she has celebrated since her earliest days.

Rabbi Shillor involved her father, who is non-Jewish, in choosing a Torah portion—"her portion"—together with our daughter, and since then, the main hurdle seems to be overcome. My shy little girl is turning into a young lady who is looking forward to and preparing with quite some gravity for her bat mitzvah next year.

I feel happy with what Rabbi Shillor has accomplished, most of all because I now can concentrate on the real tasks of a mother: planning the meal, inviting family, thinking about dresses, and being proud and nervous at the same time. And I can stop thinking about where Bette Midler might have gotten that tape.

BELGIUM

As in many countries of Europe, Jews are said to have arrived in what is now Belgium with the Roman legions in the first century. At the onset of World War II, there were 100,000 Jews in Belgium. When Nazi Germany invaded Belgium, increasingly harsh measures were enacted against

Jews. For the most part, Belgian non-Jews did not cooperate willingly in murdering the Jews. Twenty-five thousand Belgian Jews perished, a terrible number, but far fewer as a percentage than in other occupied countries. Belgium was among the first countries to establish diplomatic relations with Israel. Today, its 35,000 Jews are centered in French-speaking Brussels and Flemish-speaking Antwerp. There are more than a dozen Jewish schools, five Jewish newspapers, and more than forty-five active synagogues. Belgium is a major center of ultra-Orthodox Jewish life. Established in 1961, the French-language Athénée Ganenou, serving students from nursery school through high school, is located in Brussels and has a general and Jewish curriculum. It also sponsors a day care center for babies starting at three months.

Like in many other places around the world, bat mitzvah preparation at Athénée Ganenou involves the study of the girl's personal family history, as staff member Hava Darmon describes. Tamara Szerer's story illustrates the hardships that Jews endured during the era of World War II. Nethaly Gouray's story speaks of more ancient Jewish history: one of her ancestors was the Maharal of Prague, the famous creator of the mythical Golem. She also mentions her grandfather, a member of the Belgian Resistance, a group that was particularly effective in gathering intelligence and operating clandestine transmitters to pinpoint German positions during World War II.

Hava Darmon, Tamara Szerer, and Nethaly Gouray

HAVA DARMON

For several years, our school, Athénée Ganenou of Brussels, has organized a collective bat mitzvah at the Great Synagogue for girls who have reached the age of twelve. In order to symbolically mark their entrance into the community, they pursue an excellent course of study to learn about the history of the Jews and of their own families. Our program includes:

- a course about the duties of Jewish women, such as Shabbat candle lighting, *Taharat HaMishpacha* (family purity according to Jewish law), rules of kashrut, prayer, the status of women, and Jewish values

- family history, in which the students learn about their own families as a means to learn about the history of the whole Jewish people
- discovering aspects of the Jewish community where our b'not mitzvah live and which they are entering, through visits to community institutions
- a moving ceremony for family and friends at the Great Synagogue of Brussels, the fruit of their studies to symbolically mark their passage into the adult community
- a festive party with beautiful speeches, songs, dances, and food for the bat mitzvah girls and their teachers, relatives, and friends

The following pieces, written by members of the bat mitzvah classes of 2000 and 2002, were read at the ceremonies.

TAMARA SZERER, CLASS OF 2000

Last year, we moved to another house. As I was helping my father arrange some photo albums, I saw a picture of a young boy. He looked strangely like my father, except his clothes were from another time, and his haircut was different. But what was most unusual was that on his jacket, near his heart, was the letter J.

On the back of this photo, it said simply, "May, '42." The boy was handsome, but he looked sad. Certainly, he could never have imagined that one day a Ganenou student would come across his picture and tell his story.

In May of 1942, he would have just turned seventeen. The principal of his school in Seraing had summoned him to tell him terrible news: he could no longer pursue his studies there. The German police were coming to look for Jews in their homes to take them away.

It was time to go into hiding. His family found refuge in a little village in the country. No one could know that they were Jews. They hid for three years, deprived of everything. They were often hungry and had to steal potatoes from the fields.

When I was little, my grandfather took me to the country to show me where he had lived. I remember that he held my hand tightly and hugged me, and I understood everything. He is no longer here, and I miss him very much.

My other grandfather, whom I adore and who is here today, has also told me about this life. I want to tell him, and my grandmother also, "I

Bat mitzvah at the Great Synagogue of Brussels, Belgium, 2002. Photo by Paule Gut.

love you." I can't end this little speech without mentioning my two sisters, whom I love, and my parents, who will remain close to my heart forever.

NETHALY GOURARY, CLASS OF 2002

For me, my bat mitzvah means that as I am learning new things about Judaism and becoming a responsible Jew, I am taking my place in the history of my family. On this bat mitzvah day, I am going to speak about my family's history.

My name, "Gourary," comes from *gour ariè*, which means "little lion," the name of a book written by my ancestor, the Maharal of Prague, who lived from 1512 to 1609. "Maharal" comes from the Hebrew *Morenu Ha-Rav Loew* (Our Teacher, Rabbi Loew). *Loew* means "lion" in German.

In addition to his scholarship, the Maharal was a great humanist and defender of his people. At that time, he already had his thoughts directed toward Israel. He is especially well known in regard to the Golem. Legend attributes to the Maharal the creation of this creature made of mud, who defended the Jewish community when it was accused of ritual crimes.

My grandpa Alexandre Gourary is worthy of the great tradition of our family. During the Second World War, he was a member of the Resistance and helped survivors of the Shoah to get into Israel. I am extremely proud to take my place as a member of my family.

DENMARK

Since their arrival in the 1600s, the small community of Jews in Denmark has progressively gained acceptance by mainstream Danish society, leading to a great deal of intermarriage and assimilation. Danish goodwill was illustrated dramatically during World War II when Danes hid 7,000 Jews, ferried them secretly to Sweden, and thus saved them from the concentration camps and nearly certain death. Currently, there are about 6,000 Jews in Denmark, most of them in Copenhagen.

Bent Lexner is the chief rabbi of Denmark and the spiritual leader of the Great Synagogue of Copenhagen, an Orthodox congregation. Orthodox congregations, particularly in Europe, use the term bat chajil (daughter of valor) to denote the coming-of-age ceremony for girls, which is usually a group affair. But in Rabbi Lexner's congregation, as in many others around the world, the bat mitzvah for an individual girl is becoming more prevalent. In the second part of the essay, based on her personal experience, Hetty Kviat reviews the history of ceremonies for girls at the Great Synagogue.

Rabbi Bent Lexner and Hetty Kviat

BENT LEXNER

The bat chajil has been the normal way of celebrating young girls' coming-of-age for many, many years. Since 1814, our traditional Orthodox community in Copenhagen has had a celebration for young girls on a Sunday during the spring. Today, I would say that only 10 percent still have the Sunday ceremony.

In the last fifteen to twenty years, more and more people have been influenced by bat mitzvah ceremonies in Israel and other countries. Little by little, we have introduced the bat mitzvah, similar to the bar mitzvah, in our community, and today 90 percent of girls choose to celebrate their bat mitzvah in this way

We have the bat mitzvah ceremony in the synagogue after the service on Shabbat morning before *Adon Olam* (a hymn usually sung at the close of the service). The girl has prepared her devar Torah and, just as for bar mitzvah boys, I use the occasion to say something about her and her family, whom I usually know a little. I try then to relate my remarks to her speech. Next, I bless the girl and her family, and very often they invite the congregation for kiddush.

HETTY KVIAT

In Copenhagen, the only place in Denmark where there was an Orthodox Jewish congregation, there were two possibilities when my daughters were young teenagers in the 1990s. We could choose an old-fashioned ritual, meaning that the girl's name, daughter of so-and-so, was read aloud from the bima by the rabbi. Then, the father had a mitzvah (the honor of being called up to the bima), and maybe there was a party at home afterward. That was it. The girl herself didn't do anything active and was not allowed to speak in the synagogue.

Our daughters and most of their friends chose a more active form. The bat chajil is a ceremony a bit like the Protestant confirmation. The ceremony was held on a Sunday in the spring, in the synagogue. That year's group of girls, most of whom were about fourteen years old, had studied with the rabbi since the previous September for two or three hours each Sunday. They also had an obligation to attend all Shabbat services in that period. We, as parents, were also supposed to attend services, which, of course, we did.

At the ceremony itself, the girls entered the synagogue behind the rabbi, dressed in beautiful light dresses and looking their best. They were seated in the area behind the bima. The synagogue was filled with family and friends, and the atmosphere was full of expectation. All the mothers cried, including me. After singing, blessings, and a speech from the rabbi, each girl made a presentation to the congregation. She could choose any topic and speak for about five minutes, standing at the bima and facing the guests. (Photographs were allowed, since it was not Shabbat.)

Both of my daughters spoke about women's rights and peace, critiquing the Orthodox view of women and their role in Jewish life and the lack of possibilities for participation in Jewish ceremonies. The ceremony ended beautifully with a personal blessing, some words of wisdom to every girl by the rabbi, and presentation of a siddur from the congregation. Then, a big party with family and friends.

Starting a couple of years ago, the bat mitzvah became very popular, with even more active participation by the girls, now at age twelve. The bat mitzvah is now a part of the Shabbat service, one girl at a time. At the end of the service, the girl enters from rooms behind the bima. She stands at the bima where, facing the congregation, she offers comments on the day's Torah portion. As before, there are special blessings and extra songs, and her father is offered a mitzvah.

ENGLAND

As in the majority of European countries, Jews have been welcomed at various times in English history and expelled at others. William the Conqueror allowed Jews to immigrate to England from northern France and Germany, but once in England, Jews were victimized widely and subsequently expelled in 1290. Not until the mid-1600s did small groups of Sephardic Jews from Holland and Ashkenazi Jews from Germany return to England. Today, the largest group among British Jews has Central and Eastern European origins.

Currently, there are about 196,000 Jews in greater London—two-thirds of the total national Jewish population, which is shrinking by about 2,000 each year.[1] Older women lead most of the Jewish women's organizations as increasing numbers of younger women work outside the home and participate less in such organizations. On a positive note, women constitute 47 percent of the members of the Board of Deputies, the umbrella organization of British Jews.[2]

Anne Karpf is a London-based writer, journalist, and sociologist. After earning a postgraduate degree in the sociology of health and illness, she taught medical students at London University. A columnist for the *Guard-*

ian and the *Jewish Chronicle,* where the following piece first appeared, Anne broadcasts regularly on BBC radio and television and writes for many national newspapers on social, political, and Jewish issues, especially those pertaining to gender and health. Her article, humorous but true, documents the learning process that mothers, as well as bat mitzvah girls, must undergo.

Radlett, the home of Charlotte Olins, has the highest percentage of Jews—24 percent—of any town in England. Charlotte's story illustrates one way that many Orthodox synagogues have fashioned the bat mitzvah ceremony since the end of the twentieth century. Charlotte is now a student at the University of Birmingham in the north of England.

Rochel Zajac, whose other story appears in this volume in the section on Australia and New Zealand, is the rebbitsen of the Wellington (New Zealand) Hebrew Congregation, where she prepares girls for their bat mitzvah. In the story below, she writes about her life as a young girl in London and remembers her bat mitzvah celebration in amazing detail. An Orthodox girl like Rochel did not have a public ceremony to mark her coming-of-age. Instead, there was a party at home. As she documents in her piece, Jewish adulthood for women was recognized by new obligations in religious and daily life. Rochel's visit to the Lubavitcher rebbe in New York was a significant marker of her coming-of-age. Menachem Mendel Schneerson (1902–1994) was the worldwide leader of the Lubavitch branch of Chassidic Judaism, a movement focused on revitalizing Jewish life.

Anne Karpf

I've never understood the saying about not blowing your own trumpet. Why have one if you don't blow it? And if you blow someone else's, just think of the exchange of saliva—you may as well establish a stud farm for germs.

It's in this spirit that I can now reveal my past year's greatest achievement: I organized a bat mitzvah. Even more astounding, I haven't written about it (until now)—inhibited, I'll admit, by my oldest daughter's practice of charging me each time I mention her in an article. (If I mention the fact that she charges me, she charges me again, and more.) But now it's over, caution has gone the way of the place cards.

When my daughter first said she wanted a bat mitzvah, I dismissed it as a copycat thing. All the girls were doing it, procuring a disco and vast quantities of presents in the name of religion. But crucially, she'd failed to take note of the day of the week when most of these girls' bat mitzvahs were held—Sunday. In other words, they belonged to Orthodox synagogues where the sum total of a bat mitzvah appears to consist of making a speech about their families in English (something my daughter does every mealtime). The same seems to go, in some Liberal synagogues, even for boys on Shabbat. According to my friend Jenny, her brother only had to do a tiny bit in Hebrew and then remind everyone not to commit adultery, and for that he got three traveling alarm clocks and a set of matching luggage labels (real leather, mind). In our synagogue, on the other hand, it's the full Sabbath Monty: the girls chant maftir and haftorah, just like the boys, in Hebrew.

I hope I impress by the effortless way I slipped those [words] in, seeing as one short year ago I had no idea what they meant. Indeed, encountering the rabbi in the corridor after I first attended a bat mitzvah in the synagogue last year, I confessed that I was in a state of panic. Despite reading Hebrew, I couldn't follow a word of the service. I didn't have enough skirts for weekly Shabbat (for it wasn't just her attendance that was required weekly, it was mine too), and as for the kiddush, it was on a scale of lavishness that you only find in films based on Philip Roth novels.

The rabbi, a modern fellow, advised me to obey the first law of the *Hitchhiker's Guide to the Galaxy*: "Don't Panic." So I went out and bought a couple of skirts and, there being an intimate relationship in Judaism between religion and tailoring, soon I was mastering whole chunks of the service. And, of course, what I first chafed against (weekly synagogue attendance), I came to enjoy. Not on account of any sudden inrush of religious belief, but simply for the calming effect of the unchanging nature of the ritual, the beauty of the melodies, and the time out from the eddies of daily life.

I also concluded that in the matter of bat mitzvahs, as in that of births, deaths, and the bits in between, we would be doing it our way. We courted disapproval even with the invitations. Friends had already incurred wide-

Bianca Karpf and her teacher Louis Hirshfield, London, United Kingdom, 2002.

spread wrath when theirs represented the *o* in their son's name with a bagel. Some North London/American Jews clearly believe that the Ten Commandments were written in copperplate, and no other font can serve for a bar or bat invite.

As for the lunch, of some things I was certain. No salmon. No chopped herring in the shape of a Torah scroll. No monogrammed matchboxes or yarmulkes. No electric guitar–strummed *Hava Nagilla,* none of the stuff I've spent my every waking hour in flight from. I heard recently of an £8,000 bill for bar mitzvah flowers. Ours cost £25. As in Zen, so in Judaism—less is more.

And then there was the seating plan. A friend once invented a board game called Broigus: you had to make sure you didn't seat Mrs. Berkovitz next to Mrs. Goldenbaum, and so on. I inflamed some by splitting most couples. The gays insisted on a gay table, but there was also the intellectuals table—so where, asked another friend, did I put the gay intellectuals?

How was it in the end? Wonderful—surprisingly, amazingly wonderful. The kid done great, the choir was fabulous, the sermon wise, the cantor a friend with a beautiful voice, the food terrific. Altogether they created something else, too, shared and extra meaningful to Jew and non-Jew alike: unostentatious but spiritually uplifting.

My parents' families were ruptured by the Holocaust: this was the first bar or bat mitzvah on my mother's side for over seventy years, aptly in a synagogue founded by refugees from Nazism. It therefore also constituted a tiny gesture of repair.[3]

Charlotte Olins

My bat mitzvah was held on June 13, 1998, at Radlett United Synagogue in Hertfordshire close to London, the fastest-growing United Synagogue community in the United Kingdom. I had attended bat chayil classes with seven other girls for a year, a continuation of weekly cheder (religious school) classes. We covered a wide range of subjects, similar to most of my Jewish friends who were preparing for bat mitzvahs. Some of them would have group ceremonies on a Sunday, instead of on Shabbat, like mine.

Girls in our shul are not allowed to read from the Torah, so a ceremony has evolved that takes place at the end of the Shabbat morning service. The choir sings *Ma Tovu* and *Baruch Haba*, followed by a bat mitzvah prayer that the girl reads in English, and then a d'var Torah. My sedra was Beha'alotecha (literally, "when you step up"). I spent many weeks researching, preparing, and writing an insight into the sedra that would be interesting and informative for the congregation, with their varying levels of knowledge. My mum helped me with the research, and it was really nice to do it together. Although I didn't read from the Torah, this didn't particularly worry me; boys often learn their portion parrot-fashion, while I had the opportunity to investigate the sedra in depth. At the end of the ceremony, the rabbi addressed me and gave me a blessing.

Our shul likes to involve other members of the family. Earlier in the service, my sister had prepared and read a sedra synopsis, and my dad re-

Charlotte Olins (*left*), her parents, and her sister, Natalie,
Hertfordshire, United Kingdom, 1998.

cited the haftorah, a great achievement for him, as he had done this only once before, at my sister's bat mitzvah.

It was a moving event for my family and me. I felt proud to carry on the tradition of celebrating my coming-of-age within the Jewish religion, as my older sister had. I particularly enjoyed the intimate and friendly atmosphere of our synagogue, where I knew a lot of the congregants. We continued the celebration with a luncheon at home and a wonderful party at a restaurant on Sunday night.

Rochel Zajac

If I close my eyes and remember, I see my parents' home in London. The house stood proudly at the corner of the street. Yellow daffodils grew in the front garden, slightly bent from the wind, and a tall and not so neatly clipped hedge ran along the front. At age eleven, I was carefree. I wore only flat shoes, buckled in the front. No makeup. My black hair, neither curly nor straight, was tied back. My wardrobe consisted of school uniforms and childish clothes, no suits or imitation grown-up outfits. I think I spent long periods looking at myself in the mirror. I was a bit naive, friendly, and learning how to fit into senior (high) school.

My birthday was during the summer holidays. I never was able to have a proper birthday party with presents because my friends always were on holiday with their families. My birthdays were always spent with my immediate family, so my bat mitzvah celebration was the first proper party I ever had.

We planned the day carefully. It was the first Sunday after Succoth. The new school year had started, and the holidays of the month of Tishrei were over. I was one of the youngest in my class, so I had been to many celebrations before. Most girls had their party at home, but I remember one girl who had hers in a restaurant, the first restaurant that I had been to. They had a cake with fire in the middle. That was a dream bat mitzvah. I knew mine would never be up to that standard.

I gave every girl in my class an invitation. We set up long tables in the front room and dining room. I was a bit nervous about the black-carpeted floor and about the twenty-six girls who were coming. In addition to my friends were my two sisters and an older girl who I had asked to come as a leader, to supervise us. My aunt and uncle and parents and cousins sat in the morning room. The tables were set with flowered paperware and napkins. Every place setting had a small plastic bowl of fruit salad set in front of it.

Usually, the bat mitzvah girl would get up and say a d'var Torah, possibly a point taken from that week's Torah portion, or perhaps about the meaning of bat mitzvah. It was not unusual for the girl's father to address the gathering. I had prepared my short talk on a piece of paper. The time came to say it, and I became too shy. I asked my elder sister, and she spoke instead of me. After the food, we went into the back garden and played games. Looking back, it seems that my bat mitzvah was like a birthday party. Nothing too spiritual or public. No grand speeches, photographers, or rented halls. Just a close group of girls and family members.

But looking deeper, I recall that my bat mitzvah signaled changes in my religious and daily life. There were things that stopped happening at age twelve, and new things we were allowed to begin. One immediate change concerned Yom Kippur. Until bat mitzvah, one isn't obligated to fast, but now it was mandatory. Some girls I knew were allowed to fast before their b'not mitzvah, but my parents never allowed it.

Another change concerned Simchat Torah. When I was growing up, Simchat Torah was the only time of the year when the net curtain between the women's and men's sections of the synagogue was opened. Until bat mitzvah age, girls were allowed to go into the men's section to stand at the back or around the walls. We watched the dancing and chewed away on all kinds of sweets. We knew that after bat mitzvah we would be considered grown women, not able to go into the men's section. At community gatherings, children, both boys and girls, would be called up to the front to recite pesukim (psalms) from the Torah. Once we were b'not mitzvah, we couldn't join in to say them.

Bat mitzvah was also the point at which we were allowed to separate the portion of dough and make the blessing on it when making challah. And in our family, we were allowed to check the eggs for blood only after the age of bat mitzvah.

Some of my friends wrote to the Lubavitch rebbe for a blessing when they became twelve. They would come to school proudly waving the airmail envelope with the blue and red stripes. There was a yearly trip of bat

Rochel Zajac and her father at the home of the
Lubavitch rebbe, Brooklyn, New York, 1987.

mitzvah girls to New York to visit the rebbe. I did not go because I was
younger than most of the girls. The next year, I went with my father and
elder sister. My father, a survivor of Siberian slave labor camps, was very
proud to show off his daughters to the rebbe. We stood in line on a Sunday morning to receive a blessing and a dollar for charity. The rebbe gave
my father a blessing that we should grow up and give him Chassidishe
naches (Chassidic pride.)

On family occasions like b'nai mitzvah, weddings, and my son's brit,
my father says that when he was starving in Siberia he never, ever imagined that he would accompany his children through those stages in life.

FINLAND

Today, there are about 1,400 Jews in Finland. Approximately 1,200 live in Helsinki, the capital of Finland, and about 130 in Turku, the first capital of Finland and now the major port to Sweden, where Karmela Bélinki grew up.

A writer, journalist, and university teacher, Karmela is a senior producer for the Finnish Broadcasting Company and a columnist for several major newspapers in Finland. She is the former director of the Finnish-Norwegian Cultural Institute in Oslo, a past president of WIZO Finland, and the president of the Council of Jewish Women of Finland. She is the author of fiction and nonfiction books and many academic papers, most recently about Jewish themes.

Karmela Bélinki

When I was the right age to have one, the bat mitzvah did not exist in Finland. There were Jewish communities in two cities, Helsinki (Helsingfors) and Turku (Åbo), and a small one without a synagogue in a third city, all of them Orthodox. Girls in Turku, my community, got an excellent Jewish education from teachers imported from Israel, but bat mitzvah preparation was not included.

I was the only child of my family and had very progressive parents. My father taught me everything he would have taught a son. And my mother gave me her ample knowledge of the responsibilities and rights of a Jewish woman. So I became a learned Jew in more ways than one. I never felt the need to go through a formal bat mitzvah ceremony; I knew who and what I was.

Bat mitzvah was introduced in Finland about twenty years ago. Now, it has become as natural to our community as bar mitzvah for boys. Girls are taught by the same teachers as boys and are given the same attention. The joy felt for a bat mitzvah girl is as great as for a bar mitzvah boy.

Due to the high rate of intermarriage in Finland, bat mitzvah preparation has become an especially important learning process. The Jewish day school in Helsinki is a fully accredited, comprehensive school with nine grades. It is part of the general school system, with Hebrew and Jewish subjects included. Bar and bat mitzvah preparation is separate from the regular school curriculum, but taught by the same teacher who teaches other religious subjects. The children are taught the basics in class, but receive individual tutoring and preparation for the ceremony.

FRANCE

France hosts the third-largest Jewish population in the world and the largest in Europe. More than half of the Jewish population of 600,000 people are Sephardi Jews who emigrated from North Africa between the late 1950s and the 1970s. The rest are Ashkenazi Jews with origins in Eastern Europe. Orthodox congregations throughout the country are organized under the bureaucratic *consistoire* system, created by Napoleon in 1808. The system is composed of a central governing body in Paris and twelve other consistories around the country, each with a grand rabbi and other representatives. Liberal (Reform) congregations are comparatively few, although currently they are attracting more members.

Despite the efforts of the French Resistance, 25 percent of French Jews perished in the Holocaust as victims of the World War II Vichy government. This number is lower than that of many of the other countries occupied by the Nazis. The 1990s were particularly disquieting as the anti-Semitic National Front political party came to prominence once again.

Only 20 percent of French Jews are active participants in Jewish communal life;[4] this relatively low number is consistent with the French cultural emphasis on individuality and the nation's suspicion of subcultural community-building. Nevertheless, there are more than forty Jewish weekly and monthly publications, numerous Jewish youth movements and organizations, and a multitude of Jewish social, cultural, and educational organizations. In Paris alone, there are twenty Jewish schools in the day school system. Yabne, the school that Eliana Gurfinkiel attended when she became a bat mitzvah, is Paris's largest Jewish high school. Bnei Akiva, to which her youth group belongs, is a religious Zionist youth movement active in thirty countries, including the United States.

While some women around the world chafe against what they perceive to be a lack of equality in Jewish religious observances and public rituals, others, like Daphna Attali, accept women's traditional roles in Judaism, recognizing the importance of women's separate responsibilities.

Eliana Gurfinkiel

When I became twelve years old a few years ago, I entered the Jewish community. I come from an Orthodox family. We observe Shabbat, we eat kosher food, and since my ninth birthday, I have attended a Jewish school. When I was ten, my sister, Ora, became a bat mitzvah. I saw that that moment was very special in a Jewish girl's life.

During the year of my bat mitzvah, the Jewish education teachers at Yabne, my school, organized a bat mitzvah project. It was a record of the bat mitzvah with photos, discussion issues, and my bat mitzvah speech. We also learned about the importance of women in Jewish tradition. At the end of the year, we had a party with all the bat mitzvah girls; it was very cool.

When my bat mitzvah came, I didn't want to have a party like some of my friends had. My family just offered a kiddush, a meal in our shul. There, I made a speech to my community. It was a commentary on my bat mitzvah parasha, with thanks to my family, my friends, my teachers, and my youth movement, Bnei Akiva. I thought that thanking people was the most important thing to do, because without them, I wouldn't be the same Eliana or the same bat mitzvah Eliana.

I received presents and advice. At home, I would say that I wasn't little Eliana any more. I wasn't a woman yet, but I was changing. At school, thanks to Mrs. Geissman, our full-of-genius teacher of Jewish education, the whole class understood that now we girls had a real place in Jewish society. We don't have to put on tefilin every morning like boys, but we can do some special things to be involved in Judaism. I think that was the most important message I gained from my bat mitzvah.

I dedicate this article to my grandmother Laja Slominska Gurfinkiel, who was not able to be at my bat mitzvah.

Daphna Attali

My brother is seventeen months older than I and turned thirteen in January 1987. My birthday is in July, so my brother and I would have celebrated our bar and bat mitzvah in the same year, six months apart. Therefore, the rabbi and my parents agreed to have both celebrations on the same day, my brother's bar mitzvah day. I was eleven years old, and it was the first time in our synagogue that a bar and bat mitzvah would take place on the same day. Thursday morning would be the day of the first placing of tefilin, Saturday the reading of the haftarah, and Sunday the party. My role in those services was very small, but very significant to me.

Since the age of nine, my brother and I had attended Jewish classes at the Talmud Torah. We learned how to read Hebrew, how to lead a Shabbat service, the history of our people, and the norms and values of Judaism in the Sephardi tradition. The year before his bar mitzvah, my brother attended private sessions in addition to his usual Talmud Torah classes. There, he learned the secrets of reading the Torah. In the Jewish community where I grew up, which is Orthodox, it was normal that I did not do that.

At the Thursday morning service, while my brother practiced the duties of a Jewish man for the first time, I sat on a chair next to the rabbi's chair. At the end of the Torah reading, it was my turn to stand in front of the congregation (where, for the occasion, both men and women sat downstairs, but separated) to read a speech. In it, I expressed my gratitude to my parents and my family for helping me grow up to be a Jewish woman. I also read the *Sim Shalom* prayer at the end of the service. On Saturday morning, all the women sat upstairs, and I sang the *Adon Olam* from the top of the balcony to close the ceremony.

Although my role in the services was limited to a speech and those two beautiful prayers, the celebration of my bat mitzvah had an enormous impact on me. It made me realize the importance of passing on traditions and that being Jewish is not only being part of a people, but is a big part of identity. The practice of religion is very personal, and at some point in life you have to think about what it is going to mean to your future. To what extent do you want to practice Judaism? Is it going to be only an annual observance at Rosh Hashanah or Yom Kippur?

Will I want to have a Jewish home, with a Kabbalat Shabbat every week? Will I keep kosher? Being bat mitzvah made me think deeply about those things. I think that growing up in the Jewish tradition means understanding at a young age that everyone has responsibilities—responsibilities toward a nation and toward oneself in relation to God. I learned that I wanted to carry on the traditions and pass them on to my own children.

GERMANY

Germany is home to Europe's third-largest and fastest-growing Jewish population, a result of a massive influx of Jews from the former Soviet Union. When the Berlin Wall fell in the early 1990s, at least 200,000 immigrants arrived, joining the 25,000 aging Jews who formed the last remnant of Germany's Jewish community. The new residents have been awarded work rights and offered citizenship. They also have received a variety of social services to help them acclimate.

Ashkenazi Jews originated in the Middle Ages in communities in western Germany along the Rhine River, where they spoke a dialect that evolved into Yiddish. In its 1,700-year history in Germany, the Jewish community was sometimes accepted and sometimes subjected to special taxation, segregation, violence, and expulsion. Despite a spike in anti-Semitism and neo-Nazi activities since the late twentieth century, the Jewish community remains vital and optimistic.

In 1988, Rabbi Yisroel and Chana Diskin were sent as emissaries to establish the first Chabad center in Germany. In 2005, Chana Diskin told the *Jewish Telegraphic Agency*, "When we came [to Munich], Judaism was based on Holocaust identity and very little joy. We aimed to show that Judaism is relevant in our modern times. It is not about constantly commemorating a tragic history. We are not allowed to forget it, but there is so much more." At the Luitpold Gymnasium, the Munich public school that Albert Einstein attended, Chana teaches Jewish religion courses to grades five through eight and prepares the "future mothers and nurturers of the Jewish nation," as she describes in her contribution.

Cologne, which has been a home to Jews since Roman times, is the oldest Jewish community in Northern Europe. The synagogue where Hedvah Ben Zev's husband is cantor was built in 1899, destroyed during Kristallnacht on November 9, 1938, and rebuilt in 1959. Pope Benedict's 2005 visit to the synagogue, where he addressed the assembled congregation with respect and cordiality, was widely endorsed and praised. Hedvah's story is another illustration of the evolution of the bat mitzvah ceremony in response to changing Jewish populations and their needs.

Chana Diskin

The "traditional" way for a girl in Munich to celebrate her bat mitzvah was to have a party with disco music, dancing, great decorations, and elaborate party favors. The main Jewish aspect of this event was usually a candle-lighting ceremony, when family and friends would be honored with the lighting of twelve candles.

A group of sincere parents and community leaders approached me, as an educator in the city and in my capacity as the Chabad rebbitzen, seeking a viable alternative to this kind of superficial party. They felt that girls who are coming of age should have the possibility of celebrating their bat mitzvah with a meaningful religious ceremony that would also be halachically acceptable.

The idea we agreed upon was a Friday evening ceremony. We decided that the bat mitzvah girl, together with her mother, would light the Shabbat candles. She would read aloud a *Yehi Ratzon* prayer in Hebrew and in German, and then the guests would proceed to the synagogue where Friday evening services are usually held. At the conclusion of the prayers, the women would join the men in the main sanctuary for speeches by the rabbi and the bat mitzvah girl. Then, the guests would be invited to a festive Friday night dinner.

As preparation, we established the Bat Mitzvah Club. All of the girls who will be twelve in the upcoming year are invited to attend. The club reaches beyond the common conception of a group that simply prepares girls for the ceremony. It serves as a forum for discussion and for discovery of the true meaning of bat mitzvah. As the club's leader, I encourage

DUKE

U N I V E R S I T Y

PRESS · PUBLICITY

B O X   9 0 6 6 0

D U R H A M · N C

2 7 7 0 8 - 0 6 6 0

Laura Sell
Publicity

(919) 687-3639
telephone

(919) 688-4391
fax

lsell@dukeupress.edu
email

REVIEW COPY

INFORMATION PLEASE

Culture and Politics in the Age of Digital Machines

Mark Poster

Price:

Paper	(0-8223- 3839-4)	$ 22.95
Library cloth edition	(0-8223- 3801-7)	$ 79.95

(Please note that unjacketed cloth editions are primarily for library use. Non-library reviewers should quote the paperback price.)

Publication Date: October 3, 2006

*Please send two copies of the published review.

the girls to learn more about this unique time in their lives and to gain new perspectives on their positions as women, as adults, and as Jews. The girls enjoy a combination of learning and fun through regular meetings and occasional special activities.

We practice the prayers of the Friday night services so that the girls can be active participants at both their own and their friends' bat mitzvah celebrations. Together, we also discuss and explore major issues confronting Jewish teenagers today, sharing opinions, feelings, and frustrations in an open and honest manner. Then it is left up to the girls and their families to decide how they want to celebrate the bat mitzvah.

I encourage all the club members to celebrate in a meaningful way. Many girls do not feel comfortable speaking in public or being the center of attention. These girls opt for a more private celebration. Some choose to celebrate using the ceremony I have described and have found it to be very special and meaningful for them. As their teacher and as a guest at the celebrations, I have been moved by the spirituality of the events and the pride they have imbued in the future mothers and nurturers of the Jewish nation.

Hedvah Ben Zev

My husband is the communal chazzan in Cologne. In Orthodox circles in England, where my husband and I come from, a bat mitzvah is not usual. If it is done at all, it is on a Sunday afternoon, preferably for a whole group of girls together. Family and friends join in a little party, the rabbi comes, and the girls give speeches showing what they have learned.

In Germany before the war, I believe it was much the same. After the war, things changed a lot. Now, we have the so-called *Einheitsgemeinde*. It means that, although the rabbi, the chazzan, and the service are Orthodox, and the restaurant and mikvah are kosher, all kinds of Jews can become members and join in the services. The more Liberal members (especially their daughters) want some kind of bat mitzvah celebration in shul on Shabbes.

So, over the years, it was agreed to let the girls come down from the women's gallery just before mussaf starts. From the middle of the synagogue, the girl gives a speech with religious content about either a "female" subject or the weekly parsha. When she finishes, the rabbi addresses her, trying to find a connection between her Hebrew name and the parsha, or between the content of the parsha and women, or something like that. She receives a siddur, given in the name of the community and then goes back to her seat in the gallery. As an extra gift, she can keep this seat for a whole year without paying for it. In this way, we try to draw the girls to the services.

After the service, the girl's family gives a kiddush in the hall. She thanks the teacher, the rabbi, the community, her patient younger brother, and so on, and is given a Chumash. At moza'ei Shabbes, some families have a big party in a hotel. (Sometimes the hotel is kashered, but mostly not.) Others celebrate with a party at home.

I think girls should be given the opportunity to prove their abilities and knowledge. The way this should happen is primarily a matter of community policy. However, we know of families, mostly new immigrants from the former Soviet Union, whose daughters do not want bat mitzvah ceremonies. In these cases, we do not try to push them, as long as they join the religious classes. The bat mitzvah should never be only a glamorous, fancy party. The important thing is the religious spirit behind it.

GREECE

One of the most popular tourist sites in Athens is the Jewish Museum of Greece, which contains artifacts, photographs, a reconstructed synagogue from Patras, and a room representing the interior of a Jewish home during the time of the Ottoman Empire. Zanet Battinou is the director of the museum and a past president of Bat El, a cultural group for professional Jewish women.

The Jews of Greece have a rich, ancient, and ultimately tragic history. By the first century CE, there were flourishing Jewish communities in most of the major Greek cities. Archaeological evidence suggests that the culturally assimilated "Romaniot" Jews lived like their Christian neighbors. When Greece became part of the Ottoman Empire, Jews fleeing the Spanish Inquisition made their way to Greece, which welcomed the economic stimulation they brought. This wave of immigration by Sephardic Jews caused many Romaniot communities, such as Thessaloniki and the island of Rhodes, to adopt the customs and language (Ladino) of the Sephardic newcomers.

By 1939, there were 70,000 Jews in Greece. Despite their long history of being productive, peaceful members of Greek society, beginning in 1943 the local authorities began to deport Greek Jews to German extermination camps. Some were saved by courageous local officials, depending on where they lived. After the war, under the leadership of George Papandreou, Greece was the first European nation to return Jewish properties that had been confiscated, but fewer than 10,000 Jews remained. Currently, about 5,000 Jews are left in nine Greek cities and towns; 3,000 of them live in Athens.

Zanet Battinou

It seems strange to be asked to write about my bat mitzvah, because I never had one. In my hometown of Ioannina, the small Jewish community numbered about ninety people. I was the only girl my age, and there was no organized Jewish school or permanently employed rabbi to teach me. Rabbis used to travel to my town from other communities in Greece or from abroad to officiate during the High Holidays or Pesach. In order to have a bat mitzvah, I was told that I would have to join a group of girls my age in the town of Larissa, which had a larger community but was 200 kilometers away. As I did not really know those girls, I felt uncomfortable and declined altogether. Besides, the bat mitzvah was not considered a very important rite of passage in my family in the year 1977. My mother had not had hers, for reasons very similar to mine, and no one seemed too concerned when I decided against it.

About a year and a half later, my closest pal (and cousin by marriage), who lived in Larissa, had her bat mitzvah there with five or six other girls. I attended the proceedings and was not too impressed. The individual attention and excitement that accompany a bar mitzvah were lacking. There was no reading from the Torah, and the girls were wearing bridal-type white dresses, which looked ridiculous to my irreverent adolescent eyes! And to top it all off, they did not receive the pens, cameras, books, and cash that any boy would receive for his religious coming-of-age. Instead, they were given singularly uninteresting and even offensive items for their future trousseau, which is something that every self-respecting Greek Jewish girl is expected to amass from a young age. Since I had absolutely no use for embroidered items, doilies, blankets, and velveteen bathroom mats, I was almost glad, and secretly congratulated myself on having decided against a potentially embarrassing and possibly bothersome ceremony. When I think about it today, I can hardly believe the degree to which the spiritual and communal (if not the religious) meaning of the bat mitzvah as a rite of passage had escaped me at that stage of my life.

Years later, living in Cape Town, South Africa, as a young adult, I found myself part of a large, active, vibrant Jewish community. The bat mitzvah, as well as other Jewish ceremonies, traditions, and celebrations, took on new meaning and substance. It evolved before my eyes into an important, attractive milestone of human growth.

Then, I found out that I could still have a bat mitzvah if I wanted to, even as a grown-up. I thought about it a few times, but never really got around to doing it. More years passed. I am now back in Greece, married to a wonderful man, and expecting my first child, a daughter. Who knows? Maybe our daughter and I could have our b'not mitzvah together!

HOLLAND

When the Netherlands became a leader in world shipping and trade, it attracted Sephardi Jews who had been forced out of their homelands by the Spanish and Portuguese Inquisitions. In the seventeenth century, these Sephardi Jews were joined by Ashkenazi Jews from Germany and Eastern Europe. Portuguese Jews, especially, were successful in the tobacco, sugar, printing, and diamond industries, and Jews lived freely, without the fear of anti-Semitic violence, which was prevalent in other countries of Europe. In May 1940, when the Germans invaded and then occupied Holland, 140,000 Jews lived in communities throughout the country. Although many families, like that of Anne Frank, went into hiding, the vast majority of Jews were discovered and deported. After the war, only 20 percent of the Jewish population had survived and remained in Holland. The Jewish population has stayed stable at 25,000–30,000 in recent years.

Bettina Sanders is a co-founder of DEBORAH, an Orthodox Dutch Jewish women's group, and a founding member of Tamar, an interfaith feminist organization. A past president of WIZO Holland, she has co-edited feminist books and lectures widely on Jewish subjects. The Portuguese synagogue (the Esnoga) where Bettina's daughter participated in a creative bat mitzvah ceremony somehow remained undamaged during the war. Inaugurated in 1675, the building has had some renovation but retains its essential character. The floor is covered with sand "in the old Dutch fashion," according to the synagogue's website, "to absorb dust, moisture and dirt from shoes and to muffle the noise."

Bettina Sanders

You know the date of a bat mitzvah for a long time, from the time your daughter is born. But in our case, the kind of ceremony was uncertain. When Tsifjah was born in 1973, the feminist bug did not yet infect me. But later on, my husband and I came under the influence of Jewish Orthodox feminism. We did not want the traditional party or costly affair devoid of a meaningful ceremony. We decided that Tsifjah had to learn something from her bat mitzvah, that she had to put the same energy into learning as her brother had a few years earlier, studying his sidra for a whole year. Those were the conditions.

But what could we do? Until then, b'not mitzvah in our community were celebrated by a kiddush in shul after the service. During the kiddush, the girl would give a small d'var Torah. This was not what we liked. We wanted a special service dedicated completely to the bat mitzvah, with the same role for our daughter as was true for a boy when he reads in shul. The community should get to know the new member who is coming of age.

We did not have examples within the Orthodox scene in Holland that we could copy. We consulted several Orthodox feminists in Israel and the United States, including Pnina Peri and Blu Greenberg. They gave us advice, but a shul service where the bat mitzvah would read from the bima and the men would sit, for once, behind the mechitsa was out of the question for us. Also, reading from the Torah was not acceptable—not because we did not want it, but the bat mitzvah did not like the idea of being different from the other girls at her school. So we decided that we had to compromise.

My husband thought of a solution and went to our rabbi, a respected man with a lot of authority. We suggested that our daughter, from behind the mechitsa, read some psalms during an afternoon service. To our surprise, he was enthusiastic and willing to cooperate, saying, "It is very important that special attention should be paid to the bat mitzvah girl, because she has to fulfill the mitzvot as well." He wanted to choose the psalms for my daughter to read during the special service we would organize for her. Then he added, "If you invite me, I am very willing to come." So he was added to the guest list.

On June 16, 1985, we celebrated Tsifjah's bat mitzvah in the summer synagogue of the Portuguese community with our family and friends. Tsifjah read her part from behind the mechitsa. She was standing on a chair, because she was very short and nobody could see her otherwise. She had on a white dress and wore a white hat, which she liked a lot. Afterward, the rabbi complimented us on the meaningful service. He told us that he liked the idea, and hoped that there would be many celebrations of this kind in the future.

The reception was followed by a walk through the old Jewish quarter of Amsterdam. Afterward, we had a party in the old [beit] midrash, where our daughter told the assembled guests about her sidra, Korach (literally, "ice," "hail," or "frost"), which she could translate from beginning to end, and gave a d'var Torah.

Regrettably, we have had only two similar bat mitzvah ceremonies in Holland since then. These are people who, like us, have the opinion that there is no difference between a bat and a bar mitzvah, that a girl should get her share. For one of them, our Portuguese-Sephardic friends did it their own Sephardic way: a few nights before the bat mitzvah party, a limud (learning) was organized where their daughter learned something in public. The other celebration was similar to ours, not surprising because the mother and father are modern Orthodox like us, and hold similar ideas.

I thought that in due time my daughter would appreciate that we brought some renewal to the stuffy traditional bat mitzvah service. But today my daughter still complains that she had to endure the feminist ways of her parents!

IRELAND

Emigration, intermarriage, and assimilation have reduced the Irish Jewish population from about 6,000 in the 1940s to an estimated 1,800 today, with a slight uptick as the economy improved in recent years. Small Jewish communities existed as early as the Middle Ages, but today's Irish Jews trace their ancestry back primarily to Lithuanian Jews who fled oppression and pogroms in the 1880s, landing in Dublin and Cork. In an overwhelmingly Catholic country, Jews have always been a tiny minority, but they were never persecuted. Chaim Herzog, a former president of Israel, grew up in Dublin. Jews have been members of parliament and mayors of Dublin and Cork. (Perhaps the most famous Irish Jew is fictional: Leopold Bloom, the protagonist of James Joyce's *Ulysses*.) The community in Dublin, where most Jews live, supports a home for the aged, a museum, a mikvah, a kosher butcher and bakery, and a school. The Dublin Jewish Progressive Congregation is one of three synagogues. (The other two are Orthodox.) In her essay, synagogue president Sue Woolfson describes the bat mitzvah program as identical to the bar mitzvah program for boys.

Sue Woolfson

The first bat mitzvah ceremony was held at the Dublin Jewish Progressive Congregation in 1948. Rabbi Kokotek conducted the ceremony for four girls. Bat mitzvah ceremonies were held at Shavuoth, and the girls did not read from the Torah. This soon changed, as it was decided that girls could read from the Torah, although they still shared the ceremony.

For many years now, at least twenty-five, girls in our synagogue have been treated exactly the same as the boys. Most of the ceremonies, both for boys and girls, are individual. Girls become bat mitzvah at age thirteen, having completed a bar/bat mitzvah course, in which they build on what they have learned at cheder. They read their Torah and haftorah portions, and many of them also lead at least part of the Shabbat morning service.

Girls in our synagogue do not wear a tallith or yarmulke, although there is no prohibition on their doing so, should they so desire.

ITALY

The Jewish community of Rome is one of the oldest in the world, established by Jewish envoys of Judah Maccabee a hundred years before the Common Era. The oldest ghetto in Europe was established in Venice in 1516 and lasted until Napoleon destroyed its gates. Although the majority of Italians refused to cooperate with the Nazi plan to eliminate the Jews of Italy, 20 percent of the Jewish population perished in the Holocaust. Today, about 40,000 Jews live in Italy.

Throughout their history, Italian Jewish women have shown remarkable independence. During the Renaissance, Anna the Hebrew made and sold cosmetics to Italian noblewomen. Doña Gracia Nasi was a famous businesswoman, patron of the arts, and political leader who came to the aid of poor Jews and invited them to eat at her table daily.[5]

The bat mitzvah ceremony was established in Italy at the beginning of the 1800s. Significantly, Rabbi Mordecai Kaplan attended a bat mitzvah in Rome in 1922. Later that year, his daughter Judith became the first bat mitzvah in the United States.

Giorgina Vitale's dramatic story begins in Turin, where she celebrated her bat mitzvah. Turin, the capital of the Piedmont region of northern Italy, has been home to Jews since the fifteenth century. Between 1941 and 1943, many Jewish families, including Giorgina's, were forced to leave their homes, hiding in the country or the mountains among people who kept their secrets.

The neo-Moorish synagogue of Turin (Tempio Israelitico), where Giorgina's sister Lina was married amid the ruins, was restored soon after the war with public and private contributions. Today, it houses community offices, a private school, a home for the aged, and a library. Giorgina is a former director of the Women's Division of the United Jewish Appeal in New Haven, Connecticut, and an active volunteer with the Hebrew Home in New Haven, SeniorNet, and Yale–New Haven Hospital.

The magnificent synagogue of Casale Monferrato, where Serena Tedeschi celebrated her bat mitzvah, is also in the Piedmont region, about an hour's drive from Turin. Built in 1595, the synagogue is a rare example of late Piedmontese baroque design, with a beautifully decorated ceiling. Casale (population 36,000) shares its history with Turin as a hub of Jewish culture. Today, it seeks to maintain that heritage, despite the fact that only a handful of Jewish residents remain. The synagogue, which has been called one of the most beautiful in the world, has been restored. It now houses a museum and is open for its small congregation on Yom Kippur. Serena Tedeschi maintains a love of her mother's birthplace and helped to design the website that describes the community and its museum complex.

Giorgina Vitale

It was 1938, a year that promised wonderful things for a twelve-year-old girl. We had moved from Turin to Milan just two years before, but I was already accustomed to the change. I liked my school and my teachers. I had lots of friends, and a wonderful family life. I had turned twelve in February, the age of bat mitzvah for Italian Jewish girls, and the ceremony would take place in May, at Shavuoth, when all the girls would stand on the bimah together, recite some prayers, and receive the rabbi's blessing.

I prepared for my bat mitzvah in Milan, but I knew the ceremony would take place in Turin, where most of our relatives lived. Synagogues in Italy are Orthodox, so girls do not read from the Torah and do not chant a haftorah. They study the Bible, Hebrew, and Jewish history, and then go through an oral exam with the rabbi, who declares them ready (or not) to become daughters of the covenant.

I passed the exam and was eager and happy. My sister, Lina, just a year older than me, had become a bat mitzvah the year before, so I knew what to expect. My cousin Pina, who lived in Rome, would join us in Turin and become a bat mitzvah with me and the other twelve-year-old girls. Furthermore, our family was joyously expecting a new baby in July, and we were anxiously counting the days to the happy event.

It was a memorable day. All the girls were dressed like brides in white, a custom probably derived from Catholic communion. Pictures were taken in the synagogue (not with the rabbi's blessing, I imagine). More pictures of the group and their families were taken outside. After changing into

Giorgina Vitale's sister Lina (*left*) in her bat mitzvah outfit
with her mother and Giorgina, Turin, Italy, 1937.

regular clothing, we went to the park for more pictures, and then to a restaurant for a luncheon in Pina's and my honor.

I had lived in Turin most of my life. My grandparents, my father's three
brothers, one of my mother's sisters, and a host of great-uncles, great-
aunts, and cousins lived within blocks of each other, near the Jewish Community Center, which included the synagogue, the Talmud Torah, the
Jewish home for the aged, and the orphanage.

Near my father's and uncles' store was the park where we children played
together. As the business continued to expand and prosper, my father and
his brothers decided to open stores in Milan and Rome. So in 1935 we had
moved to Milan, where my father managed the new store, while one of his
brothers moved to Rome, where another store was opened.

It was a difficult decision to separate the family, especially for the older
generation. But Milan is only about eighty miles from Turin, and we drove
back almost every other weekend to visit our grandparents and the rest of
the family. The Rome contingent was too far for frequent visits, and only

important rites of passage brought us all together to celebrate. Pina's and my bat mitzvah was such an occasion, and our happiness was complete.

Of all the gifts I received, I remember most a beautiful brass *hanukki-yah* (menorah), which I still have and use; a gold ring with the word *Shadai* (Almighty) on it; a giant box of blue stationery, which I used for a very long time, even when I was corresponding many years later with my future husband; a ceramic figurine of a young girl washing clothes in a tub, which I still have; and a photo album, which I filled with my bat mitzvah pictures and cherished.

In July, a little sister, Emilia, named for our maternal grandmother, joined our family. Lina and I became two little mothers for her; we adored her, and so did the rest of the extended family.

But 1938, a year that began with such promise and happiness, turned into a year of despair. I cannot think of my bat mitzvah without recalling every event of that fateful year. It was probably the most important year of my life for the development of my character, my personality, and my dreams. That is why I am telling this story.

In September, the whole family was gathered, as usual, in my grandfather's summer home to celebrate his birthday and enjoy the grape harvest. One evening at the dinner table, one of my uncles opened the newspaper, showing us the headline that announced that all Jews were excluded from public schools at the start of the academic year. The Nuremberg Laws against the Jews had come into force that day, bringing severe restrictions.

With the public schools closed to Jews, the Jewish community back home in Milan worked together to enlarge the day school to accommodate every Jewish student up to college level. That school became my inspiration and my haven. What it lacked in space, it made up in the quality of the teachers and students. For the first time, I was introduced to Zionism. I embraced it with the fervor of a young pioneer. We learned modern Hebrew, sang the songs of the halutzim (pioneers), and dreamed of our return to Zion.

But it was also the beginning of years of sacrifice, danger, and humiliation. In September 1943, during the German occupation of Italy, we went into hiding, with false names and identification papers. We were in hiding for two years. I brought my precious bat mitzvah photo album with me. I hid it under the hay in the hayloft, and looked at it only occasionally, when I was up there doing chores.

One day, the Germans came, as they regularly did, going from house to house looking for guns and for young men who had deserted the army. They went through our house, then up to the hayloft, and stabbed the mounds of hay with their bayonets. They didn't find anything. But after they left, I took my album and burned it. So I don't have even one picture of my bat mitzvah, only the memories, which will always be with me.

After liberation in April 1945, Lina, who during all those years had been engaged to a young man who had joined the partisans and whose family was in hiding not far from where we were, was finally able to set a wedding date. Lina and Giorgio's wedding was the first wedding performed in the almost-destroyed synagogue in Turin, with the chuppah standing among the ruins and everyone showing signs of the tragedy they had survived.

We had celebrated Lina's bat mitzvah in the same synagogue eight years before, and mine the year after. I have a picture of the synagogue at that time, a magnificent sanctuary with marble walls, with prayers and the sayings of the fathers etched in gold. During an air raid by the Allies, it had been completely gutted, with only the outside wall remaining. Now, Lina's wedding ceremony seemed to signify the rebirth of a people who had been almost reduced to ashes by the evil schemes of a world gone mad. There wasn't a dry eye that day.

Serena Yael Tedeschi

My mother's family comes from Casale Monferrato, a small town not far from Torino (Turin), where I live. I became a bat mitzvah a few years ago, on the Sunday after Shavuot in the synagogue of the Orthodox congregation of Casale Monferrato. In the moving atmosphere of the synagogue, I was very excited. It was full of all of the relatives and friends we invited. I went inside with my father, and we reached the duchan (pulpit) while the chazan was singing *Baruch Abah* (a welcome) according to a very ancient minhag. After I read the Eshet Hayl and some other verses of tehillim (psalms) as the Italian tradition dictates, I received the bracha from both the rabbi and my father. Later, I gave a drasha (sermon) concerning the parshah of the week, and thanked my teachers and my family. I was really

Serena Yael Tedeschi at her bat mitzvah in the beautiful
synagogue of Casale Monferrato, Italy, 2000.

thrilled, and aware of the responsibilities I was accepting. I understood
that, from that day on, I had to keep alive our culture and its deep roots.
The ceremony finished with religious and traditional Jewish songs sung
by all the congregation. It was an incredible day that I think and hope I
will never forget for the rest of my life.

My family, except for my great-grandmother, z"l, has never been very
religious, but has always observed the major Jewish holidays. Months after my bat mitzvah, I began to attend more services at the synagogue and
to be involved in the activities of the Bnei Akiva youth group. I became
shomeret mitzvoth (observant of Jewish laws).

LUXEMBOURG

The joy of Vivian Rosenbaum's international bat mitzvah is captured in
the essay by her father, Harry, who describes the planning and flexibility
that were called for on the part of the family and the rabbi. The main syna-

gogue of Luxembourg is modern Orthodox. Expatriates like the Rosenbaum family make up the congregation of Liberal Or Chadash. Currently, the official Jewish census of Luxembourg is 600, mostly in Luxembourg City, the capital.

Harry Rosenbaum

Vivian is Bruno's younger sister and the Rosenbaums' only girl. Her family is half Swiss and half Brazilian. Her parents met in London, got married in Zurich, and lived and worked in several countries before coming to the Grand Duchy of Luxembourg at the beginning of 2000. There, they found a thriving Liberal Jewish community, of which they soon became active members.

Vivian's bat mitzvah, the first in the four-year history of the community, Or Chadash, was planned as a big event from the start. Since the families and friends of both parents were to be gathered in from Switzerland, Brazil, and other places, it had to be an occasion to make long-distance travel worthwhile. But most important to her family was Vivian's religious confirmation. While the Rosenbaums are no zealots, they very much wanted to give Vivian the opportunity to publicly affirm her faith and her adherence to her Jewish inheritance.

The Liberal community in Luxembourg is not large enough to have a full-time rabbi, so student rabbi Aaron Goldstein from London, who has acted as rabbi on several occasions, kindly agreed to come over especially for Vivian's bat mitzvah. He prepared her Torah text, and when he told Vivian she would not have to sing, but could speak the words in Hebrew, he won a great fan.

After careful consideration, Rabbi Aaron offered the following thoughts about Vivian's Torah portion:

> The Torah portion of the day would not be appropriate. It is all about leprosy. In the Liberal tradition, we are perfectly happy to change the Torah reading for a week. That Shabbat is also Rosh Chodesh and Shabbat Atzmaut (Israeli Independence Day). Let's choose a different Torah portion to reflect these events. It may be fairer to Vivian to read and learn more about these portions.

The leadership committee of the Liberal community kindly allowed the Rosenbaums a free hand to organize the entire Shabbat service on the day of Vivian's bat mitzvah. With that, Lucia, her mom, took control decisively, with remarkable results.

Some of the highlights of that memorable weekend were a dinner on the night prior to the bat mitzvah, with many family members and friends, and Vivian being feted by all; the Shabbat lunch at the Hotel Royal for the entire Liberal community of Luxembourg, with kosher champagne, a pianist, and splendid decorations; a guided tour of Luxembourg for the out-of-towners; and a private dinner reception in the evening. Suffice it to say that the Liberal community still talks about this more than one year after the event.

The bat mitzvah provided the background for one of the best Shabbat services the Liberal Jews of Luxembourg had ever had. There were about eighty people present, a large crowd for a small community. Rabbi Aaron's personality was an important element in the success of the bat mitzvah. He is a young man with an unconventional, youthful approach to Judaism—just the person you want for such an event. He enthusiastically encouraged the congregation to participate in the service to a degree that was new for everybody. He was particularly successful with the many children and young adults who were present, including non-Jewish school friends of Vivian and Bruno. (Two couples had baby-naming ceremonies during the service, adding to the festivity.)

Rabbi Aaron had prepared the Shabbat service based on the siddur Lev Chadash, the prayer book of the Union of Liberal and Progressive Synagogues. Since not everyone in the congregation was able to read Hebrew, he provided English transliterations of the key prayers and songs, which were given to all. Vivian read the Torah earnestly and clearly, and looked beautiful.

Shortly before her bat mitzvah, a terrorist had bombed another girl's bat mitzvah in Israel, a fact to which Vivian referred in the speech she gave. When she addressed the community and guests in German, Portuguese, English, and French, grandmothers, grandfather, aunts, uncles, friends, and guests from five countries wiped away tears and gave her a big ovation. The prayer *Od Yavo Shalom Aleynoo* (Peace Will Yet Come for All of Us) was a heartfelt and bittersweet ending. Vivian did her family proud, and even managed to enjoy the day herself.

MALTA

Rosalind Dobson, who now resides in Eilat, where she is active in the Masorti (Conservative) community, was one of the few Jews on the island of Gozo, six kilometers from Malta, a larger island in the Mediterranean south of Sicily. A Phoenician site excavated by archaeologists revealed evidence that Jewish mariners first arrived in Malta 3,500 years ago. In January 2000, a new synagogue for the twenty-five Jewish families of Malta was consecrated in Valletta, the capital, to take the place of the old synagogue that was demolished in 1979.

Rosalind Dobson

Life in Gozo, Malta's sister island in the middle of the Mediterranean, was often a challenge for my daughter, Louise, and me. We perceived ourselves as a small island of Judaism in the midst of a Catholic sea. This was understandable, as we represented two-fifths of the total Jewish presence on this small island of 25,000 people.

As Louise grew up, there were two important rites of passage for her friends: holy communion at seven years of age and *grizma* (confirmation) at twelve. The latter appeared to be based on our own bar and bat mitzvah ceremonies, as it marked the change in status from child to adult. These events were celebrated in great style. For holy communion, the girls wore magnificent mini-bridal dresses, in some cases costing many hundreds of dollars. (Eventually the church stepped in and ruled that the cost of such gowns was unfair to poor families, and only a simple—and extremely ugly—white cotton dress could be worn.) Boys wore black suits and white shirts, with a white ribbon tied around one arm. For *grizma*, the girls would wear fancy formal dresses in any color other than white. Each child would have a party to honor the occasion, where gifts of gold jewelry were often given.

When Louise's peer group reached each of these important milestones, there was nothing for her to celebrate, and as she approached age twelve, she began to ask about organizing a bat mitzvah. Although she had always had a great sense of her Jewish identity, made even stronger by various inept attempts at conversion by the nuns at her elementary school, she had never been interested in the formal side of our religion. So my first reaction was delight.

One of the few other Jewish families who lived in Malta had a daughter a little younger than Louise, and they suggested that the two girls have a joint bat mitzvah. But there were many problems caused by a combination of circumstances. For one thing, there was the difficulty of going over to Malta for regular bat mitzvah lessons, a six-hour round trip by ferry from Gozo to Malta, as well as a road journey. For another, there was the lack of time; there was always masses of homework to be done, making it almost impossible to fit in any other activities. So, sadly, in the end, a bat mitzvah wasn't possible. I felt guilty about the situation, but there was no solution.

Happily, the lack of a bat mitzvah hasn't affected Louise's sense of Jewish identity. She is now studying at the medical school of Manchester University in England, and I am delighted to say she is actively involved in Jewish student life. She works for the Aliyah Department as the Israel ambassador on campus to all four universities in the city, where her work includes promoting volunteer programs in Israel. She frequently visits Israel and hopes to make aliyah eventually.

NORWAY

Shari Nilsen's piece shows that bat mitzvah celebrations do not have to be lavish to be meaningful. The Jewish community in Oslo, where the majority of Norwegian Jews live (there also is a small community in Trondheim), has never numbered more than 1,000. Events leading to World War I brought Jews from Eastern Europe, especially Poland and Lithuania. These families form the basis of the Jewish community today. The Holocaust was disastrous for Norwegian Jews, as they were deported from German-occupied Norway under President Vidkun Quisling. Today, it appears that Shari has reason to be hopeful, as the Jewish community, under the leadership since the 1970s of Rabbi Michael Melchior, has increased slightly in size and supports a number of vital Jewish institutions from a nursery to an old-age home.

Shari Nilsen

Bat mitzvah. These words conjure up pictures of lavish spreads, generous gifts, rote memorization of incomprehensible words, DJs playing the latest hits for sweaty teenagers at a catered party. At least, that's how my bat mitzvah was in the sixties, when I lived in a well-off suburb of a mid-sized American city and belonged to a Reconstructionist synagogue. When my daughter was ready for hers, in 1993, the situation was totally different.

I had married a Norwegian man who, although not Jewish himself, generously and wholeheartedly supported my wish to give our children a Jewish identity. There aren't many Norwegian Jews. Our little community consists of about 950 members, of whom fewer than 150 are active enough to go to services regularly. There is one synagogue in Oslo, and the decision was made long ago to maintain the Orthodox ritual. When there's only one game in town, you either take it or leave it. After a good deal of soul searching, I decided to take it.

So my daughters went to cheder and sat with me up in the women's gallery during services. And when it was time for Sara to have her bat mitzvah, there was not even a ghost of a chance of her reading from the Torah at the bimah. Here, a bat mitzvah means that, at the kiddush, after Saturday morning services, the girl recites a paragraph or two from the day's Torah reading, and then gives a short summary and interpretation of it. The whole thing lasts about three minutes. Then the crowd (if you can call it that) digs into the coffee and cakes. That's it.

The mom (being me, of course) has the privilege of baking for weeks in advance to try to make the day a little bit special for her daughter. I had been in the States a few months earlier, where I had ordered pink napkins with gold printing on them, reading "Sara's Bat Mitzvah" and the date. The members of the congregation looked at these with consternation, not really knowing whether they were supposed to be used or just marveled at.

Sara worked very hard on her little speech. She practiced speaking slowly and distinctly so everyone would understand what she had to say. When the time came, she stood up, straight and tall, her dark eyes shining with pride. She was participating in a ritual that was part of her identity— her identity as a Norwegian Jew.

In retrospect, I must say that my daughter's bat mitzvah, although very different from my own, was much more fraught with meaning. Here in Norway, there are so few Jews that each bar or bat mitzvah is regarded as a small victory. One more boy, one more girl, who has defied the pressure of the majority and clutches onto his or her Jewish identity! One more girl, one more boy, who just might enable our tiny Jewish community to survive assimilation and intermarriage. One more person who, just maybe, will stay in Oslo and help to keep our traditions alive instead of leaving for greener pastures abroad. Here, having a bat mitzvah is making a statement. Sara has made hers.

PORTUGAL

Jews have lived in Portugal since the start of recorded history. Until the fifteenth century, when King Manuel I expelled them, they enjoyed a privileged status. In order to avoid expulsion, many Jews converted to Christianity "on the outside" but practiced Judaism in secret. With the start of the Inquisition, in acts of incredible cruelty, people suspected of being Jews were burned at the stake. In response, most Jews fled Portugal for other countries, accounting for the multitudes of Anousim in many nations of the world. *Anousim*—meaning "forced ones" in Hebrew—or *Crypto-Jews* are terms that refer to these people, and both are preferred over the derogatory word *Marranos*, that relates to pigs.

In the twentieth century, thousands of Jewish refugees fled the Nazis in their home countries and headed for neutral Portugal, joining those who had arrived from Morocco in the late nineteenth century. In Lisbon, there are an estimated 800 Jews who participate in one of the two synagogues, the Conservative Ashkenazi Ohel Yaacov and the Orthodox Sephardic Shaare Tikva (also known as the Lisbon Synagogue), where Isaac Assor is cantor. The Lisbon Synagogue celebrated its hundredth anniversary in 2004.

Isaac Assor

Being a Sephardi community mainly of Moroccan origin, the custom of making bat mitzvah ceremonies is quite new for us. In fact, the first ceremony was held about twenty-five years ago when my late father, z"l, was the rabbi here in Portugal. It was a ceremony for four girls. After that, there were very few. Nowadays, even in Sephardi communities, we do it. But going back some years, it was very rare.

I taught the last two girls whose parents wanted them to become b'not mitzvah. As our congregation does not have a conventional service, I chose to teach the girls about the role of women in Judaism and how to read Hebrew. It seemed to me of great value for them. The ceremony took place in the synagogue at the end of the morning prayer. It started with the girl entering the synagogue while singing *Ma Tovu Ohalecha Yaacov* (How Beautiful Are Your Tents, O Jacob). Afterward, she recited a selection from Proverbs, *Eshet Chail Mi Imtza* (A Woman of Valor Who Shall Find). She then made a speech regarding women in Judaism, finishing with a misheberach and music.

SCOTLAND

Glasgow resident Helen Wiseman's contribution is a lovely story of the bridge that bat mitzvah built between Scotland and Russia. There are few records of Jews in Scotland before the eighteenth century, prompting one historian to observe that "Jewish communities in Scotland remain somewhat of a mystery."[6] The first congregation in Glasgow was established in 1823, and the first synagogue, Garnethill, was built in 1879. At the turn of the twentieth century, Glasgow attracted Jews from Eastern Europe who settled in a tenement area called the Gorbals. Glasgow has the largest percentage of Scotland's 6,000 Jews.

Helen Wiseman

1987: The following year was to be our only daughter's bat mitzvah. She had already started the classes that would prepare her for that special day. At that time in Glasgow, there was a thriving group of advocates for Soviet Jewry. They asked our family to "adopt" a Jewish Russian family who had a daughter of a similar age. Due to the political situation, this young girl would not be able to have a bat mitzvah ceremony of her own.

Together with our daughter, Nikki, we sat down to write a brief introductory letter to send to the address we had been given. Several weeks later, much to our surprise and joy, an airmail letter arrived from Leningrad, now St. Petersburg. A Russian-speaking friend was able to translate it for us.

It turned out that we were one of the few families who kept up a correspondence for the whole of that year. I don't think we received all the letters they sent us, but among the ones we did receive were some with photos of Irina and her family. As much as Nikki learned at her bat mitzvah classes, we all learned from those letters. Mum and Dad were refuseniks who had lost their jobs. Money was scarce, life was hard, and morale was pretty low. We learned what life was like for a highly intelligent and skilled Jewish couple and their two children in Russia.

As the months leading up to Nikki's bat mitzvah sped by, her dad and I wondered what we could do to make this bat mitzvah a really meaningful one for everyone. What do you give a twelve-year-old girl who has plenty of books, clothes, jewelry, and stereos?

On the day of Nikki's bat mitzvah, Irina's photo, which we had enlarged to almost life-size, was on the back wall of the shul just behind where Nikki stood. During the moving ceremony, Irina was referred to many times. A tea party with family and close friends followed.

That evening, after everyone had gone home, we sat Nikki down. We told her that we were now ready to share with her what our bat mitzvah gift to her was. "In three days' time, you are coming with us to Leningrad for a week to see Irina." Of course, we were not allowed to let the family know of our visit, as it could put them into even more danger from the authorities. (We also intended to visit other refusenik families and were secretly taking in medicines, syringes, clothes, kosher food, and stereos.)

I can't say it was easy moving around Leningrad, nor was it easy to find the flat where Irina and her family lived. We were watched nearly all the time. However, the meeting finally took place at their home. Nikki spoke no Russian, and Irina spoke no English. But both had been learning German at school for a few months. That was their common language at first. Two hours later, they had developed their own language, that of teenage young ladies, and it was amazing to see how many traits they had in common. We met twice more, and each time the bond between the girls grew. Before we left, we gave Irina the gifts we had brought. Her favorite was a

Nikki Glekin of Glasgow, Scotland, and Irina Feldster
of Leningrad, Soviet Union, as they appeared in a
Glasgow newspaper, 1988.

Walkman with a tape recording of the entire bat mitzvah ceremony held
in Glasgow the previous week, together with many photos.

We returned to Glasgow pensive and feeling that there had been a change
in each of us because of our experiences in Leningrad. Many groups asked
Nikki to give an account of her trip. I went along to one of them to hear
what she would say. She ended her presentation by saying, "If my grandpa
had not been able to get out of Poland when he did, and my great-grandma
on the other side of the family hadn't left Lithuania when she did, I might
have been an Irina, too, and been locked into a country where I wasn't free
to celebrate my Jewishness." When I heard that, I said to myself with tears
of pride, "My Nikki has not just grown in height over the past months, but
she has grown in strength of character and in an appreciation of her special cultural inheritance."

The letters continued for another year and then stopped. Then, in December 1990, a letter arrived, in a familiar handwriting but with the post-
mark "Haifa." Irina's family had arrived at an absorption center in Israel.
Within two months, we had a new common language—Hebrew.

Six months after Irina's family arrived in Israel, they paid their first visit to the Kotel—to join our family in celebrating the bar mitzvah of Nikki's younger brother. It was a joyous reunion and one we would never have dreamed of three years before. The circle was complete when, the following year, Irina came to Glasgow to spend the whole summer with Nikki.

Irina is now called Irit, has served in the Israeli army, and is more like a sabra than anything else. Her parents have good jobs at the Technion in Haifa. Nikki now also lives in Israel, and next year she is marrying a delightful Israeli young man. We never know what wonderful moments life holds in store for us, do we?

SICILY

Jews have lived in Sicily for fourteen centuries, arriving first as traders in Grecian times and then as slaves in Roman times. Over the centuries, Jews became integrated into the social fabric of Sicily. But in 1492, despite pressure from Sicilian authorities who did not want to lose the Jews' skills, the Jews were expelled from all Spanish territories, including Sicily. The majority of Sicilian Jews, particularly the upper classes, converted rather than lose their homes and capital. Others practiced their religion in secret or fled to more tolerant countries around the world. Among the forced converts was the family of Dolores DeLuise, as she relates in her story. A teacher, researcher, and translator, Dolores received her Ph.D. in women's studies and is on the faculty of the Borough of Manhattan Community College of the City University of New York. She is writing a memoir about discovering her new family in the Old World.

Dolores DeLuise

My family is from Sicily. I am certain that at one time they were Jewish. Several years ago, I traveled to Sicily to find them. I discovered a wonderful family of about a hundred people. Since then, I have returned many times.

During my search for my family, I came across a small book called *The Jews of Castelbuono*. It described how, in 1492, when the Jews were expelled from Sicily, then a Spanish possession, the people of Castelbuono, my grandmother's town, hid their Jewish neighbors by converting them. Church records reveal many conversions to Christianity of people with Spanish surnames, the Jews of the community. There are still Jewish artifacts in the church's possession.

I converted to Judaism twenty years before my first trip to Sicily. When my teacher, Rabbi Stephen Lerner, instructed me about keeping kosher and lighting candles, it all seemed familiar. My grandmother (the one from Castelbuono) always kept a single candle lit. "At the weekend," she always lit a second candle. I subsequently discovered that, because they did not have a ninth spot on their menorahs, Italian Jews always kept a candle, the *shamash*, lit. Also, my grandmother taught me to sweep into the center of the room, as Sephardim do. And, essentially, she kept kosher. When I put these things, and much more, together with the Spanish surnames in my grandmother's family, I began to suspect strongly that they had been Jewish.

What finally made me certain was an incident that occurred two years ago, the last time I was in Sicily. I was eating (what else?) with my cousins, and they wanted me to have some cheese during lunch. I said I would eat it with the fruit that concluded every meal. One cousin looked dismayed and embarrassed because they had no fruit that day. *Siamo tutti ebrei*, she said. "We are all Jews."

"What did you just say?" I asked, shocked. It was a family saying, they explained. When something is lacking, such as food, they attribute it to the fact that they "are all Jews." A few days later, I heard it again. I was having dinner with about twenty of my relatives. I was thinking that it reminded me of Passover. Just then, one of them said, *Siamo tutti ebrei*. When they "see all the faces around the table," they told me, they invoke the family dictum, "We are all Jews."

Shortly after my conversion to Judaism, I became a bat mitzvah at Rabbi Lerner's synagogue in New Jersey. I chanted the haftorah and had planned to chant the maftir, but chickened out during the service because I feared I would stumble over a certain difficult word. As it turned out, the cantor himself stumbled over the word and another one as well. *Siamo tutti ebrei*.

SPAIN

The Jewish population of Spain has been estimated to be between 20,000 and 40,000; significant numbers of Jews have immigrated from Morocco and South America in recent decades. Residents of Spain since Roman times, Jews gained power and prestige during the Golden Age that spanned the eighth to eleventh centuries. During the Spanish Inquisition, they were forced to convert to Catholicism and were finally expelled in 1492. From Spain, these Sephardim (from the Hebrew word for Spain, *Sepharad*, which is used in the Bible) spread throughout the world, first to Portugal (from which they were expelled shortly thereafter) and then to Turkey, Greece, Palestine, North Africa, and Italy. Many traveled to the Netherlands, Western Europe (London, Bordeaux, and Hamburg, for example), and North and South America.

Currently, there are thirteen Orthodox congregations in Spain, one Reform congregation (in Barcelona), and a few congregations of Conservative (Masorti) Jews, including La Javura in Valencia, which California-born translator Alba Toscano co-founded. Every year on Tu b'Shvat, the Jewish Arbor Day, La Javura (from "group of friends" in Hebrew) celebrates its founding with a tree planting at the botanical gardens of the University of Valencia followed by a party. In March 2005, eighty-five people showed up to "eat, drink, sing, dance, and take turns reading poetry in praise of the edible fruit-bearing assortment of trees growing in the Botanical Garden."[7] Several of the guests, who included Christians, Muslims, and Jews, signed up for Hebrew lessons and invited La Javura members to give lectures on Judaism.

Alba Toscano

I was born in 1950 into a Conservative Jewish family in California. We frequented a kind of "Orthodox-lite" synagogue because the only other option was a Reform synagogue, and my father flatly refused to have anything to do with Reform synagogues. I never had a bat mitzvah, proper or otherwise, because in 1962, when I would have participated in one in a Reform synagogue, my mother, sister, and I were still making the hike up to the balcony on Saturday mornings.

When I came to Valencia in 1988, about 99 percent of the active Jewish population was composed of people from Morocco who had arrived in the late 1940s and early 1950s. The rest of the Jewish population fell into the category of "tourists." Unable to find a synagogue in Valencia, I would go to Madrid from time to time to the Moroccan Sephardic Orthodox synagogue, and climb up to the balcony. By accident, I stumbled upon a collective bat mitzvah one weekend when I was in Madrid. The young ladies, gathered on the steps leading up to the Aron Kodesh under a large, flower-decorated jupa (canopy), formed a pretty tableau. The girls sang a couple of songs, recited a little poetry, and gave short speeches: "what coming-of-age means to me." The presentation was followed by a massive bash laid on by proud parents, several of whom had evidently mortgaged off the family homestead.

In 1996, there were no Conservative or Reform synagogues in Spain. As nice as the Orthodox Sephardic Moroccan synagogues were, they just weren't my cup of tea. At the rate things were going, I would be looking down from a balcony the rest of my religious life. My options were clear and evident. Either I could give it up—stop being Jewish, close the door, get on with life—or I could found my own synagogue.

It took me a little more than a year to decide whether I was going to open or close the door. And then one day, time was up, and the thinking was over. There was no party with twinkling fairy lights, no fancy dresses, no strawberries and whipped cream, no garlands of flowers. At high noon on January 24, 1997, the Sunday closest to Tu b'Shvat, I and four other people planted a maple tree in the University of Valencia's botanical gardens. On that day, we founded the Sinagoga Conservador/Masorti La Javura. At the time, I felt neither prepared nor ready. But a beginning is a beginning, at twelve or at forty-six. And, as in all formal beginnings, there must be a formal public ceremony. Bat mitzvah means you have been instructed and are ready to take your place among the up-and-coming generation of a Jewish community. It is the moment to accept a lifetime of working for the greater good. Unbeknown to the others, I celebrated my bat mitzvah as I planted that tree. It grows there still.

Alba Toscano (*right*) and friends planting a tree at the University
of Valencia's botanical gardens, Valencia, Spain, 1997.

SWEDEN

In her essay, Mirjam Carlberg documents the evolution of bat mitzvah
through the generations of her family—from a simple confirmation ceremony, to a deeply felt but belated alternative ceremony, to a more typical
bat mitzvah ceremony.

There are approximately 20,000 Jews in Sweden, about half in Stockholm and most of the rest in Malmö, Uppsala, and cosmopolitan Gothenburg, Sweden's second-largest city, where Mirjam lives. Officially neutral
during World War II, Sweden provided sanctuary to Norwegian and Danish Jews, who were secretly transported to Sweden in fishing boats. Between 1945 and 1970, the Jewish population doubled as Holocaust survivors were brought to Sweden for rehabilitation, and others arrived from
Hungary, Czechoslovakia, and Poland. A pioneer in Holocaust education, the government sponsors a national program on Holocaust awareness and in 2000 hosted an international conference on the Holocaust attended by delegations from around the world.

Mirjam Carlberg

In our hometown of Gothenburg on the Swedish west coast, my daughter, now fifty, participated in a rather shallow "confirmation" when she was fourteen or fifteen years old (like the confirmation in the Protestant Church). This was the only religious ceremony customary for girls at that time. It took place after two years of studying twice a week with the rabbi. The girls studied only biblical history, almost nothing about religion, and no Hebrew.

But when my daughter's daughter, Anna, had her bat mitzvah at age seventeen, it was a personal and philosophical event. Anna, now twenty-three, had lived in Uppsala, outside Stockholm, since birth and had not had the opportunity to attend a Jewish after-school program. She was therefore unable to make her bat mitzvah at the usual age. When her family moved to Stockholm, she was able to study Judaism with a woman teacher for some months.

Anna's bat mitzvah was quite moving. During the service, she sang *Shir Hama'a Lot* (literally, "song of ascents," or stairs leading up to the ancient Temple, a joyful song said to have been written by King David) and made a thoughtful and mature speech about it. She spoke about its meaning for her personally (she used to spend summers at a Jewish camp where Hebrew songs were sung) and for the Jewish people. After the ceremony, we had a small party for relatives and friends at her parents' home.

My other granddaughter, Dahlia, my son's daughter, made her bat mitzvah at the age of twelve like almost all her Jewish friends of that period. They studied at our religious school in the afternoons. During the ceremony, she spoke about her Hebrew name, Dahlia Rachel, as is customary in our congregation. She explained that Rachel was meant to commemorate her great-grandmother, who was from Vienna and whom the Nazis killed together with her husband, little son, and many other relatives. Her daughter, Dahlia's grandmother, was sent to Sweden along with 500 other children, all of whom had been rescued from Germany, Austria, and Czechoslovakia.

Rachel told the congregation that her other name, Dahlia, a very popular girl's name in Israel, actually has a Swedish origin. The flower was

Mirjam Carlberg's granddaughter Dahlia, now dressed casually,
listens to her mother's remarks at her bat mitzvah reception
as her father looks on, Gothenburg, Sweden, 2002.

named the dahlia in honor of the Swedish botanist Andrew Dahl. In another part of the ceremony, she sang the *Sh'mah* with a melody she learned
from the chassen of our congregation. Like Anna's, her bat mitzvah was a
moving experience for our family. Afterward, we had a party—very nice,
but not as costly and overdone as some in our community.

WALES

The first Jewish community in Wales was founded in about 1730 in Swan-
sea. In the next century, communities were formed in other towns, including Cardiff, the capital, where the first synagogue was built in 1858.
After riots in 1911 that targeted Jewish shops in coal-mining areas, the Jewish population of Wales began to decline from 4,000 at its height to about
2,000 today, most of them in Cardiff.

The Cardiff New Synagogue, where Natalie Masters celebrated her bat mitzvah, is an active Reform congregation founded in 1948. The bat torah ("daughter of the Torah" in Hebrew) service is an apt designation for the opportunity that Reform (Liberal or Progressive) Judaism offers to women who wish to read from Judaism's sacred scroll.

Andrea Masters

Our daughter, Natalie, had always said she didn't want a bat mitzvah celebration. But when our new rabbi, Elaina Rothman, arrived at the Cardiff New Synagogue, she encouraged Natalie and gradually guided her in the right direction. Natalie changed her mind and worked hard to learn her bat mitzvah parasha, taking lessons with Alfred Moritz, a member of our community who is a professor of Greek and Latin. As she was studying Latin in school, the two of them got on well together.

We knew Natalie would have no problem reading Hebrew when not on public view. But we were a bit concerned about how she would perform on the day, as she was a quiet child and rather shy. Well, we needn't have worried. At her bat mitzvah in November 1996, Natalie led most of the Sabbath service. Her reading was excellent, and she took it all in her stride and had everyone sitting up in their seats.

The kiddush that followed was fabulous, catered by Helen Weil, a member of our community whose kiddushim are renowned. The food was also excellent at the lunch we held in celebration at a country hotel near where we live. The piano player had everyone dancing all afternoon. All the preparations—choosing the outfits, the food, the color scheme, and the music—were well worth it.

I had asked our son, Jonathan, then age ten, if he would propose a toast to his sister. He said yes, but only if I wrote it, and made it funny and in rhyme. What a challenge! Then, in the interest of equality for women, my husband, Simon, suggested that I make a speech about Natalie and also make it rhyme. Another challenge. But it went over well, and we still recite those rhyming speeches!

While the bat mitzvah was a happy occasion, it was tinged with a hint of sadness. Just three months earlier, Natalie's grandfather, Simon's dad, had died. Natalie was the apple of his eye, and he was sorely missed that day.

Natalie Masters and her brother, Jonathan, at Natalie's
bat mitzvah, Cardiff, Wales, 1996.

Three years later, Natalie had a bat torah on her sixteenth birthday.
Once again, we were immensely proud of her when she led the service
and read Torah. Natalie now reads Torah often for the community, having developed a knack for sight-reading the Hebrew text. (One of the para-
shas she has read has fifty-four verses.) Next year, on Saturday, the twenty-
second of May, Natalie will be twenty-one. And, yes, she will be taking
her place on the bimah once again.

We have been blessed with two lovely children and hope that one day they will know what it feels like to watch their own children take their place in the Jewish community.

NOTES

1. Marlene Schmool, "Jewish Women in Britain," in H. Epstein, ed., *Jewish Women 2000*, 192.

2. Ibid., 193.

3. A version of this essay first appeared in the London *Jewish Chronicle* on September 27, 2002. It appears here by permission of the author and the *Jewish Chronicle*.

4. Regine Azria, "Being a Jewish Woman in French Society," in H. Epstein, ed., *Jewish Women 2000*, 69.

5. Micaela Procaccia, "Italy," in H. Epstein, ed., *Jewish Women 2000*, 32–34.

6. "Historian Seeks Public Help with Research into Scotland's Jewish Community," media release, University of Aberdeen, January 12, 2006.

7. "Tu b'Shvat Seder Botanical Garden Stroll in Valencia, Spain," *World Council of Conservative/Masorti Synagogues Newsletter* (March 2005): 1.

Former Soviet Union, Former Yugoslavia, and Eastern Europe

In 1991, with the breakup of the former Soviet Union (FSU), fifteen new countries were formed: Armenia, Azerbaijan, Belarus, Estonia, Georgia, Kazakhstan, Kyrgyzstan, Latvia, Lithuania, Moldova, Russia, Tajikistan, Turkmenistan, Ukraine, and Uzbekistan. Many of these countries had vibrant, populous Jewish communities before the Russian Revolution in 1917. During the seventy-four-year period of the Soviet system, religion was suppressed in favor of atheism or secularism. This attitude toward religion in general, in combination with a long history of Russian anti-Semitism, made it nearly impossible to practice or study Judaism in any form in the Soviet Union.

It is therefore quite remarkable that, beginning in the 1970s, some Jews, feeling a strong sense of identity, risked their livelihoods and safety by requesting permission to emigrate to Israel. More than a million Soviet Jews did so after years of struggle, with assistance from individuals, groups, and governments in the West. Because so many people became refuseniks or demanded permission to leave, many of the countries listed above, which once had sizable Jewish populations, have seen their Jewish communities shrink. Nevertheless, some demographers estimate that as many as a million Jews still remain in the FSU. Many families have no intention of leaving. Some Jewish individuals have intermarried or lost interest in retaining their Jewish identity. Yet others have made contact with Western organizations that are helping to revive Jewish life in the former Soviet Union.

At the same time as the dramatic increase in freedom of religion occurred, other changes of equally profound significance occurred in the FSU, changes that affected Jew and non-Jew alike. Among these was post-Soviet capitalism, a new economic system that compelled people to support themselves rather than be supported by the government. Women's rights previously had been touted as a success of the Soviet Union, but it was not clear if these rights would be sustained in the new countries. In addition, the previous system of disinformation or lack of information had made the Jews of the FSU unaware of major events in the general and Jewish worlds. Alongside all of these enormous challenges was another huge problem—how to cope with the losses caused by the deaths of millions of Jews in the Holocaust and its aftermath.

Many of the countries created in the dissolution of the Soviet Union had been home to large populations of Jews who had perished. When freedom finally came in various forms, Judaism reemerged, with the help of organizations like Chabad, the Joint Distribution Committee, and the Jewish Agency for Israel. But Jews living in those countries faced a confusing challenge: how to integrate the new modernity of their political and economic lives with the traditional aspects of Judaism. Because of the sharp contrasts between modern and traditional ideas of womanhood, this problem was especially pressing for women. They had to seek out new ways to be Jewish women in the FSU.

We have bat mitzvah–related stories from nine of the FSU countries: Azerbaijan, Belarus, Kazakhstan, Latvia, Lithuania, Moldova, Russia, Ukraine, and Uzbekistan.

AZERBAIJAN

Magdalena Elishevah Agababayev's story about bat mitzvah—or, rather, its absence—is one of the most poignant in this collection. We can almost feel her tears on the page. But in addition to her despair, Magdalena imparts a beautiful idea from the Kabbalah, the mystical tradition in Judaism. She has come to understand that, although Jewish women seemingly had no power over their lives in Azerbaijan, they actually were the web that held the entire community together for generations.

A licensed psychotherapist and certified hypnotherapist, Magdalena has worked worldwide for UNICEF as a liaison on children's rights. Currently a resident of New York City, she is the director of adolescent programs at the Jewish Board of Family and Children's Services and a member of the Wellness Institute, the United Nations Coordination Committee, and the Academy of European Arts and Culture.

Magdalena Elishevah Agababayev

My initial reaction was to push this topic away, so far that the emotions would not find their way into the present. Yet the emotions are just a step away, and I am now fully in the midst of them.

The Mountain Jews of Azerbaijan are the descendants of the Babylonian exiles after the destruction of the First Temple in Jerusalem in 722 BCE. Jews have lived in this mountainous region for over a millennium. A predominantly Islamic country in recent history, the Azerbaijan of ancient times was the land of the Khazars and Zoroastrians, conquered by Mongols, Persians, Arabs, and Turks. In 1920, the region was invaded by Russia and came under the Soviet Union's rule. During all these changes, our Jewish identity was continuously threatened. For self-preservation, the community responded with isolation and with increased rigidity concerning Jewish laws. Although we survived as a community, some of these communal defenses kept us far from modernization and even sent some of the members of the community into secularism.

There are no rituals, now or in the past, celebrating womanhood for Mountain Jews; nothing that feels like a celebration occurs to mark the age of bat mitzvah. As I asked the elder females of our community if they knew of bat mitzvah rituals, I received a myriad of answers that all led to "no." When I asked my peers, I got sad or angry looks. Age twelve is typically the beginning of the end of living in one's parents' home, as young girls are readied for an arranged marriage and motherhood. Only in recent years have young girls been allowed to disagree with their parents' choice of a life partner. All this is done to ensure a *guard*, that is, a husband, for the newly fertile girl, a guard who will prevent her from falling into the non-Jewish world.

Ironically, it was during the Soviet regime that our women were partially liberated, as they were urged to complete primary school before marriage. Presently, with the fall of the Soviet Union, the community has regressed, and many girls are once again married in their early teens.

I turned twelve en route to the United States. Yet even the "land of the free" was not able to fully safeguard me. The years of battling for my choices in life began then. In a way, age twelve was the beginning of adulthood for me, for I had to learn to value my identity in the face of communal pressure to marry. The "tea ceremonies" began, as parents and sons of our community flooded into our Brooklyn apartment from as far away as Israel, Austria, and Canada. I was urged to serve them to display what a perfect wife I would make.

As I fought for time, the restrictions on me got tighter. I was no longer to be found alone in a room with a male, no matter what his age. There was no talk of a university education as it was not important for marriage and was a danger zone where I could be lost to the community through intermarriage. Yet it was those restrictions that slowly pushed me away, both from the Azerbaijani Mountain community and from Judaism as a whole. I was as emotionally isolated in our apartment in Brooklyn as many women of our community are in the Caucasus Mountains of Azerbaijan.

What do I suggest to women who did not have any rite of passage to womanhood? Study what it means, create a ritual, and celebrate womanhood at any age! For me, it started at twenty-two, in the ancient city of Tzfat in Israel. On the slopes, overlooking the valleys and mountains, among the cobblestoned roads and magical old synagogues, the Old and the New Worlds converge. Womanhood is celebrated, complete with motherhood, education, and individuality.

According to Kabbalistic teachings, woman is the white background that holds and supports the black letters of the Torah. Woman is supple and all-encompassing; she gives the space for creation. As *L'cha Dodi*, a Shabbat prayer that was created in Tzfat, confirms, Shabbat—peace and balance—is not accomplished until the bride (the feminine) enters.

The women of the Mountain Jews have been nurturing their communities with vibrant feminine spirit for centuries. Combined with education and freedom of individuality, our history and culture can provide rich material for a celebration of womanhood.

BELARUS

Anna Buchel, the author of the Belarus bat mitzvah story, is benefiting from the work of the Belarusian Union for Progressive Judaism, which is affiliated with the Reform movement in the United States. The first bar and bat mitzvah ceremonies sponsored by the Belarusian UPJ took place in 1999. Now, the movement has developed a cadre of professional b'nai mitzvah tutors who annually teach more than 30 children in Progressive congregations throughout the country. So far, more than 150 children have become b'nai mitzvah through this movement.

Two interesting elements of Anna's story are that there is no rabbi in her hometown and that both the boys and girls wear kippot and tallitot. Thus, these young people are learning not only about their Jewish heritage, but about an egalitarian interpretation of it. Anna seems to have a strongly committed family. Her parents have belonged to the congregation for a long time, and her younger brother is a bar mitzvah as well. In most cases, a family that practices Judaism together makes it easier for young people to participate comfortably.

Anna Buchel

I was born and have lived all my life in Gomel, a small city with about 400,000 inhabitants in the south of Belarus, near the border with Ukraine. Our city has always had a strong Jewish presence. Nowadays, the Jewish community numbers about 3,000.

I would like to share with you my recollections about the bat mitzvah celebration that I had in Gomel in the year 2000. I was thirteen years old at the time, and I was a part of the first group of children who went through preparation for b'nai mitzvah under the auspices of the Reform movement in Belarus.

My parents had been members of the Reform congregation Kadimah for three years before I started my bat mitzvah preparation. Once a week, I went to b'nai mitzvah class with four other kids from our congregation. We studied Hebrew, Torah and Tanach, as well as Jewish history and traditions. I also participated in youth Kabbalat Shabbat services.

The ceremony took place on Shabbat morning. The rabbi came to Gomel from Minsk, the capital of Belarus, to conduct the ceremony. During the service, we all wore kippot and tallitot. We took turns reading from the wonderful nineteenth-century Torah scroll that belongs to our community. Each of us shared with the congregation our thoughts on the Torah portion, Bechar from the book of Leviticus. I spoke about what freedom means to me. We received a personal siddur and a T-shirt with the logo of our Belarusian Union for Progressive Judaism, as well as many presents from family and friends. The whole bat mitzvah experience was very important and spiritually uplifting for me. Since then, my brother celebrated his bar mitzvah in 2002. Both of us remain very involved in our youth group.

KAZAKHSTAN

One of the few entries written by a man, this story about life in Kazakhstan today is very upbeat. Chabad rabbi Bezalel Lifshitz, who grew up in Cincinnati, Ohio, conveys a sense of a dynamic, growing community despite its disjointed past. The Chabad movement helps Jews all over the world by bringing rabbis and their families to live anywhere that there are Jews. Growing up as the eldest of a dozen children in a home that was enthusiastic and caring, this rabbi seems to have brought that same spirit to Kazakhstan and its girls and boys.

Rabbi Bezalel Lifshitz

The second-largest republic of the former Soviet Union and the ninth-largest country in the word, Kazakhstan has no native Jews. Built from a desperate hodgepodge of refugees, exiles, and deportees, the community now is rich in variety and in harmony. Sizable Ashkenazic and Sephardic communities blend naturally. Dark and light, young and old, wealthy and poor join together to celebrate the holidays and the joys of Jewish life. The Almaty Central Synagogue is a comfortable home to the entire community, featuring a social hall, a soup kitchen, a mikvah, a kosher grocery store, a multilingual library, hospitality suites, and two kindergartens.

Life-cycle events are a vital part of Jewish life in the community. Everyone joins in and participates in the celebration of such milestones, including bat mitzvahs, although there are fewer of those than bar mitzvahs. A bat mitzvah club for eleven-year-olds is in the planning stages. Currently, the bat mitzvah girl receives preparatory instruction from a knowledgeable and stimulating counselor, who introduces her to the challenges and beauty of reaching Jewish adulthood, to the responsibilities and ambitions of the Jewish woman, and to the delicacy and uniqueness of Jewish femininity. Together, they discuss the images and meanings of these themes in anticipation of their impending relevance.

At the bat mitzvah celebration, the girl who is coming of age generally conveys a timely Torah thought, expresses her impression of becoming a Jewish woman, and thanks her parents and grandparents for the education they have given her and the energy they have invested in her to help her grow in this virtuous direction. She is encouraged beforehand to announce at the ceremony a good resolution that she has made in honor of the event. Often, she will invite family and friends to join her and take upon themselves a resolution of their own. In the course of the ceremony, the bat mitzvah girl usually passes around a tzedakah box to offer everyone the opportunity to perform this basic mitzvah. The celebration typically ends with singing, l'chaims, and cheerful mazal tov wishes.

LATVIA

The words *Riga* and *Latvia* still make many Jews shudder when they remember what occurred there during the Holocaust. In a forest called Bikernieki, approximately 40,000 Jews from throughout Europe were murdered. A prominent monument now stands at the entrance to the forest. But today, there are also schools for Jewish girls and boys, not only memorials to those who did not survive.

Rivka Glazman, the writer of this story, along with her husband, Rabbi Mordechai Glazman, is a member of the worldwide Chabad-Lubavitch movement. In 1995, they founded the Ohel Menachem day school in Riga, Latvia's capital. The children in this school follow a demanding curriculum that includes English and Hebrew in addition to Russian and Latvian. The school is up-to-date, with free access to the internet, extensive video and audio equipment, and modern chemistry and physics labs. On the Jewish side, the children study Jewish history and traditions, learn to pray and read Torah, and celebrate their b'nai mitzvah. This story focuses on a group of girls who celebrated with their families in 2003.

Rivka Glazman

From March to May 2003, the Chabad Bat Mitzvah Club of Riga, Latvia, met each Sunday for three hours. This was a group of nine serious girls, the sixth group to participate since the club was organized, all from non-observant families, who had decided to explore the meaning of bat mitzvah.

Meetings began with a discussion about the big step that the girls were making in their lives, and then continued with a project or activity. Each girl had a folder for her worksheets and notes. The first topic—the essence of the Jewish soul and its purpose in this world—inspired the girls, as they listened to a beautiful song called *Neshamale*, which describes the journey every soul makes.

What is a Jewish birthday? How should it be celebrated? What is special about a twelfth birthday? After these discussions, the girls designed original Jewish birthday cards. They studied the meaning of the thirteenth psalm, which is significant to bat mitzvah girls starting their thirteenth year. Other topics included the special characteristics and strengths of women, the Torah role of women and their special mitzvot, and Jewish women throughout history.

During the three months, the girls watched videos on Jewish subjects, played a kosher card game, and—the highlight of the club—baked challah. Though the purpose of the class was to learn about the mitzvah of separating a piece of dough for God each time one bakes, the girls also

Bat mitzvah girls in Jurmala, Latvia, with their special birthday cake, 2003.

learned the art of braiding three, four, and six strands of challah dough. And the results were delicious.

At the end of the semester, the girls and their parents joined the Chabad rabbi and his family for a Shabbaton in Jurmala, at the seaside not far from Riga. The weekend was a culmination of all they had learned. The girls had a chance to show that they knew how to celebrate Shabbat and to observe other Jewish laws. Kosher food was prepared in the Chabad center and warmed up before Shabbat at the hotel. The challah and the dessert were prepared by the bat mitzvah girls.

The lighting of Shabbat candles by mothers and daughters, as the men looked on, was a beautiful moment. It was a first experience for many of the mothers, and they were very moved. The Shabbat meals were enhanced by divrei Torah prepared by each girl. There were activities for the whole family, which led to discussions about many Jewish topics. Much of the information was new for the parents, and together the families explored what it means to be Jewish. During the reading of the Torah portion, the girls who did not yet have a Jewish name were officially given a name that the family had chosen. And of course there was time for walks by the sea and through the forest, and swimming on Friday afternoon and Sunday morning.

A Sunday morning brunch was the official bat mitzvah ceremony, with speeches, good resolutions, and presents, including a silver-plated candlestick for each girl. It was an inspirational weekend for the whole family, which I hope has encouraged more awareness of Judaism in the homes and lives of those who participated.

LITHUANIA

Vilnius, Lithuania—half of whose population was Jewish before the Holocaust—once brimmed with institutions of higher learning to such an extent that it was called "the Jerusalem of Lithuania." During the Nazi invasion, the Lithuanian population cooperated with the Nazis and murdered nearly all of the Jews, many of them in the Palnieri Woods outside Vilnius. Today, there are approximately 4,000 Jews in Lithuania.

Fortunately, life in Lithuania in the twenty-first century is quite different from the days of the Holocaust and Soviet oppression. On July 6, 2005, the president of Lithuania awarded the Cross of the Order of the Knight to Misha Jakobas "for contributions to Lithuania" in his role as the director of the Sholom Aleichem Jewish Secondary School. Supported by numerous organizations in the United States and elsewhere, including the Ronald S. Lauder Foundation, the Israeli Ministry of Culture and Education, and the American Jewish Joint Distribution Committee, the school, established in the early 1990s, has become one of the best secondary schools in Eastern Europe.

Although Misha Jakobas did not provide us with a bat mitzvah story, he did send us photographs of one event, and the joy experienced by the young people and their families is evident. Not only does the community give girls a bat mitzvah, but the girls clearly in turn help to create the community through their ceremony.

Misha Jakobas

These pictures were sent by Misha Jakobas, the director of Sholom Aleichem Secondary School in Vilnius. In June 2003, sixth-grade students

Above. As part of a 2003 bat mitzvah ceremony in Vilnius, Lithuania, girls present their mothers with flowers.

Below. Parents celebrate happily at a bat mitzvah ceremony in Vilnius, Lithuania, 2003.

celebrated a joint bar and bat mitzvah witnessed by their parents, who evidently enjoyed themselves at the simcha (party) following the ceremony.

MOLDOVA

This entry is written by Vera Krizhak, the director of the Joint Distribution Committee (JDC) branch in Moldova, and Vladimir Kvitko, the JDC's regional coordinator. Since 1914, the JDC has served as the overseas arm of the American Jewish community with a mission "to serve the needs of Jews throughout the world, particularly where their lives as Jews are threatened or made more difficult."

Moldova, formerly known as Bessarabia, became an independent country in 1991. Its capital is now called Chisinau (formerly Kishinev). This city has a sordid place in Jewish history as the site of a horrific pogrom in 1903. The pogrom shocked the international community and led to massive Jewish emigration to the United States and Palestine.

Moldova's leadership has been more and more outspoken in its support of the Jewish community; in January 2007, President Vladimir Voronin delivered two speeches to Jewish audiences, unconditionally condemning anti-Semitism and promising his support in the fight against xenophobia.

Because Moldova is one of the poorest nations in Europe, there has been massive emigration to Israel and other countries by Jews seeking to escape the dire economic circumstances. In the 1980s, the Jewish population dropped from over 80,000 to 20,000. In this tumultuous environment, the JDC and other organizations are trying to create meaningful bat mitzvah experiences, as Vera and Vladimir explain.

Vera Krizhak and
Vladimir Kvitko

The celebration of bat mitzvah has been a tradition in Moldova for a long time. Lately, the spirit of Jewish community renewal has revived interest in this ceremony, as people want to return to their roots. Bat mitzvah now takes different forms. It is celebrated in Jewish schools for all the girls born in the same year, in family clubs, and in summer camps. Below is a description of one such event at a summer family camp.

Marina Endakova's bat mitzvah was a special occasion at
a family summer camp in Moldova, 2003.

"Oh! I'm gonna fall! Hold me!" the girl cried as her chair was raised
high by several young men. "*Mazal tov, mazal tov!*" the onlookers shouted
joyfully. Thus ended the bat mitzvah of Marina Endakova.

It had begun one morning in July at the summer camp on the river-
bank. There, Jewish families were gathered from all over Moldova. Marina
was there with her parents from the Jewish *shtetl* (town) of Bendery. Marina's
bat mitzvah was to be part of the evening program. During the day, children and grown-ups, not only from the Bendery family club, but even
people she had not met before, came up to her with kind words and con-
gratulations. A modest girl, she was embarrassed by all the attention.

That evening, Marina and her parents, Esther and Alexandr, were the
center of attention. In the big hall where community events take place,
Alexandr was called to the stage to read that week's Torah portion. Most

of the people at the family retreat had never had an opportunity to take part in a bat mitzvah ceremony, so the organizers included some educational elements in the ceremony.

Marina and her parents remained onstage while amateur actors dedicated their performances to her. The family could feel the benevolence and warmth of the performers and the audience, the special Jewish tone of the event. Marina's mother secretly wiped away a tear. As Marina's chair was raised, as madrihim (counselors) and children surrounded her amid the shouts of mazal tov!, Marina became Miriam.

Miriam Endakova now studies at Yeshiva Ahudat Israel in Kishinev.

RUSSIA

Our entry for Russia is unusual, as it is a collage of the words of four people: a male rabbi and three female congregants. The congregation that Rabbi Gregory Kotlyar serves is part of the World Union for Progressive Judaism (affiliated with Reform Judaism in the United States) and thus is committed to bringing women and girls into every aspect of Jewish life. In the bat mitzvah photographs of the two girls—Anna and Emma—we can see that they read directly from the Torah, make speeches, and receive gifts of Judaica from the rabbi and cantor. This particular congregation is special in that it recognizes the need that some women feel to become a bat mitzvah even if they have long passed the conventional age of twelve or thirteen. This opportunity is particularly important in places such as Russia where people sometimes discover only when they are adults that they actually are Jewish.

Each person tells a story of connection—to the synagogue community, to a "centuries-old tradition," or to "thousands of teens in Jewish communities all over the globe." Thus, becoming a bat mitzvah is about much more than what the person learns: it is also about what the person feels. Perhaps the most beautiful sentence is Luba's. She recognizes that when her daughter became a bat mitzvah, "it was the first celebration of its kind over the past three, or even four, generations." The fact that, after a hundred years, a child will choose to do again what had been skipped over for so long is remarkable. Perhaps the motivation is to feel connected and not alone in this world.

Anna Makarova receives a challah cover and candlesticks from Cantor Dmitry Karpenko (*left*) and Rabbi Gregory Kotlyar during her bat mitzvah at the Congregation for Progressive Judaism, Moscow, Russia, 2003.

Rabbi Gregory Kotlyar, Anna Makarova,
Olga Kulagina, and Luba Ioffe

GREGORY KOTLYAR

As far as I know, the only bat mitzvah ceremonies for girls in Moscow are held in our congregation, the Congregation for Progressive Judaism. In 2003, we held ten such ceremonies, not only for girls of twelve, but also for adult women aged twenty to thirty who did not have the possibility of such a ceremony before.

ANNA MAKAROVA

Shalom! I came to the congregation several months ago. Now, I always attend the Kabbalat Shabbat service. Here, I have found a caring atmosphere where there are many kind people with whom I can communicate.

My son Sergey is twelve. He studies a lot, so he is not able to attend synagogue along with me. But on Sundays he goes to *ulpan*, where he studies Hebrew and listens to lectures on Jewish history.

In January 2003, I had a bat mitzvah ceremony in our synagogue. This was an important step for me and a very solemn moment. Having undertaken the responsibility of following Torah mitzvot, it was wonderful to receive gifts from the congregation so that I can observe Shabbat, the most important Jewish holiday. The Shabbat set presented to me at the ceremony gives warmth to my home: candles, candlesticks, and a cloth for covering challah. I feel the generosity of the hands and hearts with which these presents were given. We light the candles and say the blessing over the challah. And we remember the people who gave these special presents to me and my family.

OLGA KULAGINA

Every society designates an age at which a person is considered to be adult, to be fully responsible for his or her actions and words. It is said in the Torah: "At age five, one should study holy scripture, at age ten, one should study Mishnah, and at age thirteen, one should follow mitzvot" (Avot 5:22). In our tradition, from the time a girl is twelve, she is to follow mitzvot and to bear the punishment for breaking mitzvot.

My bat mitzvah had great spiritual meaning for me. I felt the great responsibility of continuing the centuries-old tradition of my ancestors and fulfilling my duties to God. This was a peak moment in the life of a teenage girl, achieved after a long period of preparation. That day, I undertook the privileges and duties of studying Torah, following mitzvot, participating in the life of the Jewish community and the state of Israel, and tikkun olam.

The congregation provided me with the opportunity to carry out a mitzvah in public. I was called to the Torah and read a drasha (here, a weekly Torah portion). Then we celebrated, the congregation and my family. The celebration was very light and warm. It was an important family event, wonderful and joyful.

Bat mitzvah happens only once in life. Dear adults: present to your children this happy, solemn, and unforgettable day!

LUBA IOFFE

My daughter, Emma, is twelve. According to the Jewish law, at this age a girl becomes a grown-up person and takes responsibility for her choices.

Olga Kulagina with Cantor Karpenko (*left*) and
Rabbi Kotlyar at her bat mitzvah at the Congregation for
Progressive Judaism, Moscow, Russia, 2003.

Emma's bat mitzvah took place during the week of the parsha Vayechi
("And he lived"), in December 2002.

Thousands of teens in Jewish communities all over the globe go through
bar and bat mitzvah; it is a beautiful celebration. What was so special about
Emma's bat mitzvah? I will tell you. In the history of our family, it was
the first celebration of its kind over the past three, or even four, generations. The last coming-of-age ceremony was held about a hundred years
ago. The same can be said about the majority of Soviet Jewish families.

The whole of the week's parsha, especially the passage that Emma read,
was well matched to the meaning of the ceremony. In Vayechi, Yaakov
blesses his sons and Yosef's sons, Ephraim and Menashe. In her speech
after reading from the Torah scroll, Emma said, "The same thing is happening to me now: I am getting a blessing for the whole of my life."

Emma's attitude toward her bat mitzvah was very serious, contrary to
my expectations! She was both excited and a little nervous and spared no

Emma Ioffe reads her bat mitzvah speech at the Congregation for Progressive Judaism, Moscow, Russia, 2002. The banner of the World Union for Progressive Judaism is behind the cantor.

Emma Ioffe reads the week's Torah portion as Cantor Karpenko
and Rabbi Kotlyar look on, Moscow, Russia, 2002.

effort to prepare as well as she could. And she was lucky. In the course
of her preparations, she started an email correspondence with an American girl, Julia Goldstein, who was getting ready for her bat mitzvah too.
Emma says, "I am grateful to our community. Now I have a new friend in
America. I enjoy exchanging letters with Julia, though English is not easy
for me yet. But my mom helps me."

Now, I am going to share a discovery with you. Our daughter was supposed to choose a Jewish name. We started to think. She was named Emma
after my husband's mother, Emma Brodetskaya. But, although my mother-
in-law was known as Emma, the name written in her passport was Ethil.

Emma—Ethil—Ethel—*Esther!* We are grateful to our rabbi, who explained to us that Ethel is a Yiddish version of the ancient name Esther. You see that we did not have to invent anything! Wasn't it another chance to remind ourselves that nothing in this world happens by accident?

Going back to one's roots, reviving long-lost traditions . . . To tell the truth, I hate pompous wording like that. But what other terms can I use here? Actually, they describe quite correctly the meaning of the event that took place in our family, the bat mitzvah of our daughter, Emma/Esther.

UKRAINE

Two women who are linked together over thousands of miles wrote this entry. One lives in Boston, Massachusetts, United States, and the other lives in Dnepropetrovsk, Ukraine, a large industrial city that was closed to foreigners until the beginning of the 1990s. They know each other because Boston and "Dnep" are sister cities. This successful project has not only brought aid to Dnep, but has inspired the Jews of Boston.

Maxine Lyons of the Jewish Community Relations Council of Greater Boston has seen the Dnep Jewish community grow from a handful of people to 50,000, a population explosion which, she said, is "due in large part to the astute political and spiritual leadership of Chief Rabbi Shmuel and Rebbetsin Chany Kaminezki, sent from their home in New York."

Chany Kaminezki, like Rivka Glazman, the author of the Latvian entry, is the wife of a Chabad rabbi. Chany and her husband have spearheaded clinics for women and children, programs for disabled Jewish children, an assisted-living residence for elders, a Jewish Big Brother and Big Sister program, and a successful Jewish day school. As a rebbetsin, she has numerous responsibilities, but in particular she works with girls to educate and motivate them. The strategy she uses in her girls club is highly unusual: democracy and student leadership. People who know Rabbi Kaminezki consider him to be highly charismatic. No wonder that the Dnep Jewish community has grown to 50,000 people, and no wonder that his wife ends her entry by musing that, although some people have forgotten their Judaism, as time passes increasing numbers of people are attempting to learn more about who they are.

Maxine Lyons and Chany Kaminezki

MAXINE LYONS

Boston's Kehillah Project has coordinated ongoing educational and cultural exchanges between the Dnepropetrovsk Jewish day school (which today boasts 600 students, the largest in all of Europe) and more than thirty Hebrew schools and Jewish day schools in the greater Boston area. Many bat mitzvah girls have participated in the Kehillah Project by making contributions to needy Dnepropetrovsk children, performing the mitzvah of giving at the time of their simchas (happy occasions).

CHANY KAMINEZKI

When we first got here, we were both like young children, not knowing the language, with no minyan, and no kosher Torah. People were actually afraid to come to shul. They had been deprived of their Jewish heritage for over seventy years. Some who changed their nationality are now returning to their roots. Others have forgotten. But as the years pass, more and more thirst for the truth, and come closer to Judaism.

Bat mitzvah is a very special time for girls. They learn that they have grown up, and are beginning a new stage of life as young women. We had an idea to start a bat mitzvah program for girls in Dnepropetrovsk. Girls who are eleven and twelve years old get together to learn and develop their own programs. They set and arrange the tables and decide what they would like to do. Because they make their own plans, they feel good.

For bat mitzvahs in our community, we bring the girls to our synagogue, where they are given Jewish names. They love that. Every girl says a d'var Torah, speaking about a law, a holiday, or about the portion of the week. We sing songs like *Simen Tov*, and sometimes they get candies or confetti thrown at them. Then, we have cake, fruits, and drinks. We have bat mitzvahs at our summer camp, too. And after the bat mitzvah, we have a continuation program in our school.

UZBEKISTAN

Bukhara, the fifth-largest city in Uzbekistan, has been home to Jews since Roman times. Not only Jews from the city itself, but those from other

Students at the Dnepropetrovsk Jewish day school,
Dnepropetrovsk, Ukraine, 2001. Photo by Emily Corbato.

places in Uzbekistan (as well as from the countries of Tajikistan and Kyrgyzstan) are known as "Bukharan Jews." When the Russians closed the synagogues in the 1920s and 1930s, many left for Palestine, joining those who had emigrated at the turn of the century. After independence from the Soviet Union in 1991, the rise of Islamic fundamentalism caused another wave of emigration to Israel.

Lana Levitin was born in Samarkand, the ancient capital of Uzbekistan. After years of mental torture and frustration, her family was allowed to leave for Israel in the early 1970s. A few years later, she came to the United States. She has now come full circle by founding World of Women Immigrants to help Bukharan women, who, she says, "typically devote themselves to their husbands and their children and neglect themselves." Lana also manages Maqam, a unique Bukharan music group that has performed throughout the United States and Europe. As a single mother, Lana feels particular pride in her daughters' accomplishments.

Lana Levitin

When I was growing up, boys would have bar mitzvahs. They would be tutored by a rabbi and have a ceremony, almost in secret in those days. We never dreamed of a bat mitzvah for a girl. When a girl got her period, some mothers would make a small dinner of congratulation. But for girls, weddings really were the main celebrations. (Bukharan Jewish weddings are wonderful, with singing and dancing around a bonfire and many rituals for the bride before the wedding.)

My family has always been religious, and I've tried to set a good example for my girls. I became a member of the Conservative synagogue in Great Neck, New York, where my daughter Anya attended Hebrew school three times a week and had her bat mitzvah when she was thirteen. Anya's bat mitzvah was the first ever in my family. Relatives and friends came from Vienna and Israel, as well as from other parts of the U.S. For me, my daughter's bat mitzvah was a celebration of equality and freedom, a recognition that a woman can learn Torah and be the equal of a man.

To understand bat mitzvah in the former Yugoslavia today, one must begin with the past. One must consider the heart-wrenching words found in the following entries, words such as *extermination* and *destruction*. But there are also new words, such as *return* and *revitalization*.

Jews have lived in Yugoslavia since the tenth century. After the decimation of the Holocaust, only 14,000 Jews returned, of whom more than half had left for Israel by 1952. In the early 1990s, Yugoslavia divided into five independent countries: Bosnia and Herzegovina, Croatia, Macedonia, Serbia and Montenegro, and Slovenia. Currently, only 5,500 Jews live in these countries. We include here stories from two of these new nations: Croatia, and Serbia and Montenegro.

CROATIA

Judith Kaplan is credited with being the first bat mitzvah in the United States, in 1922. Apparently, the same phenomenon was occurring in Croatia in 1918, according to Ana Lebl, an archaeologist by profession and one of the leaders of the small Jewish community in Split, Croatia.

Croatian Jewish girls had their b'not mitzvah ceremonies as a group—ten girls in 1918 and fourteen girls two years later. Their b'not mitzvah were not on a birthday, but tied to the spring holiday of Shavuot, which celebrates the Jews' receiving of the Ten Commandments and the Torah. Between 1941, the onset of Nazism in Croatia, and 1991, when Croatia became an independent country, there were no b'not mitzvah of any kind as far as we can tell. Now, as interest in and opportunities for Jewish practice are beginning anew in Croatia, mothers and daughters are working together to bring Judaism back into community life.

Ana Lebl

In the early twentieth century, many girls studied in Jewish schools in Croatia and celebrated their b'not mitzvah. A picture from 1918 shows the first generation of girls who had their bat mitzvah ceremony in Kopriv-

Bat mitzvah girls in Koprivnica, Croatia, 1918. Photo from
J. Domas, ed., *Obitelj—Mishpaha* (Zagreb, 1996).

nica, a city in northern Croatia. Among the girls was Lizzy Kollman. Her
memories of that event were documented in a book published in 1996.

> Dr. Hirschberger, the rabbi and our professor at high school, prepared us
> for the Bat Mitzvah ceremony. He taught us Hebrew for a year, which was
> also important for our strong and active Zionist organization. For the Bat
> Mitzvah, we were all given white dresses and white shoes. It was so beau-

tiful when each of us was invited up to the Torah and had something to say. There was a big parade organized on that occasion in Koprivnica. Everyone was talking about it for days.

Today, there are no Jews in Koprivnica.

The ritual of bat mitzvah in the former Yugoslavia (of which Croatia was a part until 1991) began in the nineteenth century and was associated with the festival of Shavuot. There are similar descriptions from different cities of girls wearing white dresses and white gloves, holding white roses, which they laid in front of the Torah, or baskets full of flowers, which they would scatter at the entrance to the synagogue. The languages in which the girls recited were Hebrew and Croatian, or other ones used locally, like Hungarian or Italian. The last of those bat mitzvahs took place in 1941.

After World War II, the small number of Holocaust survivors rebuilt their communities with the main attributes of Jewish tradition, but no religion. This explains why there were no bat mitzvahs for more than fifty years.

Since the fall of communism, there has been growth in national and religious feelings in the newly established state of Croatia. Little by little, the Jewish community in Croatia is strengthening its religious identity. As a part of the revitalization, the first modern bat mitzvah celebration took place in 2001. A prominent member of the community asked the rabbi to help her organize a bat mitzvah in Croatia for her granddaughter living in Switzerland. A beautiful bat mitzvah celebration took place in Zagreb, the capital, on Shabbat, November 2, as members of the family and the community looked on.

The community in Split, where I live, is a tiny one, with only about a hundred members. My daughters, now twelve and fourteen, and another girl from Split participated in a group bat mitzvah at the international Jewish summer camp in Szarvas, Hungary. Still, we would like to organize a bat mitzvah celebration for them in our Jewish community center here in Split. The girls would have a more personal memory of their bat mitzvah, and their families, their non-Jewish school friends, and the community members would have a chance to share with them the excitement of this special event and to learn from it.

SERBIA

Milica Mihailovic is a retired curator of the Jewish Museum of Belgrade. Her essay includes two stories about b'not mitzvah of the past. They took place in Subotica, a city in northern Serbia founded in 1775, which was home to 6,000 Jews before the Holocaust. One of the elements of the ceremony—the laying of wreaths—seems to reflect the community's Christian surroundings. The beautiful art nouveau synagogue is still owned and used by the 200 Jews who live there today. The second story is extremely personal and may reflect the intense emotionality of the bat mitzvah day.

Milica Mihailovic

Before World War II, bat mitzvah rituals were observed in Ashkenazi congregations, usually near the festival of Shavuot. During the Holocaust, 80 percent of the Jewish population of Serbia was exterminated and most synagogues were destroyed. After the war, as religious Jews moved to Israel, the Jewish community of Yugoslavia remained almost completely secular for fifty years. Now, young Jews, like those in the town of Subotica, are trying to return to traditional practices and the observance of Jewish customs. The beautiful synagogue in Subotica was not destroyed during the war, and bat mitzvah ceremonies are again taking place there today.

The following testimonies are from V. Radovanovic and M. Mihailovic, *Jewish Customs: The Life Cycle* (Belgrade, 1998). They were collected for an exhibit at the Jewish Historical Museum in Belgrade in 1998 that was curated by V. Radovanovic.

EDITA DERI

In Subotica in 1941, my sister Ruža had her bat mitzvah, along with fourteen other girls. The bat mitzvah was celebrated on the day of the festival of Shavuot. Then, the war broke out. I never had a bat mitzvah.

POSLEDNJA BAT MITZVA, MAJ 1944.
U SUBOTICA

1. BANJAI MARTA (AUSTRALIA)
2. BECK LEA (ISR.)
3. FRIED EVA (ISR)
4. KLAUS ŽUŽA (ISR)
5. FENYVES ESTI (WAČINGTON)
6. FISCHER MARTA (ISR)
7. BECK ANNI (SLOVENIJA)
8. GLÜCK (LEBOVIC) ANC (ISR)
9. DONAT LILI (AUSTRIA)
10. FÜRST LUCI (ISR)
11. SPITZER KLARA (ISR)
12. RADELBURG MARTA (ISR)
13. FRANKL MARIANA (YU)

Above. Bat mitzvah, Subotica, Serbia, 1944. A few days after this picture was taken, all of these girls were transported to Auschwitz. Photo from V. Radovanovic and M. Mihailovic, *Jewish Customs: The Life Cycle* (Belgrade: Jewish Historical Museum, 1998).

Right. Bat mitzvah, Subotica, Serbia, 1994.

All fifteen girls wore white dresses and white gloves and held one white rose each. Three of the girls spoke. The first recited by heart in Hebrew, the second in Serbian, and the third in Hungarian. They had two huge wreaths with many roses and other flowers, which they laid in front of the Torah. After the benediction, they each received a book of prayers to remember the day. That afternoon at four o'clock, they were invited to the rabbi's for refreshments.

My sister took that book of prayers with her to forced labor and managed to bring it back home. I hope she still has it. She lives in Subotica and I live in Israel.

JELISAVETA DINIĆ

In June, there was a celebration in the synagogue in Subotica. Fourteen-year-old girls, myself among them, were dressed solemnly in brand-new dresses. We held baskets full of flowers, which we scattered at the entrance to the synagogue. We walked in pairs, then formed a line and walked inside and upstairs to the Torah, where Rabbi Geršom was waiting, and where we all said a prayer. The synagogue was jam-packed because this was a very important ceremony.

In the afternoon, the rabbi invited us for a snack. Unfortunately, I never went because a friend insulted me so gravely that I fainted. This sad event was covered by the daily press. Her words hurt me still today, and I can still cry as I cried then whenever I think about it. My early childhood was very painful. Later on, there was a period of serenity.

EASTERN EUROPE

Not everyone agrees on which countries comprise Eastern Europe. The United Nations includes Belarus, Bulgaria, the Czech Republic, Hungary, Moldova, Poland, Romania, Slovakia, and Ukraine. We have included some of these countries in the section on the former Soviet Union. This section includes testimonies from Bulgaria, the Czech Republic, Hungary, Poland, and Romania. Jews from these countries are mainly of Ashkenazi origin, descendants of Yiddish-speaking Jews who lived in Germany and northern France in medieval times. After the decimation of the Holocaust, some communities of Eastern Europe are experiencing a modest resurgence of Jewish life, including the celebration of the occasional bat mitzvah.

BULGARIA

Compared to the Jews in other Eastern European countries, the Jews of Bulgaria have coexisted relatively peacefully with their non-Jewish neighbors throughout history. In 1909, for example, the government elites and the czar himself attended the consecration of the beautiful synagogue in Sofia. During the Holocaust, the lives of Bulgarian Jews were spared thanks to the opposition to Nazism on all levels of Bulgarian society. Nonetheless, many Bulgarian Jews have emigrated to Israel. From a population of 50,000 Jews at the end of World War II, only about 3,500 Jews remain in Bulgaria.

In 1993, Tania Reytan-Marincheschka, a human rights activist, began her work on behalf of the Jewish community of Sofia. In the year 2000, she tells us, the first "public bat mitzvah celebration" took place. Her use of the word *public* probably reflects decades of needing to hide Jewish rituals from the communist regime, which was intent on stamping out all religion.

Jewish life is full of questions, most famously the four questions of the Passover Haggadah, each of which focuses on one way that the seder is different from other nights. Similarly, Tania's essay is a reflection on a question she finds most pressing: Why is adult bat mitzvah interesting to women in Bulgaria today?

Tania Reytan-Marincheschka

In October 2003, a small group of Jewish women, aged twenty-one to sixty, gathered in Sofia to start an adult bat mitzvah study group. We were aware of the difficulties ahead: institutionalized community support is not expected in the near future; the daily lives of local women do not encourage such endeavors; and spiritual know-how is not readily available. So why does adult bat mitzvah engage the interest of women in Bulgaria and other Eastern European countries? What is the message behind this idea? Is it really feasible to implement the practice of bat mitzvah in the chaotic and contradictory reality of Eastern Europe?

To explore the answers to these questions, we must look at broad social and historical influences. Today in Bulgaria and elsewhere in Eastern Europe, we carry within us lingering, terrifying memories of the twentieth century. Currently, we suffer the social problems inherent in restoring a market economy. In this crisis of modernity, we feel vulnerable. Increasingly, we are realizing that the messages we have received regarding equality and human dignity are problematic.

Living with inequality, uncertainty, and risk, we are also in the process of reclaiming our traditional wisdom for survival. For Jews, some major themes find great resonance in our consciousness. We listen to and appreciate the beauty of the subtle melodies of our life cycles. Time is an essential component of Jewish observance. We have daily cycles and cycles of the week, month, and year; cycles of every seven years and every forty-nine years. These cycles contribute to the sense of continuity in Jewish life and also provide an ongoing way of recharging our optimism and allowing us to participate actively. They provide a wealth of blessings and themes that help to center us.

The growing relationship of women to spirituality is a well-recognized fact, and it has not bypassed Eastern Europe. Jewish women in Bulgaria have connected their search to existing rituals. These include the monthly ritual of Rosh Chodesh and the once-in-a-lifetime event of bat mitzvah, which is part of the lifetime process of increasing spiritual maturity.

Part of the magic of adult bat mitzvah is the process of adding acquired ritual knowledge later in life, and passing it along to the next generations, a wiser mapping of time than in the past. But there are many challenges on the way to women's claiming our place in Jewish life. In the process of the reconstruction of Judaism in Eastern Europe, women are not often seen or heard in the performance of communal rituals, if at all. Of the three living generations of Bulgarian Jewish women who came of age in the twentieth century, none had the possibility of formally becoming a bat mitzvah until 1989. The first public bat mitzvah celebration of a twelve-year-old girl took place in the Sofia synagogue in 2000.

The bat mitzvah of an adult woman is more complex and difficult to implement than that of a young girl. Women are busy and exhausted by their economic struggles as they try to protect themselves and their families from the extremities of the hastily introduced market economy. They can allocate time for serious Jewish studies only with great difficulty. And there is an additional challenge: how to reclaim our traditional wisdom, share it with others, and share the wisdom of our neighbors' faith and traditional lore. How can we attain these kinds of adult maturity? The ultimate answers are far from certain, but we are taking the first little steps.

"We started from the same ground twenty or so years ago," stated an American friend, when she learned about the adult bat mitzvah group I founded. One collateral effect, I told her, might be the birth of a *havurah* (a group that learns about and observes holidays together) of the Reconstructionist type. I hope that the experience and wisdom accumulated in this process can be shared and compared. The process of bridge building, if undertaken formally, would be mutually enriching.

CZECH REPUBLIC

Since the mid-1990s, the Czech Republic has helped to restore Jewish life through educational efforts, such as teacher-training seminars and programs for students and young children on tolerance and the history of the Jews, and cultural events, such as concerts, lectures, and film screenings. In 1999, the Ronald S. Lauder Foundation, one of the major sources of strategic and financial support in these endeavors, brought to the stage *Jonah and Others*, written and directed by Vida Neuwirthova, the author of the brief entry below. Vida's play acquaints preschool children with Jewish history and traditions.

Vida Neuwirthova

During communism, our chief rabbi, Efraim Karol Sidon, was a well-known Czech writer and playwright. Because of his contacts with political dissidents and his criticism of the regime, he had many troubles and left the country. After the revolution, he returned and became our rabbi again. In 2002, the president of our republic, Vaclav Havel, gave state honors to some people who are important for this country and its history. One of the honors was given to our rabbi.

Our Jewish community is Orthodox. Therefore, girls in Prague cannot read from the Torah scrolls in the synagogue. The bat mitzvah girl is given a new Hebrew name, and our rabbi reads it during Shabbat prayers in the synagogue. The community usually organizes a party at the Jewish community center for the bat mitzvah girls.

HUNGARY

In 1859, the Neolog community (a Jewish Hungarian reform movement) built the magnificent Dohány Synagogue (also known as the Great Synagogue) in Budapest with seating for almost 3,000, making it one of the largest synagogues in the world. Theodor Herzl celebrated his bar mitzvah in the Dohány Synagogue. In 1996, the community completed the renovations that repaired the damage that the synagogue had suffered in World War II. Once again, Dohány is the main synagogue of the Jewish community of Budapest.

The fortunes of the Jews of Hungary have risen and fallen through the centuries. At times, Jews were protected, and at others they were expelled. The Holocaust took the lives of about two-thirds of the Jews who lived in Hungary before the war, and it is estimated that 20,000 Jews left following the 1956 Hungarian Revolution. Since the fall of communism, Jewish communities are being revitalized, and today 100,000 Jews live in Hungary.

Katalin Olti is a professor at Semmelweis University's College of Health Care in Budapest. While it avoids the over-the-top nature of some individual celebrations, the group bat mitzvah Katalin describes may leave girls feeling less engaged in a ceremony that, she suggests, lacks the gravity of a boy's bar mitzvah.

Katalin Olti

Dating from before World War II, a public collective bat mitzvah is an old custom at Dohány Synagogue in Budapest. Held on the first evening of Shavuot every year, thirty to forty twelve-year-old girls take part after several weeks of a preparatory course to learn the rules and commandments that apply to Jewish women.

The ceremony is always the same. In front of the main entrance of the beautiful synagogue, two students from the Jewish secondary school await the girls with lighted candles in their hands. With their symbolic lights, they lead the bat mitzvah girls into the synagogue, showing them the way to the ark and to the Torah.

In front of the ark, the rabbi and the hazan are waiting. The rabbi gives a short speech, speaking of the importance of bat mitzvah and the responsibilities and duties of membership in the adult Jewish community. The girls give testimonials concerning mitzvot, Israel, and charity. Then, standing under taliths, the rabbi blesses them.

The parents give a kiddush, and the girls get presents. But here in Hungary, a girl's bat mitzvah is not as serious a celebration as a bar mitzvah.

POLAND

Before World War II, Poland was home to 3.3 million Jews, the second-largest Jewish population in the world. Not only were Polish Jews rich in numbers, they were steeped in culture, thus earning that community the title of "cultural center of world Judaism." Many Jews led comfortable lives, but others lived in squalor. Centuries of anti-Semitism and pogroms paved the way for Polish collaboration with Nazi Germans in killing 85 percent of Poland's Jews. Currently, between 5,000 and 10,000 Jews live in Poland, and there are signs of renewal.

Bella Szwarcman-Czarnota is a scholar of philosophy, a linguist, and the editor of the Jewish-Polish magazine *Midrasz*. Her daughter's decision to become a bat mitzvah was a bold step, which was supported by her rabbi, Michael Schudrich. Born in New York, Rabbi Schudrich was appointed chief rabbi of Poland in 2004. He is credited with the small but remarkable renaissance of Jewish life in Poland, which includes a Jewish primary school in Warsaw; youth, social, and cultural organizations; newspapers; synagogues; charities; and a few kosher restaurants.

Bella Szwarcman-Czarnota

In communist Poland, Jewish girls did not know what a bat mitzvah was. Their parents were nonbelievers, sometimes totally assimilated, and the older generation had died in the Shoah. Who was there to take care of their religious education?

I did not have a bat mitzvah, so I was doubly happy when our daughter, Róża, announced that she would like to prepare for this important moment of assuming religious responsibility. Róża was to become only the third girl in our small community to experience the ceremony.

Rabbi Michael Schudrich, whom Róża has known and liked since early childhood, helped her in her studies. Róża worked on a commentary on the reading of Nicawim (Standing before God). Just before Tisha b'Av, Róża asked us if she could fast for twenty-four hours like the grown-ups. "After my bat mitzvah, there is Yom Kippur, and I am afraid that if I don't try now, later I won't be able to persevere," she said. Listening to these words and looking at her work on the commentary, my husband and I saw that she knew what she wanted and was persistent. We saw that the ceremony meant something more to her than an occasion to get presents and a new dress.

A week before the ceremony, she started daily rehearsals of reading her commentary aloud. It seemed to me that Róża spoke too softly and too quickly. Frankly put, I was nervous. She was not.

When the moment came, Róża delivered the commentary in a stentorian voice, so unusual for a twelve-year-old girl. She was self-assured and did not have the jitters. Listening to her with motherly pride, I thought about what my mother had told me about my grandfather. My pious grandfather, whom I did not know because he died during the war, did not worry that he did not have a son who could recite kaddish after his death. He adored his daughters (and there were seven of them), and used to say that, to him, they were like crown jewels.

There is one more thing. We had never experienced such support, warmth, and help from the whole community. Facing the crowd of guests, I felt a tide of real good will coming in our direction.

Eventually, customs in our community liberalized. Now, girls also learn to read from the Torah, something that Róża was not taught. Sometimes I am sorry that it was not possible earlier. But Róża has her whole life before her. There will be time for reading lessons.

Róża Czarnota and her parents on her bat mitzvah day,
Warsaw, Poland, 1998.

ROMANIA

Bat mitzvah celebrations are rare in Romania, so it should come as no surprise that Iulia Deleanu, a well-known journalist and publicist who writes for a Jewish publication launched in 1956, mentions them in her magazine. In 1870, a Hasidic mutual aid society founded the Gah Synagogue in Suceava in northeastern Romania, where there already were ten synagogues. Few Romanian Jews survived the Holocaust, but several thousand Jews from various places settled in Suceava after the war. When emigration to Israel became possible, the town emptied of Jews once again. The Gah Synagogue is the only one that remains. Given these extreme population shifts, it is remarkable that a Talmud Torah teacher was available to train the bat mitzvah girl and that a bat mitzvah actually took place there.

Iulia Deleanu

Bat mitzvah ceremonies are celebrated rarely in our community. But whenever they take place, they are always noted in our bimonthly magazine, *Realitatea Evreiasca* (Jewish Reality). Based in Bucharest, the magazine covers Jewish cultural, religious, and social life in the country. I write editorials, interviews, essays, and literary criticism.

One bat mitzvah we wrote about occurred in September 1999. It was the bat mitzvah of Marcela Gold, the daughter of Professor Sorin and Dorina Gold from Suceava in northern Moldavia. The ceremony was held in the Gah Synagogue in Suceava.

Along with family and friends, the president of the community, Soil Pietrariu, congratulated the new bat mitzvah. Marcela thanked her parents and grandmothers, the community leadership, and the local Talmud Torah teacher for giving her a Jewish education. She read from her prayer book the *Shema Israel*.

Latin America

Geographers usually include twenty-one countries in Latin America: thirteen in South America, seven in Central America, and one in North America (Mexico). Most of the residents of these countries speak Spanish, with the exceptions of Brazil, where Portuguese is the official language, and Belize, where English is the main language. Sometimes, the island nations of the Caribbean, which have a separate section in this volume, are included in Latin America.

The history of Jewish communities in Latin America is not as thoroughly researched as that of some other areas, but it appears that the first Jews came to Latin America to escape the Inquisitions of Spain and Portugal. Most of these immigrants were Conversos who had been converted forcibly to Christianity. Jews were marginalized and stigmatized in their new homes, and through the generations most of these early settlers lost their Jewish identity.[1] For the most part, the current communities of Latin American Jews did not arrive until the nineteenth century and early twentieth. There are now about 450,000 Jews in Latin America, with the largest number in Argentina and other large communities in Brazil, Mexico, and Uruguay.

Living for the most part in urban centers, Jewish women in Latin America have fewer children and tend to be more highly educated than their non-Jewish compatriots. Although there are increasing numbers of professional Jewish women, male prejudice and anti-Semitism have presented challenges to women's achievements in the workplace. Until the 1970s, almost all congregations in Latin America were Orthodox. After the opening of a Progressive rabbinical seminary in Buenos Aires in the 1960s, the number of Liberal congregations grew. Today, there are more than fifty Liberal congregations in Latin America. In these Liberal congregations, b'not mitzvah are the rule, not the exception.

ARGENTINA

With 185,000 Jews, Argentina has the seventh-largest Jewish population in the world. Irene Lubasch de Münster, the author of the following essay, recently moved to the United States to become the librarian for the Iberia and Latin America collection at Duke University.

Irene attributes the renewal of Jewish life in Argentina to one charismatic individual: Rabbi Marshall T. Meyer, an inspirational American-born Conservative rabbi and human rights activist, who encouraged women's participation in public and private Jewish observances. But perhaps he was ahead of his time and ahead of his community. Irene's parents had to fight their community's attitudes to help her become one of the first girls to have a bat mitzvah in Argentina. Ultimately, it was her skills and abilities, and not an abstract argument about what was "right," that won the community over.

Following the bombings of the Israeli embassy in 1992 and of the Jewish community headquarters in Buenos Aires in 1994 and after a significant economic crisis in 2001, nearly 10,000 Jews left Argentina. With greater economic stability today, Argentina's Jewish community may feel more secure than in the past, although significant new issues, such as increased street crime, still present challenges.

Irene Lubasch de Münster

Led by Rabbi Marshall T. Meyer z"l, Conservative Judaism came to Argentina in the 1960s. Rabbi Meyer was able to infuse a new spirit into the

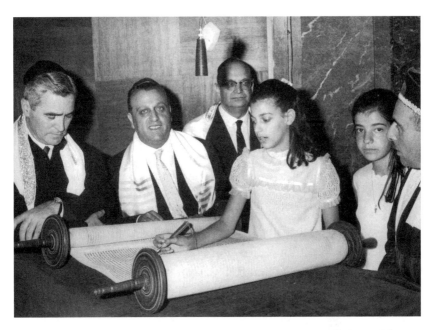

Irene Lubasch de Münster reads the Torah surrounded by (*left to right*)
Rabbi Hirsch, her father, her friend Gabriela's father, Gabriela,
and Cantor Vogel, Buenos Aires, Argentina, 1968.

dying Argentine Jewish community by founding Bet-El Synagogue and
the Rabbinical Seminary of Latin America, an institution to train religious leaders. Thanks to his contributions in the field of spiritual music
and the enthusiasm he exuded as a Jewish leader, Judaism revived, and as
it did, Jewish girls had the opportunity to be part of and participate actively in Jewish festivals and minhagim. Women started to acquire the
same rights and obligations as men. They obtained a broader religious
education and were able to better prepare themselves for both the Jewish and secular worlds.

In 1967, my parents decided that I needed to assume my duties as a
Jewish adult, as my brother had done two years earlier. Accordingly, they
organized one of the first b'not mitzvah to be held in the country. This
wasn't an easy task for them or for me. They had to fight for their ideals
and beliefs. I had to study and understand the parashah and haphtarah,
and what was happening around me. I had to understand that my par-

ents, as they had done before and would do so many times, were laying the foundation for future Jewish generations.

My bat mitzvah took place on November 30, 1968. I shared it with my friend Gabriela. Both of us were studying at Tarbut Hebrew School, so it wasn't difficult to read from the Torah. We attended a year-long instruction program at Lamroth Hakol Synagogue with Cantor Vogel. He had the patience to teach us and the virtue to trust us, since teaching girls was a new experience for him.

My father wanted us to understand what our commitment was about. Therefore, we had to read aloud an essay each of us had written on our parashah. I recall how unhappy I was about this. Not only was I afraid of having to take this big step—reading in front of my friends and my parents' friends—but I was also afraid of having to convey my thoughts about pesukim (psalms) I hardly understood. I say "hardly understood" because I didn't know if my thoughts and feelings were in accordance with what my father wanted me to express. I wanted him to be proud of me. And I was terrified!

The day arrived, and I could hardly speak. How embarrassing! All those months of preparation, and suddenly I was faced with a reduced capacity to sing and read aloud. But I was committed to go through with it; I was prepared to take this big step in my life and in the life of my family.

And suddenly, it was all over. I still recall the faces of my parents and my grandfather: their smiles, their pride, and their fortitude. I had read the parashah, the haphtarah, and given my speech. Gabriela and I had conducted the whole service, to the astonishment of the congregation. They had never thought that women could perform as men did; they had never questioned the status quo. Looking back, I believe it was all worthwhile. I believe that this effort allowed me to become more conscious of my Judaism and my duties as a Jewish woman—not only as a Jewish mother, but as an equal member of our Jewish community.

BOLIVIA

The first Jews to come to Bolivia, escapees from the Spanish Inquisition, went to work in the silver mines. Over the ensuing centuries, the community never grew large, and in the 1930s there were only thirty Jewish families. The population increased in the next decade, when Bolivia granted asylum to German, Polish, and Russian Jews fleeing Hitler's genocidal program. After the war, still more Jews settled in Bolivia, along with Nazi war criminals, who, ironically, were also given a haven. Between the 1950s and the '80s, the majority of Jews left Bolivia in response to political upheaval in the country. The Jewish population of Bolivia today is estimated to be about 600 people. There are two synagogues in La Paz, one of which is the synagogue at the highest elevation in the world.

Leslie Nebel lives in La Paz, the administrative capital of Bolivia, while his ex-wife and daughter live in the third-largest Bolivian city, Cochabamba, which has a beautiful white synagogue with a stained-glass Star of David above the door. Although the family does not live together, they are united with regard to Jewish observance. In Leslie's story, we once again see the significance of a Chabad emissary rabbi for a small, struggling community.

Leslie Nebel

The city of Cochabamba has a very small Jewish community, no larger than a couple of hundred people. When my daughter, Vanessa Noemi, wanted to celebrate her bat mitzvah, her mother and I agreed. It was Vanessa's decision to take this step to signify her sense of belonging to the Jewish community.

Bat mitzvah has never been a tradition in Bolivia. We are not religious, but we have always tried to maintain a traditional Jewish home. We both come from German Conservative Jewish families. This was the first and only bat mitzvah in either of our families.

I live in La Paz, and my ex-wife and daughter live in Cochabamba. Despite our separation and divorce several years ago, we have kept close family relations.

We decided to extend an open invitation to the whole community to share the event with us. Many came, including Chabad rabbi Yossi Smierc's family, whose presence was one of the highlights of the celebration. During the Friday evening service, Vanessa recited some lines from Rambam's Thirteen Principles of Faith as well as some psalms. On Saturday morning, she repeated her part and recited the *Sh'ma*.

Leslie Nebel showed his daughter, Vanessa Noemi, how to
put on tefillin, Cochabamba, Bolivia, 2002.

My daughter and I keep in very close contact by telephone. I visit every now and then, and her mother and Vanessa visit me as well. Vanessa is proud to be the only Jewish girl in her class and one of the few in her school.

BRAZIL

Jews arrived in Brazil in 1497, fleeing the Portuguese Inquisition. Throughout the centuries, Jews suffered discrimination in Brazil, but today they are active participants in most arenas of life, including politics, business, and the arts. There are forty Brazilian synagogues—both Ashkenazi and Sephardi—serving the Jewish population of 150,000. Brazil also has Jewish publications, university-based Jewish studies centers, kosher restaurants, and more than 200 charitable, cultural, and educational organizations. In 2001, Kahal Zur, a synagogue in Recife that had been closed for 350 years, was reopened, and in 2004, São Paulo was named a sister city to Tel Aviv. Recife is famous as the point of departure of the first group of Jews who came to North America and settled in New Amsterdam, the forerunner of New York.

In her beautiful story, writer Monica Guttmann tells about her two bat mitzvah ceremonies and the differences between them. She shares this unusual experience with very few Jewish women. A psychologist specializing in art therapy and art education, Monica has written numerous essays for magazines and newspapers and ten books for children, including a world atlas. Monica has a private clinic and gives lectures and workshops on developing Jewish identity through art therapy.

Monica Guttmann

I was ten or eleven years old when the girls who attended my Jewish day school in São Paulo began to think about their b'not mitzvah. I belonged to a traditional Jewish family. My father's father was a chazan (cantor) and a teacher of Judaism at the Congregação Israelita Paulista, the biggest and most important Liberal synagogue in the city. My mother's father was one of the Torah readers during High Holidays in a Hungarian synagogue. For a whole year, we studied, learning about the matriarchs and other important Jewish women, rehearsing the brachot and chants we would sing during the ceremony, discussing what we would wear. Then, the ceremony took place.

What has remained of it? I remember my dress, my shyness when reciting a bracha all alone with everyone looking at me. I remember wondering what my Jewish commitment would be from then on. What would be different? What should I change, add, transform, and know?

The years passed. In my family, the presence of Judaism remained strong, and Shabbatot and holidays were celebrated with much love. But, like many others, I had a hard time in adolescence. I questioned my Judaism and searched for God in other religions and cultures.

When I was sixteen, I had my first experience in Israel. Something touched me. I slowly began to find God inside myself. I wanted to return to Judaism in a different, more personal, creative, and transforming way. Eight years later, I lived in Israel for nine months. After that, I felt the need to study more deeply the tradition that had so strongly influenced my paths, my choices, and my relations with the world.

In one of the many courses and Jewish groups I attended, I met the man who would become my husband. Together, we began to attend our synagogue, Comunidade Shalom. We became more and more involved, and today, besides attending its services and activities, we contribute as lay leaders. Once a month, I offer an art therapy activity linked to a Jewish subject. I find that Judaism is a constant source of artistic inspiration and opportunity for self-knowledge.

In this personal, emotional, and spiritual environment, I wanted to give myself a second chance and celebrate my bat mitzvah once again, this time on the eve of my Jewish wedding. After ten years of being together, we decided to stand under the chuppah (wedding canopy), and I made a commitment to read the Torah, inspired by my community and my personal development as a human being, a woman, and a Jew.

My studies for reading the Torah brought back strong remembrances of my grandparents dipping their hearts and voices into such a magical world (as my grandpa used to say) of letters, sounds, images, and symbols. I felt united with other times and, in some sense, beyond time. Standing before the Torah scroll, I vividly felt the presence of my father of blessed memory, of my grandparents, and the sum of all our traditions.

Here in São Paulo, there are many pathways to the ritual of bat mitzvah. Orthodox synagogues and schools do not organize religious ceremonies, only symbolic ones sometimes. In the Conservative synagogues, girls participate together, praying, singing, and making speeches, but they do not read the Torah. After the ceremony, it is common to have a huge party with family and friends.

Our Comunidade Shalom is an egalitarian community where women have the same rights as men and participate in all activities. Some women wear kippot and many wear tallitot. Women are counted in the minyan and read the Torah as men do. A girl has her bat mitzvah alone, not with a group. Girls study for two years, and on the bat mitzvah day they have their first aliyah and read from the Torah for the first time. Their parents take an active part in the ceremony.

My real bat mitzvah took place on March 9, 2002 (25 Adar 5762). At that moment, I celebrated the sealing of a search and a profound choice. I don't remember the clothes I was wearing. There was no shyness—only happiness, reverence, love, and gratitude for being a daughter of this people, this tradition, and this family.

CHILE

Jews have been present in Chile since the time of the Spanish conquest in the sixteenth century. With Chilean independence in 1818, Jews gained positions of influence, which they have maintained to this day in spite of the latent anti-Semitism that some observers claim lies beneath the surface. Nearly a third of the Jewish population left Chile in the 1970s during the time of the Marxist Allende government. Some returned when military dictator Augusto Pinochet came to power and stabilized the economy, while others were forced into exile. Today, Chile has about 20,000 Jews.

Born in Argentina, Cantor Anibal Mass describes b'not mitzvah in Santiago, Chile, where he prepared girls for the ceremony during his years there, following his studies. His essay shows the diversity of attitudes and practices in one urban community and suggests the difficulties of initiating change. Now the cantor at Congregation Shaarey Zedek Shofar in Winnipeg, Manitoba, Canada, he was honored by the Manitoba legislature in 2003 for his work in the Jewish community.

Anibal Mass

It is strange to be writing from Winnipeg, Canada, about how a bat mitzvah ceremony is conducted in Chile. But if I am certain of one thing, it is that my time in Winnipeg has made me appreciate this subject from a different point of view. I want to make clear that the opinions expressed in this commentary represent my own particular viewpoint, and do not in any way constitute the official attitude of any social or religious institution in Chile.

I worked full time as a cantor and bar/bat mitzvah teacher during my almost nine years in the Israeli Community of Santiago, Chile, a Conservative congregation numbering 600 families. During that time, I prepared about 200 b'not mitzvah.

Despite Chile having advanced significantly in the general area of women's rights, only one of the four Conservative synagogues in Santiago is egalitarian. Therefore, the bat mitzvah ceremony—including the one at the Israeli Community of Santiago—is often carried out during a Kabbalat Shabbat service or during Havdalah. As a consequence, many girls make the choice to forgo the bat mitzvah ceremony because it is considered less important than the bar mitzvah.

Girls in the Israeli Community of Santiago begin their preparation about a year and a half in advance of the bat mitzvah by attending group classes. Once a week, they study "theory," including the significance of being Jewish, the festivals, and how they are celebrated. Then comes three months of group preparation in liturgy and studying the prayers involved in different religious ceremonies with the cantor. Three months before the ceremony, they begin individual practice sessions with the cantor, during which they learn the specific prayers they will chant on the day of the bat mitzvah ceremony. They also prepare a summary of the week's parashah and their commentary on it. During the ceremony, the obligation of assuming mitzvot in their lives is sealed by the reading of a dissertation of obligation in front of the Aron Hakodesh and receiving the blessing of Aaron Hakohen from the rabbi.

The process of preparation also includes two or three meetings with the rabbi, who speaks with the family and the girl about the bat mitzvah as an enriching experience of family growth. At the same time, he tries to convince the family that the celebration should not involve extravagant expenditures, that they can make a lovely party combined with tzedekah. Despite the efforts of the rabbi, however, the parties are usually lavish affairs, with large orchestras, performers, and dancers, at which the food is not kosher 90 percent of the time, and the donations of tzedekah are minimal. (In contrast, in Winnipeg, boys and girls prepare the same way, and the emphasis is on the ceremony and not on the party that follows.)

A noteworthy result of the Chilean experience is that, during the months of group study, the girls have the opportunity to get to know Jewish girls from other schools. From these meetings, great friendships have been born, including plans to have joint b'not mitzvah instead of individual ceremonies.

COLOMBIA

Since the 1960s, Colombia has been plagued by kidnappings and violence at the hands of extremist paramilitary groups, guerrillas, and drug traffickers. Although the country now is more stable than in the past, many of its upper-middle-class Jews have left, primarily for South Florida. Only about 3,300 Jews remain in Colombia, and most of them live in Bogotá, the capital. The current population of Jews arrived in the early twentieth century from Sephardic communities of Greece, Turkey, and Syria. Others came from Ashkenazi communities of Europe, many after the rise of Hitler. There are nine synagogues in Bogotá and many Jewish organizations.

Ethel Schuster, originally from Barranquilla, is one of the Jews who left for the United States. With a Ph.D. in computer and information sciences from the University of Pennsylvania, she has taught computer science in many U.S. universities and is now at Northern Essex Community College in Massachusetts.

Ethel and her friends—Noemi Rais and Claudia Gontovnik, both of Florida, and Margie Milhem and Rachel Safdeye Nasser, both of New York City—focus on the contrasts between the bar and the bat mitzvah, between group and individual ceremonies, and between real learning and superficial partying. These brief testimonies show how geographic change and the passage of time can rewrite the religious and social rituals of bat mitzvah.

Maribel Schuster, Ethel's sister-in-law, still lives in Barranquilla, a community that illustrates the shrinkage of the Jewish population in Colombia. She is the vice president of the board of Colegio Hebreo Unión, a private Jewish school for children from nursery through high school.

Ethel Schuster and Friends

ETHEL SCHUSTER

My family belonged to a Conservative synagogue in Barranquilla, where bat mitzvahs were celebrated in a group ceremony. We were a group of ten friends of about the same age. All of us except one attended the Colegio

Hebreo Unión, the Jewish day school. In May 1972, we all participated in a bat mitzvah service that consisted of readings, traditional prayers, and group singing. It included a "Kaddish for the Jewish Mothers," as well as a reading about Jewish mothers. I was the last one on the program, and I read "A Personal Invocation."

Our bat mitzvah was a joyful event, and we prepared for it with all our hearts. We practiced the songs, our respective reading parts, and parading. Since the bat mitzvah was held on a Sunday morning, the service did not include reading the Torah. Thus, none of us was taught to read trope (the marks that indicate the melody when chanting). After the ceremony at the synagogue, there was a festive breakfast organized by our parents and served to the community. I remember that we did not have any dancing or music, which is traditionally a part of any Colombian celebration.

The same traditions continue in Barranquilla today. Girls have their group bat mitzvah, while boys have an individual bar mitzvah. Girls are not taught to read Torah and trope, while boys are given that instruction. From a logistical point of view, it is easier to plan a group event since the tasks involved in the planning and organization, as well as the costs, are divided among the families. But there is a different cost: I remember having to agree on the color of the cloth, the design of the dress, the reception, and every other detail.

None of the girls in my bat mitzvah group live in Barranquilla today. One of us lives in Cartagena, Colombia; eight of us live in the United States; and one lives in Argentina. We keep in touch through our parents and grandparents who still live in Colombia. And the memories are always sweet.

NOEMI RAIS

I like the idea of a group bat mitzvah, even if it sounds old-fashioned. Bat mitzvahs have become important and a big to-do nowadays. If there were a group of girls with whom my daughter could celebrate her bat mitzvah, I'd go for it.

CLAUDIA GONTOVNIK

I don't remember many details about my bat mitzvah. I do remember that the boys studied the Torah and we did not, that they had their own very

Ethel Schuster reads her piece during her bat mitzvah
in Barranquilla, Colombia, 1972.

important studies and ceremony and we did not, that it was their families'
most important and proud day and ours was not. Of course, we learned
some songs and sang them. Some had solo pieces. We had pretty dresses
in a pretty fabric. I remember having a good time, but it was not an important part of my life.

I still ask myself, now more than ever, why was there that difference
from the boys? I would love to see the day when, in our Jewish communities in Colombia, we have the opportunity and honor to start lives of
mitzvot as Jewish women.

MARGIE MILHEM

Margie Milhem woke up with chicken pox on the day of the bat mitzvah, and she could not participate. The rabbi read her parts. A few days
after she recuperated, her father made her get dressed up and had pictures
taken of her in her bat mitzvah dress.

RACHEL SAFDEYE NASSER

In 1972, I was the only member of the group who did not attend the Hebrew school. That made it all the more difficult, as Rabbi Angel demanded that I learn to read Hebrew if I wanted to participate. I remember finding this unfair, as the rest of the girls had grown up with the language. But he tested me, and I passed!

It was not common in the Sephardi tradition for a girl to be a bat mitzvah, and to a degree, it is still not common today. It took some talking with my father, but eventually he agreed.

As I prepare for my daughter, Emilie's, bat mitzvah, I am dealing with cultural and traditional differences between how I grew up and how she is growing up. How do you explain these to your child? You cave in and plan a celebration like her brother's two years ago. Born in New York City, Emilie is not Colombian and has not been in Colombia for the past five years. My daughter will not have a group bat mitzvah, nor a Conservative service. She will do a d'var Torah, followed by a disco party. In our circle of friends, girls have bat mitzvah celebrations as elaborate as the boys.

Maribel Schuster

I live in Barranquilla, where I belong to the Centro Israelita Filantrópico, an Ashkenazi community that is nearly eighty years old. My husband's family comes from Poland and Romania. Today, we have 150 families, but twenty years ago we had 350. We have a Jewish school, a social community center, a synagogue, and a cemetery. It has been five years since we had a rabbi at our synagogue, so our children have their religion classes at the Jewish day school, where there are two Lubavitch rabbis.

The tradition of celebrating bat mitzvah in our community is well established, and every girl looks forward to that day. My daughter, Yael, had her bat mitzvah in 2002. When girls in Barranquilla are twelve, the wife of one of the Lubavitch rabbis helps them to prepare. They go to classes every Sunday afternoon for four or five months at the Lubavitch library.

Usually, there is an activity that goes with the lesson of the day. For example, each girl had to learn about her Hebrew name and why it was chosen. Then the girls made their own presentation cards. When they learned

Yael Schuster celebrated her bat mitzvah at Centro Israelita
Filántropico in Barranquilla, Colombia, 2002.

about kosher meal preparation, they created a menu, prepared a meal, and
invited their mothers to enjoy the food and the occasion. They learned
how to prepare challah for Shabbat, and each girl made two of them for
the next Shabbat dinner with her family.

She teaches them about the mikve and talks a little about the laws of
nida (family purity) if the group is interested. She also complements what
they are learning at school about the daily tefila. Three times a week,
they practice the songs they will sing. Yael's group prepared *Shehejeyanu,
Aishes Chayil, Hine Ma Tov, Shein Vi DiLevune, Mi Ma,* and *Bat Mitzvah*

Meidel Mazel Tov (Hebrew and Yiddish songs), which they sang at the end of the ceremony as they came out of the synagogue. Let me tell you, it was so beautiful that people wanted to clap. They looked like professionals!

The ceremony usually takes place on a Saturday after Shabbat has ended, so it does not correspond to any of the services at the synagogue. The girls wear the same dresses, which the mothers approve after the girls pick the style, but in different colors. They enter the synagogue by the central aisle and sit facing the congregation, with the Aron Hakodesh at their back. Between songs, each girl reads her interpretation of the parasha that corresponds to her birthday date. At Yael's bat mitzvah, we included blessings from the mothers and grandmothers of the b'not mitzvah.

I know some people will wonder why the girls do not read Torah, as they once used to do in our community. From my point of view, mothers do not feel strongly that the girls should receive this honor. Besides, our rabbis are Lubavitch and they are not interested in teaching girls the reading of Torah. That is the way things are, and at the moment no one is interested in making the effort to change the ceremony. But I am sure that if a family were interested in their daughter learning to read Torah and wearing a tallit, and could find someone to teach her, the synagogue would be happy to have a girl conduct a service.

After the ceremony, there is always a big party at the community center across from the synagogue. We have a beautiful, yummy buffet and the most amazing desserts you will ever eat. Every mother spends weeks making her best recipes for the party. Since we are such a small community, every member is invited to the celebration. We all dance until late at night.

COSTA RICA

The Jewish community of Costa Rica has been called "a peaceful community in a peaceful land."[2] Costa Ricans are committed to education for all, have no standing army, are ecological activists who preserve their natural wonders, and are tolerant of minorities, including Jews. One wave of Sephardi Jews lived in Costa Rica as Conversos (Jews who were forced to adopt Christianity, at least publicly) after the Inquisitions in Spain and Portugal. Another group came as merchants in the nineteenth century. The majority of today's Costa Rican Jewish community arrived before World War II from Eastern Europe, nearly half from two villages in Poland.

Located in the capital, San Jose, the Instituto Dr. Jaim Weizman, which is named for the first president of Israel, is a mainstay of the community. The high academic level of the institute and its intensive Jewish education program are partly the result of the school employing teachers sent from Israel for multi-year stints.

Karen Ponchner, a graduate of the University of Costa Rica with a degree in chemical engineering and of MIT's graduate business school, is a Boston-area resident who remembers fondly the communal nature of her bat mitzvah preparation, which was different from boys' bar mitzvah instruction, but nevertheless of great value to her.

Karen Ponchner

Bat mitzvah in Costa Rica is a school event. Not an old tradition, it has probably been done for about twenty years. I went to a British school in the early years, but in the sixth grade my parents sent me to the Jewish day school, Instituto Jaim Weizman, so that I could have a bat mitzvah. The other girls had been taking Hebrew for five years, and I hadn't, but I caught up. I knew most of the girls from before—there are about 3,000 people in the Jewish community of San Jose—so it wasn't a difficult adjustment.

In the middle of the school year, all the girls were prepared together. There were fifteen girls, everyone about twelve years old. We met every week for six months. We did crafts related to Jewish homemaking. I remember that we made a matzoh plate and a scrapbook. The teachers were from Israel, so we learned Israeli songs and dances. Once, we went to a teacher's house, and I remember seeing her pull a chicken out of a pot of salted water, where it had been koshered.

The bat mitzvah itself was in the hall of the community center, near the synagogue. Every girl was allowed to invite twenty people. In addition to singing and dancing, we put on a performance as part of the bat mitzvah. I played the part of a bride. The boys in our class also took part, doing a mariachi performance. They brought silk flowers for the girls.

On the Shabbat before, we had gone to services in the synagogue. There, the bat mitzvah girls lit candles with our mothers, and our fathers went to the Torah. The parents had prepared refreshments for a reception after the service.

The bat mitzvah in Costa Rica is simpler than a bar mitzvah. It is a nice community event to ensure that girls don't feel left out. But the really elaborate coming-of-age ceremony is a girl's wedding.

EL SALVADOR

Marga Biller is an educational consultant who now lives in the Boston area. Her entry about bat mitzvah shows that the resilience of the tiny Jewish population of El Salvador rests in great measure on the determination and courage of its women, including her grandmother. It is heartening to know that the small community has established a community center and now has two synagogues (Conservative and Reform), a kindergarten, a youth group (the same one that Marga led as a teenager), a university students organization, and a monthly newsletter.

Marga Biller

El Salvador is in Central America, a small, densely populated country about the size of Rhode Island. In the early 1900s, Jewish German and French immigrants came to Central America seeking a better life than they had known in Europe. One of those immigrants was my grandfather Max Freund, who came from Strelitz in Germany (now Poland). Five years after his arrival, my grandfather went back to his native town to find a wife. My grandmother Herta Freund, then eighteen, accepted his marriage proposal and returned with him to El Salvador. She was one of the many brave women who became pillars of the Jewish community.

Eventually, the Jewish families numbered about seventy. During my childhood in the 1970s, only three girls were b'not mitzvah. These girls were considered pioneers. They studied with a rabbi and with their own mothers, learned women who taught the children of the community about Jewish traditions, as well as Hebrew.

The Jewish population began to grow again in 1992, after the end of a twelve-year civil war that had forced many families to emigrate. Services are now held in a house that once belonged to a family from the congregation that moved to the United States. The house has been transformed into a welcoming community center housing the sanctuary, a gathering place for Jewish youth, a stage for presentations, and a wonderful garden where many community celebrations are held.

It wasn't until 2001 that girls started to have bat mitzvah ceremonies again. These days, girls study with the rabbi and his wife to prepare for their bat mitzvah day. They lead the entire service on Friday night and on Saturday. As part of their bat mitzvah experience, the girls do community service projects. My cousin Michele chose to collect clothing, which she distributed to children who live in a poor section of the city.

Since our family now lives all over the world, Michele's bat mitzvah offered a reason for many family members to return to San Salvador. After participating in the service and listening to Michele's interpretation of her Torah portion, the guests enjoyed a happy celebration. For some of the non-Jewish guests, this was their first exposure to the Jewish community.

There may have been some doubt during the 1980s and '90s about whether the Jewish community would survive. But thanks to the efforts of those families who continue to make Judaism a priority in their lives and who pass on the traditions that were given to them by their grandparents and great-grandparents, that doubt no longer exists.

GUATEMALA

Few traces of the original Converso (Jews forced to convert to Christianity) settlers of the Spanish colonial period remain in Guatemala. Assimilation has also wiped out the remnants of the German Jewish community of the mid-nineteenth century. The current population includes German and Middle Eastern Jews who arrived in Guatemala at the beginning of the twentieth century, and Jews from Eastern Europe who arrived in the 1920s. After World War II, Guatemala allowed entry to European refugees. In 1948, it was the first country in the United Nations to recognize Israel.

Deedie Karake's story shows the unusual history of bat mitzvah in Guatemala: individual ceremonies similar to boys' b'nai mitzvah have given way to group bat mitzvah ceremonies that seem less like those of boys. This change probably reflects the closing of the Reform synagogue and the influence of more traditional Orthodox groups, which encourage gender differences in religious practice. Deedie paints a picture of acceptance and of the cherishing of the bat mitzvah ceremony—however it is conducted—as part of Jewish life in Guatemala. Deedie and her husband, Miguel, were among the founders of the Gan Hillel preschool in Guatemala City, where she was the first administrative director.

Deedie Karake

The Jewish community of Guatemala is very small. There are roughly a thousand people, and sadly, not all of them are active as Jews. We have two synagogues in Guatemala City, one Ashkenazi and one Sefaradí. Everyone is welcome in both, and in general, we feel at home in either of them. We have a kosher mini-market, El Kolbo, on the premises of the Jewish Community Center (JCC). The community also runs a nursery and preschool that has been recognized as one of the best in Guatemala. At the Tarbut school, children learn about Judaism three afternoons a week until their bar or bat mitzvah.

The first bat mitzvah in Guatemala took place in 1965 in a Reform temple, Beth El. This temple, which no longer exists, started the tradition of preparing young girls for their bat mitzvah in the same way young boys prepared for their bar mitzvah. The girls had to study for about a year, and on the day of their bat mitzvah they read a parashá, followed by a haftará. They also did all the corresponding tehfillahs during the service. Afterward, there was always a reception with friends and family members.

When Beth El disappeared, bat mitzvah ceremonies switched over to a collective format. In 1974, the first group of thirteen young girls got together to celebrate their bat mitzvah. This bat mitzvah was held on a Saturday night. The girls wore dresses of the same color. Each read something that she had learned and found interesting, and together they sang Jewish songs. Following the service, there was a reception that all JCC members attended.

Twenty-eight years later, I spoke with some of the girls who participated in that first group bat mitzvah. They all said that their bat mitzvah helped them to learn about religion and united them with Judaism. It also

Bat mitzvah, Guatemala City, Guatemala, 1988.

created close bonds among them. They cherish those times. I have witnessed how these women have transmitted Jewish values and knowledge to their families, especially to their daughters.

The most important thing about bat mitzvahs in Guatemala is that the girls in our community keep on celebrating them. Sometimes, bat mitzvah ceremonies are held with large groups together, sometimes with only two girls. They are usually held on Thursday mornings or Saturday nights, followed by a large party or an intimate celebration with close friends and relatives. Since 1965, the tradition of bat mitzvah has prevailed, and the girls of Guatemala continue to pass on their knowledge of Judaism to other generations.

HONDURAS

In the 1920s, immigrants from Europe established two Jewish communities in Honduras, one in Tegucigalpa and the other in San Pedro Sula. In the 1970s and 1980s, many Israelis arrived to work in engineering, agriculture, and security. Today, there are about fifty Jewish families in Honduras. A new synagogue, Shevet Achim, was inaugurated in Tegucigalpa in 2003 after Hurricane Mitch devastated the country and destroyed the original synagogue.

Rosario Losk took the name Ruth at her conversion to Judaism, an appropriate name for this mother of four children. Many women who convert to Judaism strengthen the entire Jewish community in which they live, as well as their own families. This seems to be the case for Rosario, who became the honorary consul of Israel in Tegucigalpa and who organizes celebrations of Israeli Independence Day. Formerly the assistant director of the Peace Corps training center in Tegucigalpa, she is the founder of Conversa, a Spanish-language school, and a member of the board of directors at Shevet Achim.

Rosario Losk

We are a State Department family that has moved frequently, and synagogues have been a stabilizing element in our lives. We lived for many years in Tegucigalpa and were long-time members of that small Jewish community. My husband, David, was president of the community, led services for years, and pushed for the purchase of a modest house that eventually became its first community-owned synagogue and meeting place. Our daughter Rebecca had been going there since the first grade with many friends. So we decided that that was where her bat mitzvah would take place.

We realized that it was unusual for such an event to take place in Tegucigalpa. The fact that we are so few in the community means that one

Rebecca Losk at her bat mitzvah in Tegucigalpa, Honduras, 2000.

Rebecca Losk and her father after her bat mitzvah service,
Tegucigalpa, Honduras, 2000.

is, in many senses, alone. In the U.S., where one's friends observe their b'nai mitzvah almost every week at age thirteen, it is easier to assume the burden of study and carry it through. The incentive is almost built in. Not so here, where we have, at the most, one bar or bat mitzvah ceremony per year. One must find the motivation and the incentive from within.

Rebecca's bat mitzvah became a family project. Her brothers, her sister, and I provided full support and studied with her, especially the Torah portion. Given the difficulty of the endeavor, we decided to share her parasha with two friends in the community. Each would read three aliyot, and Rebecca would read the final aliyah, which contained the Ten Commandments.

Of course, Rebecca responded appropriately, adding her own drive and energy to the effort. If it were not for that, no amount of encouragement or insistence from family or friends could have compensated. We sensed that she wanted to please her family, but at the same time, she did it because she wanted to do it for herself. If she is like her father, who continues to think with awe about the meaning of his own bar mitzvah, and like her mother, a converted Jew who finds extraordinary comfort and joy in Judaism, Rebecca will take her place as a Jewish adult who will spend her life seeking the hidden and not-so-hidden treasures of our faith.

MEXICO

In Mexico, as in many countries of Latin America, the first Jews who arrived were fleeing the Inquisitions of Spain and Portugal. When the Inquisition came to Mexico itself, Jews were again forced into exile. It was only in the late 1800s, after the official separation of church and state in Mexico, that Jews came in large numbers, mainly from Russia, followed by Sephardic Jews from Turkey and Syria. For the most part, Mexico's 40,000–50,000 Jews, 95 percent of whom live in Mexico City, have encountered little anti-Semitism and have attained respected positions in politics, journalism, business, and the arts.

Eva Ginsburg Resnikoff, an English literature teacher and translator, documents her efforts to find a bat mitzvah girl in the sprawling and divided Jewish community of Mexico City. This was not easy. Despite the fact that "most Jews in Mexico consider themselves Jews first and Mexicans second,"[3] most are not religiously observant. The intermarriage rate is low, and most children attend a Jewish school. At the same time, because Mexican culture values tradition, the modern innovation of bat mitzvah has only now become more common.

Ada Smoler, the bat mitzvah girl Eva finally found, was encouraged by her mother to study for her bat mitzvah. The determination and influence of mothers to create change for their daughters is a theme that runs through many of the bat mitzvah stories in this book.

Eva Ginsburg Resnikoff

The Jewish community of Mexico City, where most Mexican Jews live, is unique in more ways than one. I believe it is the only (or one of the only) places in the world in which we are divided not only by different levels of religiosity but by places of origin. There are four different communities, and each has its own traditions, synagogues, schools, cemeteries, newspapers. The four groups are the Ashkenazim, who came from Eastern Europe; the Sfaradim, who came from Spain and Turkey; the Shami, who are originally from Damascus in Syria; and the Halevi, who also come from Syria, but from Aleppo. Intercommunity cooperation does exist, but relations are distrustful and strained. If you add to this the distance between places and the traffic of our overpopulated city, you get an idea of the apathy that plays a big role in our lives, as in the lives of all those living in this immense urban mess.

I experienced this pervasive division among Jewish groups when I tried to find someone who would help me with this essay. I couldn't write from experience because I didn't have a bat mitzvah and neither did any of my acquaintances. I wrote a small article for the newspaper of the Jewish Sports Center, which caters to members of all of the communities. I asked for help, but no one got in touch with me. I went to a synagogue near my house to see if there were any b'not mitzvah scheduled so I could witness one, but there weren't. I contacted some people at an important magazine called *Tribuna Israelita*. They gave me email addresses for two rabbis, but they did not respond. Mexico is a wonderful, magical country, but it is also one where it is difficult to get things done.

I was about to give up and write only about my difficulties when some friends who live in Chicago came to visit a cousin of theirs who lives in Mexico City. I asked if she'd had a bat mitzvah and if she'd help. She had, and she would! So I am very grateful to Ada Smoler for granting me an interview and for welcoming me into her home, where I met her beautiful twin daughters. This is what she said:

My mother's family was Orthodox and my dad's wasn't religious at all. When they got married and lived in the United States for a while, they came into contact with the Conservative branch of Judaism. My mother liked the Conservative movement because things were done differently from the Orthodox, and men and women could sit together in the synagogue. My parents were among the first members of Beth El, the Conservative temple in Mexico City, and we children grew up there.

My mom studied medicine in a class that had twenty women out of a hundred students. It was very important for her that men and women be treated equally. If my brothers had a bar mitzvah, why wouldn't I? And if they had it at thirteen, why not I?

I had my bat mitzvah at a time when girls got to choose between that, a trip, or a big party for *quince años*, an important and symbolic celebration for young ladies here in Mexico, when they come of age and are presented to society. The father dances a waltz with his daughter and makes a speech; girls are given high-heeled shoes and their last doll.

As far as I know, the idea of having b'not mitzvah in Mexico started at Beth El just before mine. When I did my bat mitzvah in the mid-1980s, I studied for a whole year with many boys and a few other girls. I learned the haphtarah, not a parashah, because women did not read Torah, and I did all the tfillah during the ceremony, which took place on a Saturday morning.

Family came, those living in Mexico and elsewhere, and I felt really important reading in front of everyone. My parents offered a big breakfast, and in the afternoon we invited close family and friends to our house and served the leftovers. It wasn't a dance party. My mom, who was very proud of me, believed that spiritual is spiritual, and it has nothing to do with wild parties. So we had a nice, simple, quiet get-together.

Nowadays, it is fashionable to celebrate a bat mitzvah; it's like a fad. Orthodox girls in Mexico now also have b'not mitzvah, although I imagine that the ceremony is different. There are collective b'not mitzvah at some of the Jewish schools. But I think that when my daughters, who are now a year old, have their b'not mitzvah, things will be very much the same. Change in the Jewish community comes slowly and reluctantly.

PANAMA

We offer two stories about b'not mitzvah in the 7,000-member Jewish community of Panama. Jews have been firmly entrenched in Panama's economy and society since the end of the nineteenth century, when Sephardic Jews from Syria and Turkey and a smaller number of Jews from Europe arrived. Panama is one of the few countries in the world where a small Jewish population is growing, aided by a booming economy that has attracted more than a thousand Israelis in recent years. It is the only country other than Israel that has had two Jewish presidents in the twentieth century. In a country where three-quarters of the Jewish community is Orthodox and 85 percent keep kosher, Panama City has the largest kosher supermarket outside of Israel.

The first story, by Ivette Zebede, describes the group bat mitzvah ceremony created by the Jewish school that the girls attend. Instituto Alberto Einstein, established in 1955, is one of three Jewish day schools that together educate 1,300 students in Panama City. The bat mitzvah is a meaningful occasion that is distinctly different from the bar mitzvah.

The second story, by Roslyn Zelenka, takes off from the point at which Ivette Zebede's story ends. Kol Shearith Israel, under the umbrella of the World Union for Progressive Judaism, encourages girls to participate in bat mitzvah ceremonies. With 180 families, the Reform congregation has struggled to gain the acceptance of the majority Orthodox Jewish community. It dedicated a new house of worship in 2006. The opportunity for Katie Zelenka to hold the Torah and the chance for her grandmother to

Instituto Alberto Einstein students at their bat mitzvah
celebration, Panama City, Panama, 2003.

receive an aliyah are unusual in Panama. In this symbolic way, membership in the Jewish community was passed from grandmother to mother
to daughter, just as the Torah was passed from one generation to another.

Ivette Zebede

The Instituto Alberto Einstein, a Jewish school of the Panamanian community, devotes two hours a week to bat mitzvah preparation as part of
the regular sixth-grade curriculum. The school prepares the young people
because the synagogue to which the majority of the Jewish population in
Panama belongs is the Sephardic congregation, Shevet Ahim, which does
not usually celebrate b'not mitzvah.

The preparatory courses are about the duties and responsibilities of the
Jewish woman, including tending to a Jewish home, knowing the impor-

tance of Jewish women in history, practicing tefila, knowing the laws of kashrut, and learning to make *jalot* (challah) with the *rabisa* (rabbi's wife) of the community. In other words, the courses teach important topics for Jewish women.

Moreover, along with the academic activities, we pick a date to celebrate with all the b'not mitzvah girls from the school. This is a very exciting day for the school community. Each year, we select a different theme that has to do with the importance of Jewish women, our beliefs, and our faith. We invite parents, family, and community members, and the girls put on a show in which they dance, act, light candles in honor of Jewish women, and otherwise rejoice in this important day. They all get certificates of recognition as b'not mitzvah.

In conclusion, we desire to instill and impress upon our young women basic Jewish values. Thus, we can be content in the knowledge that we have done our job.

Roslyn Zelenka

As the majority of the Jewish community in Panama follows the Orthodox tradition, women are not permitted to go to the bimah in the synagogue. It is considered a sin. Only in the Reform congregation are bat mitzvahs performed in the same manner as bar mitzvahs for boys. My daughter, Katie, went to the Instituto Alberto Einstein and participated in the collective bat mitzvah ceremony at school. However, she also had her bat mitzvah at Kol Shearith Israel, the Reform Sephardic synagogue.

Katie's story is an unusual one. The rabbi who was preparing her passed away two months before her bat mitzvah. There was no one in Panama to continue to train her, and our congregation did not have a new rabbi yet. So Katie listened to a tape prepared by our deceased rabbi. And on her own, at twelve years old, she basically trained herself for her Torah portion, assisted only by her father.

It was an emotional time for us all. Katie conducted the service on Friday night and was called to the Torah on Saturday morning to recite her portion—the entire portion, not just the haftorah. Our services at that time were conducted in three languages: Spanish, English, and, of course, He-

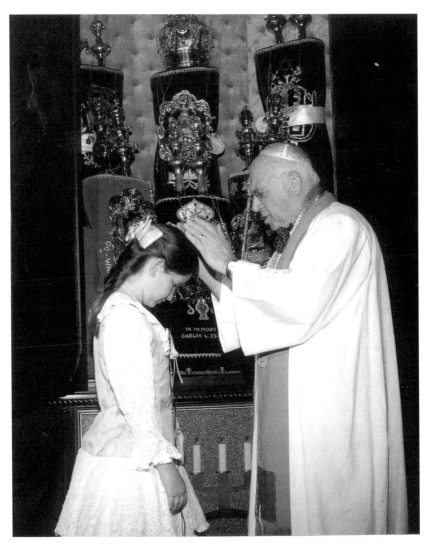

Katie Zelenka receives a blessing from Rabbi Bernard Zlotovitz,
Panama City, Panama, 1995

brew. Our close family friend Rabbi Bernard Zlotovitz came from New York to officiate. He incorporates into his services a beautiful tradition of physically passing down the Torah from parents to child, so the child truly feels she is receiving something precious, which of course she is. The day was also very special, as it was the first time my mother, z"l, had ever been called up for an aliyah. So there were three generations of women on the bimah at the same time—my mother, my daughter, and myself. And Katie was great!

PARAGUAY

Paraguay, a landlocked country sandwiched between Argentina and Brazil, has been isolated for much of its history because of political unrest and instability. Although there is a large non-Jewish German population, many of whom were given a haven after World War II, there has been little overt anti-Semitism directed at the Jewish community of about 1,000 people. Today, the main challenges, according to Jewish leaders, are assimilation and intermarriage.

As in many small Jewish communities worldwide, Paraguayan Jews have been helped by outsiders, in this case headmaster Aron Zar, who came from Israel and initiated bat mitzvah preparation at the Colegio Integral Estado de Israel. Diana Varzan-Laufer documents the changes that have occurred as the ceremony has shifted from its school-based origins and provides loving details of her own bat mitzvah. As Diana's story shows, although they may live thousands of miles apart, girls who become b'not mitzvah together can become lifelong friends.

Diana Varzan-Laufer

Bat mitzvah began only in the mid-1960s, when the Jewish school in Asunción, the only one in Paraguay, hired a director from Israel who introduced the custom. At first, the school was responsible for teaching and preparing the girls. There was no religious ceremony, but portions of the Torah were recited, songs were sung, and candles were lit. In short, there was a simple ceremony that was generally followed by a little party for family and friends.

Diana Varzan-Laufer (*right*) and other bat mitzvah girls
bless their candles, Asunción, Paraguay, 1972.

Now, religious institutions take the responsibility for preparation. Conservative Jewish girls take a course in which they learn about Judaism, its symbols and their significance, and the role of the Jewish mother. (Girls who attend the Orthodox Habad Lubavitch do not participate in a bat mitzvah ceremony.) The ceremony itself takes place in the temple on Kabbalat Shabbat. Whether or not to celebrate as a group is up to the girls and their parents. The next day, they perform the Havdalah ceremony, accompanied by stories and songs. Some families give a big party at the end of the ceremony.

Going back in time, I remember my own bat mitzvah. It corresponded to the first era, when the organization and preparation for the event were in the hands of the school and we celebrated as a group. Since the community is very small, we had only five girls coming of age. The ceremony coincided with the time that the youngest became twelve years old. Ours took place on May 20, 1972, in the function hall of the Hebrew Union, which, even today, is used as a school.

Each of us entered on the arm of her father, who took her to the stage on which we performed the ceremony. We read and commented on the Torah portion Beresheet ("In the beginning," the first portion of the Torah). Then we sang and recited the blessing over the candles that each of us had in her little candelabra. It was a simple and emotional ceremony, during which each girl secured her bonds to her heritage and reaffirmed her Jewish faith. At the end of the ceremony, our parents gave a little party in the same room.

Our collective bat mitzvah is a deeply fixed and treasured memory. During the succeeding years, the five of us would get together on the twentieth of May to remember and celebrate the anniversary. Finally, time broke up this custom. Today, each of us has taken her own path. Two live in Israel, one in the United States, and one remains with me in Paraguay. I am certain that each of us carries with her traditions that she will pass on to the generations to come.

PERU

After reaching a peak of 5,000, today there are fewer than 3,000 Jews in Peru, as young people leave the country for education and as intermarriage and economic downturns have taken their toll. Eliane Karp, a Hebrew University–educated Jewish woman, was married to former president Alejandro Toledo and served as the first lady of Peru from 2001 to 2006.

As Sandra Behar reports, the efforts of the rabbi of the Sephardic community led to the creation of the bat mitzvah ceremony in Lima in 1998. In a city with a limited Jewish population and three separate synagogues (Ashkenazi Orthodox, Sephardi Orthodox, and Conservative, plus a Chabad center), the rabbi's work to bridge the Ashkenazi-Sephardi divide seems especially worthwhile and possibly groundbreaking. By attending Friday night services, which Sandra describes, the girls no doubt help to build bonds among the parents and help to strengthen the community itself.

_____

Sandra Behar

Eveinu Shalom, aleijem . . .

November 1998. Singing, with gleaming smiles on their faces, we see twelve girls entering the main sanctuary of the synagogue, ready to assume their responsibilities as Jewish women. Among them is my daughter, Eliane, who has prepared a speech about Israel's fiftieth anniversary that she will present during the ceremony.

It began eight months before. The rabbi of the Sephardic community of Lima called eleven-year-old girls to encourage them to become b'not mitzvah. The girls were thrilled and organized a meeting. It was decided that Ashkenazi and Sephardi girls would study and perform the ceremony together as friends.

The girls made a commitment to study, but they also enjoyed themselves. They got together twice a week with the rabbi, always learning something new, always bringing home their knowledge of Jewish values, and having one of the best times of their lives.

The families attended Kabalat Shabbat at the synagogue, and each Friday one of the girls would give a speech about the weekly parasha. We parents felt immense pride as we watched our daughters identify more and more with our faith and our community.

URUGUAY

Uruguay has a relatively large and cosmopolitan Jewish community, primarily located in Montevideo, the country's capital. Although there are fifteen synagogues in Uruguay (fourteen Orthodox, one Masorti or Conservative, and two Chabad centers), most Jews are secular in their outlook. Jewish culture, rather than religious observance, forms the core of Jewish identity, although some, such as Sylvia Ascher, the author of the following story, work to foster traditional Jewish practices. Uruguay has eight strong Zionist youth organizations and is the only South American country authorized to administer Israel's university entrance exam.

Less than 1 percent of the total population of Uruguay, the Jewish population has undergone a serious decline since the 1960s and 1970s. At that time, emigration soared as the economy worsened and political repression increased. Between 1998 and 2003, more than half of the community's remaining Jews emigrated, mostly to Israel. Currently, there are about 23,000 Jews in Uruguay.

From Sylvia's description, it seems clear that the forceful personality and strong talents of one individual can create a new definition of how b'not mitzvah are celebrated for a whole community. Unique among the stories we have collected, the b'not mitzvah ceremonies of Uruguay seem ready for Broadway.

Sylvia Ascher

In Uruguay, girls who are about to become twelve years old learn about the importance of their position in Judaism. They study for a whole year and perform special mitzvot, including tzdakah, hachnasat orchim (hospitality), tfila, and bikur cholim (visiting the sick). Then, they prepare a musical production with song, video, and dance for their families, friends, and the whole community.

I have been in charge of these bat mitzvah productions since 1973. I work in three Jewish schools as the coordinator of Jewish education through the performing arts. I love my job. It is a privilege and a zchut (right) for me to prepare the girls—usually more than forty in a class—for this special time in their lives. The productions are quite professional, with lights, audio, and a huge video screen, like in a theater. Through song and dance, the girls learn much more than they would in a regular class.

The themes have varied throughout the years. One year, it was women in Jewish history. The video showed momentous times for Jewish women: the desert after Egypt, Spain before the Inquisition, Europe in the time before World War II, and the creation of the state of Israel. The girls on-stage interacted with the video with special songs and choreography created for the production.

For another group, I chose the theme of the yetzer hara and the yetzer hatov, the inclinations that live inside each of us to do bad or good. The video showed different situations in which the girls are supposed to do a mitzvah. In three-dimensional animations, the yetzer hara tries to convince them not to do it, and the yetzer hatov argues with him. Finally, the

Bat mitzvah production, Montevideo, Uruguay.
Sylvia Ascher, producer, 2002.

girls decide to do as the yetzer hatov says, and they perform the mitzvot and become b'not mitzvah the way God wants them to.

For the bat mitzvah of my younger daughter, Tamar, a few years ago, I wanted to do something very special, as I had for Cecile, my older daughter. I wrote a script in which Tammy goes to the computer and starts to chat with an Israeli girl her age. She tells her that she is about to be bat mitzvah, and that her dream is to go to Jerusalem. The Israeli girl tells her that she knows a special magic, that if Tammy closes her eyes and puts

In a bat mitzvah video, girls must choose between *yetzer hara*
(the inclination to do evil) and *yetzer hatov* (the inclination to do good),
Montevideo, Uruguay. Sylvia Ascher, producer, 2002.

her hands on the computer screen, she will be in Jerusalem with her in
two seconds.

Tammy does as she says and suddenly finds herself in Jerusalem. The
Israeli girl meets her there. She shows her all the important places, like
the Kotel and Yad Vashem (Holocaust memorial). They go to Hadassah
Hospital and do bikur cholim there. They walk through the streets of our
past, and they touch the stones of our present. It is magical and beautiful,
and they sing together.

Then they have to say goodbye. Tammy comes back to her computer
here in Montevideo to discover that it has all been a dream. It has been a
dream that has touched her soul, though, making her realize the importance of her commitment to perform mitzvot today, and her responsibility

for the future to become a *bat Yisrael ne'emana* (faithful daughter of Israel) to her people and her God.

The chief rabbi in Montevideo has a niece named Norior in Jerusalem who was about to be bat mitzvah. We talked to her on the phone, and she was happy to be in the film. So we flew with Tammy to Jerusalem, where we shot all the scenes and did the sound at a recording studio. I made the film here in Uruguay when we returned.

The day of Tammy's bat mitzvah, we invited all our friends and family to the cinema in Punta del Este, a summer resort. We showed the film and then had a seuda (meal) in a restaurant, a kosher barbecue. It was beautiful, and Tammy was very proud of her work. It may have been a crazy idea—but it worked!

The bat mitzvah ceremonies/productions that I have described have been my life for a long time. Bat mitzvah is the beginning of a new period in the lives of our Jewish girls, the opening of a door to new identities as active Jewish women. The productions will remain in their memories, but the most significant aspect is the message about their importance to the survival of the Jewish people—their connection to the past and their commitment to the future.

VENEZUELA

Jews began to settle in Venezuela at the beginning of the nineteenth century, but the community did not fully develop until the 1920s and 1930s, when Ashkenazi Jews arrived from Eastern Europe and Sephardi Jews from North Africa. Before and after World War II the population increased with arrivals from war-torn Europe, and increased again in the 1950s with the arrival of Jews from Egypt, Lebanon, Syria, and Turkey. Current Jewish population estimates range from 15,000 to 35,000, split between the Ashkenazi and Sephardi communities.

The range of ways in which bat mitzvah is celebrated around the world is extended yet again when we read the story provided by Sonia Weisselberger. Unlike other countries, where b'not mitzvah may be based in the school or in the synagogue, in Venezuela, the local branch of WIZO (the Women's International Zionist Organization, founded in England in 1920) is in charge. The sheer size of the group Sonia describes, the presence of the Israeli ambassador to Venezuela, and the enormous collective party must have made the day memorable, if not overwhelming, for many of the girls. WIZO does a great service to the community by taking on this important role.

Sonia Weisselberger

Since the mid-1970s, all the bat mitzvahs in Venezuela have been organized by WIZO. Among its multitude of projects in Venezuela and Israel, WIZO aids families who cannot afford to pay the fee for the bat mitzvah preparation and ceremony. Every girl in sixth grade has the opportunity to take part.

In 1996, my daughter, Valerie, celebrated her bat mitzvah. The previous year, all the mothers were invited to attend a meeting to learn more about the program in which their daughters would participate for the next five and a half months. Because there were ninety-eight girls, they were divided into two groups. Every Tuesday and Thursday after school, they went to the Unión Israelita de Caracas, the main synagogue for the Ashkenazi community in Caracas, which is also where the ceremony took place. The girls came from different places, including Margarita, Miami, and Maracaibo, but they were expected to work together. By doing activities together, they got to know each other.

One group had classes with a mora (teacher), who taught the brahot as well as such details as the manner in which they should enter the synagogue and how to approach the bima and stand adjacent to the Aron Hakodesh. Simultaneously, the other group had classes about Judaism, Shabbat, and women in Judaism. They also painted a cup for Shabbat and created a cover for halah bread. These were exhibited at the entrance of the synagogue on the day of the bat mitzvah.

WIZO members were there every Tuesday and Thursday, supervising all the details of the ceremony. We took care of the invitations that were sent to the families and friends, sometimes as many as 2,000. Other WIZO members were responsible for making sure all the girls were dressed properly in the same outfit.

Bat mitzvah group in Caracas, Venezuela, 1996.

Throughout the five and a half months, the *mora* watched over every detail so that the girls would be prepared for the ceremony, which consisted of several prayers that the girls would sing. One of the *mora's* responsibilities was to help the girls perform, as not all of them had vocal talent. Obviously, this was not an easy task, and the *mora* should be thanked for doing a difficult job well.

The day of the ceremony, the girls arrived early at the synagogue to take pictures with their families. We joined the girls to calm them down, because many were nervous. After the guests arrived, including members of the board of the community and the Israeli ambassador, the pianist began to play. The girls made their entrance, walking down the aisles until they reached the bima and took their places. Next, they began to sing and pray together. There also was a moment in which the parents stood up and said a prayer for their daughters.

The ceremony continued with songs and prayers that the girls sang with the cantor. The previous November, Yitzhak Rabin had been killed, so they sang *Shir la Shalom* in his memory. They also recited the *Shema Israel* and said a prayer for Israel. At the end of the ceremony, there were a few short speeches by the principal rabbis of the Ashkenazi and Sephardi communities and the president of WIZO in Venezuela. After the speeches, the girls left in order, accompanied by music.

Everybody was invited to a party in another room in the synagogue. Each girl had a table with hors d'oeuvres and wine. Most of the people in the community know each other, so people went from table to table congratulating the families. Although they had been nervous before the ceremony, now that it was over and they had completed their duties, the bat mitzvah girls enjoyed the party with no worries, sharing the great event with their friends and families.

NOTES

1. Judith Laikin Elkin, "Latin American Jews," in H. Epstein, ed., *Jewish Women 2000*, 39–48.

2. Jerusalem Center for Public Affairs, Daniel Elazar Papers Index, 1989, www .jcpa.org/dje/articles2/costarica.htm.

3. Paulette Kershenovich, "Jewish Women in Mexico," in H. Epstein, ed., *Jewish Women 2000*, 105.

Middle East and North Africa

This section includes bat mitzvah descriptions and stories from three Middle Eastern countries—Iran, Israel, and Yemen—from Kurdistan, not a country but an area in the Middle East with a unique culture; and from Turkey, which borders Iraq, Iran, and Syria and is ambiguously located between Europe and Asia.

People from the Arab states of the Middle East and North Africa are often referred to as Mizrahi Jews and are generally of Sephardi origin. Before 1948, approximately 900,000 Jews lived in the Middle East and North Africa. The great majority of the Jewish population was persecuted after 1948 and the creation of the state of Israel and subsequently driven out of their homes and countries.[1] Now, only a small number remain, estimated as fewer than 8,000 in the entire area.

IRAN

The Iranian Jewish community is ancient, dating back to the sixth century BCE. The story of Esther, commemorated each year on the holiday of Purim, took place in Persia, current-day Iran. Under Persian and then Muslim rule, the welfare of the Jews waxed and waned. Iran was a monarchy ruled by a shah or emperor from 1501 until the Iranian revolution which began on April 1, 1979, inaugurating Iran officially as an Islamic republic. Before then, for a while, Jews had lived in relative peace in Iran, but with the onset of the Islamic revolution tens of thousands of the 80,000 Jewish inhabitants left the country, leaving behind vast amounts of property. Today, the Jewish population in Iran, estimated to be the second largest in the Middle East after that of Israel, is isolated and suffers from the suspicion of the majority population and restrictions on Jewish education and travel. The current president of Iran is actively hostile to Israel and its Jewish community and denies the existence of the Holocaust.

The two Iranian Jewish women who tell stories of b'not mitzvah now live in the United States. Their stories are about the contrast between the life of Iranian Jewish women as they knew it growing up, and the life of Iranian-American Jewish women as they experience and create it now. Soraya Nazarian is part of a large and thriving Iranian Jewish community that has taken root in Los Angeles. Her story concerns her journey to a bat mitzvah celebration for herself and for other women. Farideh Goldin, the author of the second story, believes in the necessity of making personal choices. What is right for her is not necessarily right for her three daughters. Farideh, a member of a Conservative synagogue in Norfolk, Virginia, recognizes that she is part of a transitional generation between the restrictions of the past and the opportunities of the present. In 2004, Farideh's book, *Wedding Song: Memoirs of an Iranian Jewish Woman,* was published in the Hadassah-Brandeis Institute Series on Jewish Women.

Soraya Masjedi Nazarian

We did not have bat mitzvah in Iran, where I grew up. Women and girls could not even touch the Torah. When I came here to Los Angeles, I became a member of my temple and then a member of its board. Board members sit on the bimah and are given an aliyah. Our gabbai is a nice gentleman who likes to joke and make you feel good. After an aliyah, as a habit, he says to everyone, "Mazal tov on your bar/bat mitzvah."

Hadassah Southern California's first adult bat mitzvah class,
initiated by Soraya Nazarian, Los Angeles, 1997.

After my first aliyah, he asked, "Wait a minute, did you have your bat mitzvah?" I said, "No, Sid, in Iran girls cannot go to the Torah." He replied, "Well, mazal tov. You just had your bat mitzvah."

That feeling was so great that I wanted to share it with everyone, especially those who had no experience of reading from Torah or having a bat mitzvah. One Shabbat morning, our rabbi gave a sermon about Rosh

Chodesh. He explained that it was traditionally a day of rest for women, and that women can read the Torah on days other than Shabbat. Aha! That is what I was waiting for.

As the education chair of Hadassah of Southern California, I got together a group of thirty-two women from twenty to ninety years old. Together, we learned all the prayers and how to read the Torah, even though at first some of us didn't know aleph from Chinese. On Rosh Chodesh, the Sunday of Thanksgiving 1997, Southern California Hadassah had a most inspiring bat mitzvah event. The women conducted the full service. Since then, the program has continued, and groups of women conduct a service every year. Some of the women have continued their studies of Torah and Hebrew until this day.

Farideh Goldin

I never had a bat mitzvah. The idea was inconceivable for a woman growing up in Iran. Then I came to the United States. And now, with each adult bat mitzvah celebration at our synagogue, I invariably receive a call from the cantor or a friend, encouraging me to join the group. Even my husband, and especially my three daughters, urge me to participate in a ceremony that was forbidden to me thirty-seven years ago. Once, I went as far as attending classes. Halfway through, I quit.

Do we women really want to imitate this age-old ceremony of men? Or should we search for a ritual that is ours, women-centered, women-oriented? If so, how can we find one when there is little written of our mothers? Or should we try to make ourselves comfortable within the ceremonial garb of men, adding creative designs, pastel colors?

Women's uneasiness about embracing the roles we expect to be ours is one reason for my ambivalence about taking part in a formal bat mitzvah.

Nevertheless, the best aspect of bat mitzvah ceremonies, I believe, is creating an occasion for young women to affirm their dedication to study the Torah. Even though I was denied the opportunity, even though I am uncomfortable with a bat mitzvah ceremony for myself, I wanted my daughters to have choices, to learn, and to be proud of their accomplishments.

Lena Goldin at her bat mitzvah, Norfolk, Virginia, 2003.

When my eldest daughter, Lena, had her bat mitzvah, I saw the face of the Torah for the first time, standing next to her, watching her read the impossible words. I remember being in awe of touching the Torah with a tallit, kissing it, shaking from joy and fear—the fear that I might in some way desecrate a holy book because I am a woman. Our Israeli cantor, who knows about my background, whispered in my ear, "Don't worry! God won't strike you!"

In many ways, Lena's bat mitzvah was mine as well. After each class, we discussed her lessons. I sat with her as she practiced her readings. We went through her speech together. I wore a tallit, even if awkwardly, an obligatory practice in our synagogue for anyone who takes an aliyah. I followed the words of the Torah, and as Lena chanted them, I read them quietly in my mind. I felt God's presence as surely as I had on childhood Fridays with my grandmother, as she prayed standing in front of two handmade oil lamps. Perhaps I don't aspire to a bat mitzvah ceremony of my own because I cannot imagine another one as meaningful as the first time I stood by my daughter, facing our ancient text.

ISRAEL

In Israel, religious coming-of-age ceremonies have been the provenance of boys. Often, girls from non-Orthodox families make a trip or have a party to mark their twelfth birthday—a special celebration, but not a religious one. Girls from Orthodox families usually do not participate in bat mitzvah ceremonies either.

Because Orthodox women are not allowed to read the Torah in front of men, having a women-only service is a creative compromise that some girls' parents have arranged. Tanya Zion's parents developed such a service for her when she was twelve years old. Now in her twenties, an activist for gay and lesbian and women's issues, she remembers her own bat mitzvah and writes about two women she tutored for unusual adult bat mitzvah ceremonies in Jerusalem.

Schulamith Chava Halevy, who was born in Switzerland, is a well-known researcher, historian, ethnographer, and international expert on Anousim (Jews forced to convert to Christianity). She writes about her painful segregation to the upstairs women's section of the synagogue and about her adult bat mitzvah in the United States. Her family is descended from the great Spanish poet Yehudah Halevy.

Tanya Zion

I woke up early on a winter morning, overwhelmed by the exciting thought that the long-expected day of my bat mitzvah had finally arrived. Today, I can recall reading the Torah to women in our Orthodox synagogue and teaching the words of Torah to the entire community. I remember the joyous family meal, the Saturday night party, the dancing, the celebration, the gifts. Yet, my most vivid memory is not of those events, but of the moments preceding them. Most of all, I remember walking early in the morning alongside my father on our way to the synagogue. Perhaps I remember this walk because of the quiet tension that preceded the storm of celebration, or perhaps because something in this experience symbolized the entire event.

I am reminded of the verse "and the two walked together" from the biblical story of the binding of Isaac. Abraham and Isaac journey to Mount Moriah, toward a point of no return. I felt that, like Isaac, the chosen child, I had earned a moment of togetherness with my father, who was accompanying me to an event that would transform my life. I realized that the bat mitzvah ceremony is a transitional one, after which I would no longer be a child, but an almost-woman, committed to mitzvot, an equal. I felt that my parents had educated and prepared me for life as best they could, but that on this day they were setting me free. (Surely, many feel like this on their first day of army service or college.)

During the bat mitzvah ceremony itself, my parents blessed my independence, reciting the traditional blessing over the fact that they were no longer responsible for my actions: Baruch she-p'taranu m'onsha shel zo. For the first time, the adult world, which every child dreams of joining, turned its full attention to me, and I had to prove that I was worthy of my new status. Through this ceremony, I acquired a voice.

Unlike many other families, it was clear to my parents that when I arrived at the symbolic age of twelve, they would celebrate my bat mitzvah publicly, and there would be no discrimination based on my gender.

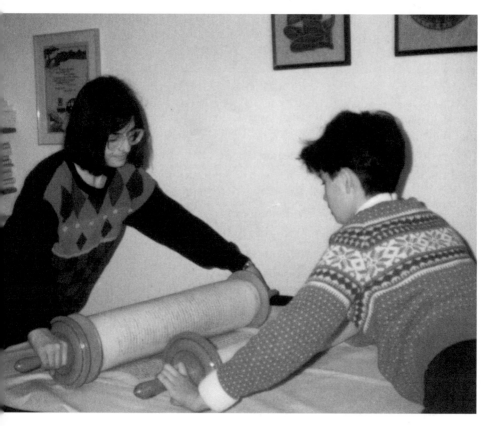

Tanya Zion practices opening the Torah scroll with the aid of her aunt, 1992.

My parents saw this coming-of-age as an opportunity for me to assume an adult identity. They designed a multifaceted bat mitzvah preparation plan: I was to participate in a tzedakka project of social action, to study some Zionist history, to prepare a speech (a commentary on my weekly Torah portion), to learn how to read from the Torah and haftara—and wouldn't I like to prepare a dance piece to perform before the guests at the party? On one hand, my parents' master plan was derived from their determination to cultivate a mature individual, dedicated to Israel, Judaism, social justice, and creativity. On the other hand, the entire bat mitzvah—from its initial planning to its realization—was an expression of my own personality. It became one of the most significant moments of my life.

For Bat-Ami Schulman,
the bat mitzvah ceremony in
Jerusalem at age twenty-eight
was a personal milestone,
2003.

Over the years, I have come to realize that my bat mitzvah celebration, especially its public aspect—reading Torah, teaching the words of Torah—is not typical in Israel. As a bat mitzvah tutor, I have often helped women who wish to perform bat mitzvah ceremonies at a later age. Two of those women, Avigail Antman and Bat-Ami Schulman, have generously shared their experiences and reflections with me.

Bat-Ami, born Bethany Joy, was raised in Los Angeles. While her family belonged officially to the Reform movement, as time went on, the family's connection to Judaism was all but forgotten. Years later, she found herself and her spouse lighting Hanukah candles beside the Christmas tree. After a traumatic life event, Bat-Ami decided to join a tour of Israel sponsored by Birthright Israel. The trip to Israel opened her to a new-yet-old world of meaning stemming from her cultural and spiritual Jewish heritage.

A few years later, Bat-Ami made aliya. In honor of her twenty-eighth birthday, she invited friends to hear her read Torah at a Conservative synagogue in Jerusalem. She thoughtfully described her motivation for a bat mitzvah ceremony: "This was a moment of reinvention. I realized that this ritual, this milestone, was so much more meaningful to me at this juncture in my life than it would have been at age twelve, because here I was

Avigail Antman with daughter Ruth, who was born soon
after Avigail's bat mitzvah at the inclusive Orthodox
synagogue Shira Hadasha, Jerusalem, 2003.

actually living a life embracing mitzvot, truly deserving of the name and
honor of being a 'daughter of mitzvah.'"

For Bat-Ami, the bat mitzvah ceremony served as a personal milestone,
symbolizing her inner transformation and choice of a new identity and
lifestyle. In contrast, Avigail's decision to have a bat mitzvah was connected to her desire to claim a public space for herself.

Avigail, the mother of three, was born and raised in Israel in a modern
Orthodox family. She dates her inner revolution to the time of her par-

ents' death. At that time, she joined the innovative and inclusive Orthodox synagogue Shira Hadasha in Jerusalem, where women take an active part in prayer and where it is acceptable for women to say the mourner's kaddish: "I suddenly wanted a place of my own. . . . I had lost my link to the past. I sought a public element to my mourning process. I wanted people to recognize that I wasn't the same as before."

It was difficult for Avigail's Orthodox family to understand and accept her decision to have a bat mitzvah on the occasion of her thirty-sixth birthday, a special age—three times the age of the usual bat mitzvah. Even her friends worried that her voice would sound too "feminist," angry, or demonstrative. Instead, the attendees heard an authentic female voice:

> It still feels a little strange for me to see a woman wearing a kippa, a tallit, or holding a Torah scroll. I am still ambivalent; these are "male" images, at odds with the world I grew up in. On the other hand, now that the female voice is heard in the synagogue, I couldn't bring myself to pray in any other synagogue. Going back to the silence would be impossible. The bat mitzvah was one of the rare moments of my life when I felt uncharacteristically whole and at peace with everything that happened. It's very significant that it's so natural for my sons to have Mom be the one who leads the way to the synagogue.

Today, I am perhaps a little envious of Avigail and Bat-Ami. I, too, would like to celebrate my bat mitzvah again, this time as an adult. I, too, would like to redefine my identity, born of commitment and life experience. To me, it is an advantage that the bat mitzvah ceremony is not fully codified and dictated by the establishment. This allows for the freedom to create more dynamic, divergent, and meaningful ceremonies. I hope that the sense of responsibility that parents feel toward their daughters' bat mitzvah preparation will continue to grow, and I hope that communities' acceptance and openness will also grow.

Schulamith C. Halevy

I was not yet twelve years old when I was banished from the men's section of the synagogue in Moshav Hazorim in northern Israel. Before that,

I remember often going with my dad to the early daily services, when the synagogue was not crowded and I was allowed my space. I would approach the ark with awe, touch the parokhet, the velvety, richly but rather primitively adorned curtain. I would touch it, caress it gently, feel the softness, let my lips touch the velvet and sometimes the metallic thread from the embroidery, shifting it just enough to smell the unusual mix of dust and parchment within. When the ark was opened, I would touch the Torah scroll in its velvety dress and kiss it. During this time, I made pacts with God, prayed for prophecy or, at least, a sign of my purpose here on earth. Sometimes, I chose certain verses or chapters from psalms I had memorized to say there; sometimes, I asked him about my sorrows, seeking to understand their cause and purpose.

All this came to an abrupt end one morning. Some man—I have no memory of who he was—simply sent me upstairs to the ladies' section. Stunned, but obedient, I climbed up, where I was all alone—no other woman ever came—and without access. I began to try to follow the prayers of the men downstairs, who prayed very rapidly, challenging myself to actually say every word before the prayer leader reached the end of the stanza, which proved impossible with almost all prayer leaders. This is also when I began to follow the Torah readings, listening with the book open before me, trying to learn how to chant. It was not simple, because—as I soon found out—many men go up and read unprepared, committing errors that complicated my self-imposed task. (Still, today, it irritates me when the men cantillate carelessly.) But by the time I was twelve, I could read correctly both the typical "Israeli" Ashkenazi chant and the German (*Yekkish*) cantillation.

The only mark of my bat mitzvah was a small party, with the kids in my class in Jerusalem, where we were living at the time, coming to our home, and the boys making me miserable. It was not really on my birthday, which falls just before Passover, and the party had nothing in it to indicate that I was coming of age. No program, nothing. Although the possibility of reading the Torah before the community did not even enter my mind at that time, I had hoped to give some kind of speech, say something about the Torah, which, along with the interpretive literature, I read avidly.

But eventually I did have my bat mitzvah. I was thirty-six, three times the usual age. We were living at the time in Urbana, Illinois, where women were regularly sharing their insights on the Torah portion read in the Orthodox services of the Hillel Foundation. By then, I had spoken before countless crowds of every type and size, including the congregation before me. Yet when I went up there, before the ark, my heart was racing and my knees were shaking. I had had no idea I would become so emotional, no idea how deeply I still longed for this closure.

As I was born on Passover eve, my Torah reading was on the interim Sabbath of the holiday. In it, Moses—my favorite biblical personality—ascends Mount Sinai yet again, to receive the greatest closeness to and comprehension of God that any human ever has or will. My voice quaked and my hands were pasty with sweat when I was done, as if I were still twelve. Afterward, I could no longer feel the sorrow, only the beautiful closure that I had attained. That moment still symbolizes for me that I had not been hindered beyond remedy. Ultimately, whatever barriers there may be, the path to God is not in any man's hand to leave open or to bar.

I have read the Torah for women at women's services, and I have read for women on Simhat Torah. Few Orthodox synagogues accept such practices yet, innocuous as they are. The access I strive for in the public religious arena is motivated by my inner dialogue with God. Like all members of the Jewish people, I would like the public aspect of Jewish ritual to enhance and express my private spiritual journey. It is lonely out there on the road we traverse in our quest for intimacy with the divine, and the obstacles are many. But the rewards are beyond words. And to the mundane eye, they remain mostly hidden.

KURDISTAN

Kurdistan is a mountainous area that includes parts of Turkey, Iran, Iraq, and Syria; in sum, it is the area inhabited by the Kurds, a distinct ethnic group. The origin of the Jews of Kurdistan is unclear, but they are believed to have lived in the area for almost 3,000 years. Some scholars believe that, in the first century CE, the ruling family of Kurdistan converted to Judaism, as did many of its inhabitants. With the birth of the Jewish state in 1948 and the rise of Islamic fundamentalism, many Kurdish Jews have emigrated to Israel, where Kurdish culture remains largely intact.

Through the ages, Kurdish Jewish women have been well known for having relative equality with men. Some consider a Kurdish woman, Asenath Barzani (1590–1670), to have been the first woman rabbi. The daughter of a rabbi, Asenath studied Kabbalah (a body of mystical teachings) and became the head of the prestigious Jewish academy of Mosul in what is now Iraq.

Mazal Fishman's family emigrated to Israel from the northern Iraqi portion of Kurdistan in 1951. She now lives near the Hudson River in New York state, where she assists her U.S.-born husband in his dental practice and teaches Kurdish dancing.

Mazal Fishman

When girls reached twelve years of age in Kurdistan, there would be a big celebration, like a wedding. I was born in Israel, but my mother remembers her bat mitzvah in Kurdistan. The women would gather together in a hall outside the synagogue. They would sit on beautiful carpets. Inside, the men would hear the rabbi give a drasha (speech) in honor of the girl. It would be in Aramaic, the language of the community. The women could hear it from where they sat.

People don't understand that, in Kurdistan, women had high status. The bat mitzvah was as important as a bar mitzvah, except the girl wouldn't read from the Torah. My mother, fortunately, still has the white dress she wore, with gorgeous hand embroidery. (When her family left for Israel, the Iraqis took almost everything, including a Bible that had been in our family for generations. I look for my family's possessions when I go to museums.)

The bat mitzvah girl was presented with poems that the women wrote for her, and the women would also dance and sing for the bat mitzvah girl, beautiful Aramaic songs about growing up and finding her soulmate. This wouldn't be far in the future, because girls were usually married at age fourteen. Jewish girls were really beautiful. If not married at a young age, a girl might be kidnapped by a Muslim neighbor. This happened to my mother's cousin. There could be no celebration in Kurdistan without a big meal. The women would prepare a feast, just like for a wedding. They wouldn't do anything more for a boy's bar mitzvah than they did for a girl.

TURKEY

The community of nearly 25,000 Turkish Jews maintains synagogues in Ankara, Istanbul, Bursa, and Izmir. Unlike the dying Jewish communities in other parts of the Islamic Middle East, the one in Turkey has remained vibrant, albeit vigilant. Jews have lived in the area for 2,000 years, mostly in peace with their neighbors. Turkey welcomed Jews following the Inquisition in 1492 and again during the Holocaust. Nevertheless, the area is volatile and the future uncertain.

Eda Birol lives in Istanbul, where she teaches yoga to children and trains others to do the same. Like several of the other authors, Eda mentions the close ties of friendship, some lasting a lifetime, that group bat mitzvahs promote. Families like Eda's seek to assure the continuance of Judaism by passing on their traditions to their children.

Eda Birol

I had my bat mitzvah in 1983. At that time, groups of girls would do them together during the summer. Our group was the first to have their bat mitzvah in this particular synagogue. (Before this, bat mitzvahs were performed in another one.) So our bat mitzvah was an important event for us, and also for our synagogue.

We were a group of six girls who knew each other from childhood. We studied with a respected rabbi who taught us prayers, lessons from the Torah, plenty of songs, and how to read basic Hebrew. We studied together, sang together, had fun together, and bonded very strongly.

We were all very, very excited. I was especially over the moon, as my family had prepared me emotionally long before the date. My bat mitzvah was extremely important for my father, whose grandfather was a rabbi and who came from a conservative family. My father was good at motivating me, making me understand this as a significant turning point in my life.

With all the support and preparation, I was ready to go out in front of so many people. Guests of six bat mitzvah girls sure do fill up a synagogue.

On the day of our ceremony, we all wore white dresses and hats. We sang our songs, and each of us was called to the tevah (pulpit). We were invited with our dads to read a few lines from the sefer Torah as the rabbis stood beside us. This was amazing, because women are never invited to do this.

After the synagogue, we had small parties where everybody danced and sang and had lots of fun. I cannot say if it was the bat mitzvah itself or how people treated me, but I felt more mature afterward.

It has been many years since my bat mitzvah. I do not remember many details of that day. But the details are unimportant. What remains and what will remain throughout my life are the feelings that that day inspired. I was affected deeply. There was something spiritual about it that I can understand only now. It is said that between Rosh Hashana and Yom Kippur, God opens the doors to heaven. But I believe that on that day, also, those doors were open for us.

I now have a three-year-old daughter. My goal is to prepare her for this lovely, meaningful ceremony, and I hope that she will share my feelings. My father has already started to tell her about the bat mitzvah and to rehearse dances with her.

YEMEN

Increasing violence against Jews led to the emigration of virtually the entire Yemenite Jewish community—almost 50,000 people—between June 1949 and September 1950 in Operation Magic Carpet. It is estimated that 200 Jews remain in the mountainous regions of northern Yemen. They are allowed to practice Judaism, but remain isolated and are treated as second-class citizens. American-born Renée Levine Melammed is a professor and assistant dean at the Schechter Institute of Jewish Studies in Jerusalem, as well as the director of its women's studies program. A desire to sustain her husband's Yemenite traditions led to a new bat mitzvah ceremony for their daughter, as Renée describes in loving detail.

Renée Levine Melammed

When my daughter, Shira, approached bat mitzvah age in 1997, I was faced with a serious challenge. My husband's family was not only Israeli and Orthodox, but Yemenite as well. Their tradition was different. At most, a meal might be arranged where the girl could give a dvar Torah. This would not suffice for us. Thus, I needed to figure out how to satisfy halakhic demands and yet allow my daughter to express herself and attain a sense of accomplishment. Not an easy task.

Since my husband, a seasoned Torah reader and gabbai at his synagogue, had stated that he had no objection to women reading Torah if this takes place among women only, I put him to the test: "Will you teach our daughter to read in the tradition of your ancestors?" He agreed without hesitation, and the lessons began—painfully at first, for our children did not speak with the guttural ayin and het [letters of the Hebrew alphabet], which are essential parts of proper Yemenite reading.

Then, the next questions loomed. When and where could we arrange to have a Yemenite girl read Torah? A friend had the perfect suggestion: Rosh Hodesh during Hanukah. Since school is not in session in Israel during Hanukah, we wouldn't conflict with classes. Moreover, Rosh Hodesh is a traditional women's holiday and an occasion that requires the use of a Torah scroll, so Shira would have a respectable amount to read. I called the Reconstructionist congregation in Jerusalem to reserve their hall and Torah scrolls that day. All I needed to supply were the prayer books.

Our invitation listed prayers at 9:30 in the morning and a meal at 11:00. Whoever called us received an explanation: there was going to be a women's prayer group. Some traditionalists balked and said they would come only for the meal. Meanwhile, we set up the hall with a makeshift mehitza in the back, in case any men chose to attend. They did! The boys from our daughter's Orthodox co-ed elementary school sat *behind* the mehitza, as did my husband with a Yemenite college friend, and other men, including my mother's rabbi, who was visiting from New York.

By hallel (a part of the service that expresses joy), the strength of the women's and girls' voices was beautiful and empowering. My friend Debbie stood on one side of the lectern, and another friend who had never seen a Torah up close was stationed on the other side. I chose the daughter of a Kohen (traditionally, one of priestly descent who is called to the Torah first) for the first aliyah, myself (daughter of a Levite) for the second, my mother for the third, and my daughter for the fourth.

Shira read each line in perfect Yemenite trope, and her seven-year-old brother, Benjamin, chanted the same line in Aramaic after her. This Aramaic translation, the Targum of Onkelos, is a custom still observed in Yemenite synagogues today. Benjamin was the only male on our side of the partition. Mother and daughter teams were chosen for hagba (the honor of raising the Torah after the reading) and galila (putting the vestments on the Torah). Musaf was chanted by a friend who sings in the Zamir Chorale. The best part was that we could record everything on video because this bat mitzvah was not held on Shabbat!

The experience was incredibly moving. Not only did I watch my daughter chant with proficiency in a hauntingly beautiful melody, but I also enjoyed the participation of other women. Most—especially the Yemenite and Moroccan women and the youngest girls—had never participated in a women's prayer group before. My mother's rabbi said that he planned to deliver a sermon upon his return to the States, and he would call it "Behind the Mehitza." My husband's friend said he had never heard a more beautiful reading. And he has heard hundreds of Yemenite men read in his lifetime.

I hoped that this rite of passage would not be the end of Shira's Torah reading, as it is for most bar mitzvah boys. Fortunately, there was a Torah reading every Rosh Hodesh at Shira's high school, and almost every month during her four years there, Shira volunteered to read. She was asked to read a new portion at a friend's Shabbat bat mitzvah, and learned to read Megillat Esther (the book of Esther, which is read on Purim).

This year, Shira was chosen to be kallat bereshit (literally, "bride of Genesis," the person who reads the beginning of the Torah) on Simhat Torah, and was challenged to prepare forty-five lines. So, six years later, the bat mitzvah girl was still chanting in her breathtaking style. The women and children in the room were enraptured as they listened to, quite possibly, the only woman who has ever chanted Torah publicly in the Yemenite style.

Shira Melammed reads from the Torah at her women-only
bat mitzvah, Jerusalem, 1997.

NORTH AFRICA

At one time, the countries of North Africa hosted vibrant Jewish communities. Sadly, none of these exist today. The Jewish populations of North African countries were traditional in their observance of Judaism. Thus, girls who grew up in North Africa were mostly unaware of bat mitzvah, and it is not surprising that we were unable to find bat mitzvah stories from Algeria, Morocco, Sudan, or Western Sahara, nor from the wealthy Arab states of Bahrain and Kuwait, which had small, little-known Jewish communities before the establishment of Israel in 1948. But we were able to get bat mitzvah accounts from Egypt, Libya, and Tunisia. They describe the unusual experiences of women who later moved on to live in different parts of the world.

EGYPT

Jews have been residents of Egypt since ancient times. Jews from other Arab lands and from Europe swelled the Jewish population of Egypt to about 80,000 by 1948. With the formation of the state of Israel that year, virulent governmental and public anti-Semitism erupted. About half the Jews left. By 1956 and the outbreak of the war between Egypt and Israel, Jews were no longer welcome or safe in Egypt. All but a tiny remnant emigrated to Israel, France, Brazil, the United States, Australia, and Canada. In recent years, some synagogues have been restored, and efforts are under way to save religious articles and the archives of the once-thriving Jewish community of Cairo. But the Jews have not returned and are not welcome.

Racheline Barda has lived in Australia since the 1950s. At the University of Sydney, she conducted her Ph.D. research on the immigration experiences of Jews who left Egypt for Australia and other countries. Racheline and her husband, Joe, an Egyptian Jew of Italian descent, began the Jews of Egypt Foundation at the University of Haifa, whose mission is to study their native community.

Racheline Barda

In 1951, I was attending the Lycée français d'Alexandrie, a nondenominational institution, when I heard of this practice of bat mitzvah, or "com-

Racheline Barda and her bat mitzvah group at the reception after their ceremony, and Racheline on the verandah of Eliahou HaNavi Synagogue, Alexandria, Egypt, 1951.

munion," as it was called then. I liked the idea and convinced my parents to let me enroll in the program. I attended classes where I learned the songs and prayers with a group of about forty girls, mostly from the Jewish community school, L'école Aghion.

The group ceremony was held at the synagogue Eliahou HaNavi in Alexandria on a Sunday. We were not allowed to wear fancy outfits, as some of the girls in the group were from disadvantaged backgrounds, and their parents could not afford anything elaborate. We all had to have the same long white dress with the same veil, which looked very much like a Catholic communion outfit. The ceremony was followed by a communal luncheon attended by our families and guests. Although it was quite modest by today's standards, it was a joyous celebration.

In the course of numerous interviews for my research, I encountered only six girls who had bat mitzvahs in Egypt, among them a mother and daughter. The mother must have been one of the first girls to have a bat mitzvah in the mid-1920s. Others were in 1932 and 1937, and two were of my era. As for me, the spirit of community and equality that I remember from my bat mitzvah has stayed with me to this day.

LIBYA

Malaka Bublil, who also uses the name Gina Waldman, is a community activist who lives in San Francisco. Among her accomplishments is the co-founding of JIMENA, an organization that raises awareness about the history of the Jews of the Middle East and North Africa, particularly with regard to the injustices they have suffered. The dramatic occasion that she calls her bat mitzvah did not occur in a synagogue, but it did involve prayer. Clearly, this very specific coming-of-age experience has shaped her life.

Gina Malaka Waldman

The Jewish community has lived in Libya for more than 2,500 years, since before the Arab Islamic conquest in the seventh century. My family has lived in Tripoli, one of Libya's two capitals, for as long as my great-grandfather can remember. In 1948, when I was born, our small Jewish community numbered 6,000. We were deprived of Jewish education. There were no social and cultural events for Jews, and the Arab population often targeted us for violence and harassment. Thus, Jewish families practiced religious rituals in a clandestine manner.

I flash back to the time when my brother Tino was preparing for his bar mitzvah in 1961. I was thirteen years old at the time . . .

It's nine o'clock in the evening. The curtains have been drawn; the dinner table has been cleared. A white, freshly ironed tablecloth has been thrown on the small wooden table. Nonna (Grandma) Regina is in the kitchen brewing Turkish coffee. She sets down a tray with *kak* (round cookies) and two demitasses. One is for Nonno (Grandpa) Bramino and one for the rabbi, Rav Yehuda. The aroma of the coffee is so powerful, it engulfs the house. I love the smell, but I can never understand how adults drink this ink-like brew. *Che schifo!* (Disgusting!), I say in Italian, my second language.

My mother is rushing to get my sister, Vera; my youngest brother, Ever; and me to our beds. An atmosphere of excitement mixed with fear surrounds us. My father acts nervous and paces the floor. He is holding his pipe without any tobacco in it. He pretends not to be afraid, but in truth he is the barometer of the feelings in the small dining room. The more he paces the floor, the greater the fear. The more he touches his pipe, the quieter my sister and brothers get.

Tonight, the rabbi is coming to give a Hebrew lesson to my brother. Tino is twelve, a year younger than I am. His bar mitzvah is approaching. He must be coached in his Torah reading. The lessons take place in the semi-secret atmosphere of our dining room. The lessons must be gotten over quickly. We have to conduct our Hebrew studies in a very quiet and hushed-up manner in order not to attract attention from the authorities, who barely tolerate the Jews living in their midst. After all, the Jews are Dhimmis, subjects who are "tolerated" by our Muslim rulers. As Dhimmis, we are subjected to humiliation and harassment and are treated as inferiors. We are not permitted to practice our religion freely and openly. We cannot pray or sing Hebrew melodies too loudly.

There is pressure on Tino to memorize his parasha as quickly as possible and not subject the family to additional danger and hardship. Tino is not taking the pressure very well. He is burdened by the responsibility to memorize so much and in such a short time. He is afraid, but also scared to show that he is afraid. Nonno puts a yamalka on Tino's head and hands him a small prayer book.

The hour is drawing closer to nine o'clock and Rav Yehuda is due any minute now. I beg my mother, "Ma, please, please, I will be real quiet. Can't you let me just sit in and listen to the lesson?" "No, no," my mother answers. "You know that it is *haram*—a sin—for girls to have a bar mitzvah or touch the Torah."

There is a quiet tap on the door, which Mother opens. "Rav Yehuda, please come in. Tino is ready for you." Rav Yehuda is a short, stocky man in his early fifties. He has a short, neatly trimmed beard. He looks much older than his fifties to me. I manage to sit in the kitchen with Nonna and eavesdrop on the lesson. "Repeat after me: *Baruch ata Adonai* . . ."

My brother's bar mitzvah takes place in 1961 in a small synagogue in Tripoli. The event is without fanfare. It passes by as a normal Shabbat.

Shortly after, I decide that I want to go to Switzerland to get an education. I am fourteen years old. I am coming of age, and since I cannot commit the "sin" of touching or reading the Torah, I am determined to study books which I *am* allowed to touch and read.

My father, a Middle Eastern man of his time, will hear none of it. He is not going to be ridiculed by his friends. "Why would you spend all this money to give an education to a girl, when she is going to end up washing dishes and having babies?" my father's friends say to him. "You know that if you study too much, nobody will marry you," he tells me.

But I was determined. So what did I do? I went on a hunger strike. During my lonely hunger strike, I repeated this prayer over and over: *Baruch ata Adonai, please make my father change his mind. Baruch ata Adonai, please get him to send me to Switzerland to get an education. Baruch ata Adonai, if you truly are a just God, please show your greatness.* I would sit up in my bed, crying, and repeat again and again, *Baruch ata Adonai* . . .

The hunger strike lasted four days before my father gave up. Those days seemed interminable. I never found out whether it was the fact that I was not eating that got to my father, or the prayer that I concocted, half in Judeo-Arabic and half in Italian. I am sure there is no such prayer in any of the Hebrew prayer books. Surely, Rav Yehuda would have had me excommunicated for such a sacrilegious act. But sacrilegious or not, it worked.

I was finally leaving for a Swiss boarding school. The preparation for my self-made bat mitzvah was about to begin. I would be able to read from books that would not be forbidden to me, either as a Jew or as a woman.

At long last, I arrived in Geneva. A customs official pulled me aside. He told me to wait in the adjacent room. Hours went by before he came back. "Why don't you have a passport? Why do you have only a travel document? Why are you traveling alone, when you are barely fourteen years old?"

Jews were not given passports, only travel documents. I didn't know how to speak French or English at the time. I spoke only Arabic and Italian and was not able to respond to his questions. I was nervous and didn't really know the answers to his questions. I just sat there, crying. I was desperate and petrified.

More time went by, and the officer came back to tell me, "We cannot allow you to enter Switzerland with this travel document because it is not recognized as a valid passport. We are sending you back to Tripoli on the next flight!" The officer left the waiting room. "Send you back . . ." "Send you back. . . ." Those words echoed in my head, over and over again. They sounded like a death warrant.

Baruch ata Adonai . . . I started to pray. A few minutes later, I realized that I had to take control of my own destiny, my own *maktub*. I jumped the line at passport control, walked up to the officer, grabbed his sleeve, and in very poor English, I shouted while sobbing, "Me no passport because me Jewish! Me no passport because me Jewish!"

I stared at him with teary eyes, unable to continue. A lump was stuck in my throat. The officer looked at me, stamped my travel document, and said, *"Alors, bienvenue en Suisse, ma petite!"* (In that case, welcome to Switzerland, my little one!)

Everyone in the line started to clap. It was the first time in my life I could say I was Jewish and not be afraid. It was at that moment that I became a bat mitzvah. I had come of age by making a commitment to my people. I had fought for my right to be a Jew. Isn't that what becoming a bat mitzvah is all about?

The lesson I learned at passport control in Switzerland would later define my career as a human rights advocate. The few words in Hebrew I learned sitting in Nonna's kitchen are to this day the only words I say when I pray. *Baruch ata Adonai . . .*

TUNISIA

Tunisia, an area with a Jewish minority since Roman times, was the only Arab country to come under direct German occupation during World War II. When this occurred, Jews suffered under a forced-labor and random execution policy. After Tunisia's independence from France in the 1950s, most of the Jewish Tunisian population of 100,000 left for Israel and France. Only an estimated 1,500 Jews remain. But this small remnant supports several Jewish primary and secondary schools, two yeshivas, two homes for the aged, and six rabbis. An annual pilgrimage to the island of Djerba, just off the southeast coast, takes place during the holiday of Lag b'Omer and attracts Jews from around the world.

The accounts of Lori Chemla of New York City, who writes about her daughters' unusual bat mitzvah in Tozeur, Tunisia, and Rabbi Steve Greenberg, who officiated, show that lavish celebrations can be meaningful culturally and religiously. It seems certain that no one who was there will ever forget the events described.

Rabbi Greenberg's remarks concern the benefits that bat mitzvah preparation can bring to young women and their families. An award-winning writer, researcher, and speaker, Rabbi Greenberg is Senior Teaching Fellow at CLAL: National Jewish Center for Learning and Leadership. He is the author of the groundbreaking *Wrestling with God and Men: Homosexuality in the Jewish Tradition.*

Lori Chemla and Rabbi Steven Greenberg

LORI CHEMLA

My husband was born in Tunis and lived there for the first eight years of his life, until the family emigrated to Paris. As a celebration of this heritage, a few years ago our American daughters celebrated their bat mitzvah in Tunisia. Alexandra was thirteen and a half, and Alison was twelve. We spent the bat mitzvah weekend in the town of Tozeur. It is a very beautiful area, and the hotel was the perfect size for us and our hundred guests.

Bat mitzvah guests ride camels before the festivities
in Tozeur, Tunisia, 2000.

Although there are few Jews remaining in Tunisia, we found a kosher restaurant, and the owners catered the event for us.

We had some incredible moments during that memorable weekend.
The bat mitzvah was in a deserted old city neighborhood just opposite
the hotel. We arrived there on camels and horses. Torches lit the entire
dry riverbed that separated the hotel from the old city. The night before
had been so windy that we couldn't keep a candle lit, but on this night
miraculously there was no wind. We set up large pillows in the sand and
small tents for the food, fortune tellers, and entertainment—all under the
stars. It was magical.

The Tunisian non-Jewish people were respectful of our event, particularly during our religious ceremonies. Muslims and Jews have always lived
together in harmony in Tunisia. I hope that this will remain the case as
the situation in the world worsens.

RABBI STEVEN GREENBERG

Several weeks ago, I had the great fortune to attend a bat mitzvah in Tozeur,
Tunisia. More than a hundred family members and friends from the U.S.,
France, and Israel converged upon this unlikely destination for a double

bat mitzvah. Tozeur is a dusty little town six hours south of Tunis on the edge of the desert. About an hour's drive from the center of Tozeur is the Palatial Hotel, facing the rising mountains on one side and a flat expanse of desert on the other. In the valley below the hotel are the ruins of a twelfth-century village. The hotel itself is magical and mysterious, a luxury fortress in the midst of an arid wasteland.

This event was not just a bat mitzvah. It was also a travel experience, a boisterous family reunion, a kosher catered feast, and an extravaganza. For example, after Havdalah in the ruined village, Arabian horsemen rode up into the valley with torches and swords.

Now, extravagance is hardly a new phenomenon when it comes to bat and bar mitzvahs. The competition between affluent families for the most outrageous theme party still rages from Los Angeles to Great Neck. However, there are important differences between the Jurassic Park bar mitzvah and this celebration that led me not only to attend, but to help plan the event and to serve as the family's rabbi for the occasion.

Many people bemoan the fact that the meaning and significance of the bat/bar mitzvah ceremony are in flux and clearly not what they used to be. For me, however, the current state of affairs presents us with an opportunity to be creative. For this reason, I have taken recently to "doing" bat and bar mitzvahs. Though I am an Orthodox rabbi by training and orientation, I have worked (and am working) with families who are not affiliated with synagogues, and even with youths who have never attended Hebrew school. In each situation, the impetus to have the bat mitzvah has come from the teens themselves. Having attended their friends' bat and bar mitzvahs—and the wonderful b'nai mitzvah parties—they too want to become a bar or bat mitzvah. My involvement has come at the parents' request. Unsure of how to proceed in unfamiliar territory, they have sought me out for guidance.

What I suggest in each case is that the family hire a young and talented tutor to work with their child for the entire year preceding the bat mitzvah day. While the precise focus of the training has varied from child to child in accordance with their unique interests, each has learned to read Hebrew and has become familiar with the basic contours of Jewish life.

Alexandra and Alison Chemla's teacher Rivka (*right*) took part in their unusual outdoor bat mitzvah ceremony, Tozeur, Tunisia, 2000.

I also pay a lot of attention to crafting a bat mitzvah ceremony that harmonizes with the prospective b'nai mitzvah's unique capacities and interests. At the bat mitzvah event in Tozeur, the girls orchestrated the family Shabbat, focusing upon its beginning and end, upon erev Shabbat and Havdalah, rather than upon mastering a once-in-a-lifetime Torah recitation. The result was a Shabbat of great power and beauty.

Let me add a few more words about the ceremony in Tozeur, a ceremony that was so affecting and compelling, despite the rather surreal setting. It surely trumped the typical *Goodbye, Columbus* affair in terms of sincerity and meaningfulness. The Sephardi (and originally Tunisian) roots of the family were visible. After kiddush, Papa Penot, the girls' grandfather, blessed them on the balcony that overlooked the desert, and for a full minute did not open his eyes while he opened a channel to the heavens for the blessing of his dear grandchildren. The assembled crowd fell silent and was moved. While the family is hardly Shabbat observant, their eighty-

Alison (*left*) and Alexandra Chemla during their dual bat mitzvah
ceremony under the stars, Tozeur, Tunisia, 2000.

eight-year-old grandmother—the graceful and beautiful Maman—asked
me to let her know when Shabbat would be over so that she could have a
smoke, this after spending Shabbat afternoon on a prearranged jeep tour
and hike.

A few days after the celebration in Tozeur, I found myself in Paris having dinner at one of the kosher restaurants in the Marais. A man sitting at

the table opposite was eating a dish that looked interesting. I asked him what he had ordered. He motioned to me to come to him, dipped his fork in his dish and raised it to me, offering a taste. This directness was surprising and pleasant. After taking a taste, I said to him that he must be North African, because offering to share food with strangers is a common Moroccan and Tunisian custom. He said that he was from Tunisia, and so I shared with him my recent experience in Tozeur. His son overheard us and came running to the table. In French, almost too fast for me to understand, he implored his father: "This is where I want to have the wedding," he cried, "in Tozeur at the palace in the desert!"

His father then turned to me. "So, tell me, do you do weddings?"[2]

NOTES

1. See *Jewish Women from Muslim Societies Speak,* available from the Hadassah-Brandeis Institute.

2. This essay was excerpted from "Bat Mitzvah Bonanza," an article written for *eCLAL: An Online Journal of Religion, Public Life, and Culture* in 2000. It appears here with permission from CLAL: National Jewish Center for Learning and Leadership and the author.

North America

*T*here are approximately 6 million Jews in the United States, making it the country with the largest population of Jews outside Israel. In fact, the United States and Israel are nearly equivalent in the size of their Jewish populations. The population of Canadian Jews is much smaller, about 370,000. In contrast to most of the world, the Jews of both the United States and Canada have been free to practice Judaism without persecution or infringement by the government. While the doors of some professions and institutions have been difficult to open because of a genteel type of anti-Semitism, Jewish women and men have risen to positions of influence in virtually every area of society.

This section contains stories about one bat mitzvah in Toronto, Canada, and seven in the United States. (Mexico, also in North America, is represented in the section on Latin America.) The first U.S. story is, appropriately, about the first bat mitzvah in the United States, which took place in New York City in 1922. Three of the entries—authored by the Cohen and Nemzoff mothers and daughters and by Shula Reinharz, one of the editors of this volume—come from the Boston area. Sara Aftergood wrote from Los Angeles, and Geri Garfinkel-Gershon from North Carolina. The late Brandi Fenton lived in Tucson, Arizona.

CANADA

It is not easy to distinguish Canadian Jews from their American counter-parts. Yet "Canadian Jews are not carbon copies of American Jews."[1] One difference is in their histories. Jews first came to Canada as members of the British army during the French and Indian War of 1760, and during the next two centuries, waves of additional Jews sought refuge from po-groms in Europe. But a restrictive immigration policy between the world wars in the twentieth century meant that the Jewish population remained under 100,000 until after World War II, when the majority of Canada's 370,000 Jews emigrated from war-torn Europe, northern Africa, and, most recently, Israel and the Soviet Union in search of economic opportuni-ties. The majority of Jews settled in Montreal and Toronto, and there are substantial communities in Ottawa, Vancouver, St. John's, and Winnipeg. The religious establishment is mainly Orthodox (Montreal has only one Reform congregation, for example) and, thus, there are few women rab-bis or cantors in Canada.

In a country where "linguistic and ethnic differences are the norm" and "there is no overriding patriotic fervor,"[2] Jewish women have made their marks as members of a distinctive minority community. In doing this, they have been supported by the wider society. For example, the "Ca-nadian Coalition of Jewish Women for the Get" has been successful in passing legislation for the protection of women seeking Jewish divorces, the first national legislation of its kind anywhere in the world.

Ali Feldman writes about her bat mitzvah in Toronto, which is home to 150,000 Jews, the largest Jewish population in Canada. Like many girls, Ali admits that her bat mitzvah was a "performance." She has prominent memories of her clothing and makeup, the friends who attended, and be-ing the star of the show. But the bat mitzvah experience also had a deeper meaning and a profound effect on her life. In 2005, Ali co-authored (with Penina Adelman and Shulamit Reinharz) *The JGirl's Guide: The Young Jewish Woman's Handbook for Coming of Age*, which she began as a Lily Safra summer intern at the Hadassah-Brandeis Institute.[3] With a master's degree from Hebrew University and the Pardes Institute of Jewish Stud-ies in Jerusalem, Ali now conducts classes and tutorials to prepare girls

Ali Feldman at her
bat mitzvah, Toronto,
Canada, 1989.

for their own bat mitzvah ceremonies. She is the mother of three "Jgirls,"
including a set of twins.

Ali Feldman

On September 23, 1989, in front of an enormous Conservative congregation in Toronto, I rose from my seat, ascended the bimah, and performed
a theatrical piece I had been working on for months. As my voice was that
of a budding twelve-year-old girl, it was as sweet as sugar (or so remarked
my great-aunt Bessie!).

I use the term *theatrical piece* because that is what my bat mitzvah represented to me. I had starred in plays as a child and the whole bat mitz-

vah experience was similar. Endless practices, searching for the perfect costume, hair and makeup specialists. And, of course, stage fright, proud family members, and all my friends cheering me on. How different was my bat mitzvah from when I had the role of Dodger in *Oliver Twist*?

While chanting my portion, I glanced at the crowd to find the most important person there—Jaime, the cute boy from my math class. I'd had a crush on him the whole year and I was so flattered that he came to my performance! My parents sat close by, holding their breath, praying that I didn't make a mistake. My grandparents (in typical grandparent fashion) had sheer nachas (joy) from simply seeing me stand next to a rabbi. Having memorized my portion from an audiotape (it could have been a Beatles song), I sang it in front of the crowd and felt like taking a bow when the congregation responded with "Amen." My performance was excellent. No mistakes, beautiful smile, gorgeous outfit, and an all-around nice girl.

The rabbi was pleased. He stood up and told everyone about how I volunteered with developmentally delayed children, how I was involved in synagogue life, and about my love for Israel. He mentioned that my Hebrew name, Miriam, represented a Jewish foremother. Miriam in the Bible was a proactive leader who loved to sing and dance. So was the modern-day Miriam. Just as Miriam in the Bible was helpful to her siblings, so too was the modern-day Miriam. I thought that was pretty cool!

I recall feeling accomplished. I worked hard and prepared for months. I studied with the rabbi, attended synagogue with my parents weekly, and was involved in volunteer projects.

My parents had rented a huge tent for our backyard, had hired a band and a caterer, and had spent an exorbitant amount of money on our clothing. At the party in the evening, there were speeches and toasts. Friends and family had come from all over to celebrate my coming-of-age.

Amid the glitz and glamour, I do remember feeling something special, very deep in my soul. There was a lot of talk about my ancestors who perished in the Holocaust. Everyone kept mentioning my new responsibility, and the most repeated phrase of the entire weekend was *Today I am a woman!* The weekend ended, and I found myself a bit dumbfounded. What did *Today I am a woman* mean exactly? How was I different from who I had been last Friday? What made me more of a woman today? I couldn't exactly figure it out.

Although my bat mitzvah wasn't immediately life-changing, it launched me on a quest for meaning. My quest had little to do with ballroom gowns, blasting music from the DJ, and delicious food. I learned that becoming a Jewish woman was much more than chanting a haftorah. My bat mitzvah experience helped me to discover a deeper and more beautiful understanding of Judaism. It showed me that deep down in my heart, my Judaism mattered to me. Looking back now, it truly made a difference in my life. And that's why I decided to write a book for girls so that they could experience the spiritual part of bat mitzvah in the preparation and during the day itself, not only after the fact.

UNITED STATES

The descendants of Jews who had fled the Inquisitions of Spain and Portugal in the 1400s were the first Jews to arrive in North America. Arriving in New Amsterdam in the mid-1600s, the group included men, women, and children. These women took an active role in building Jewish life in the colonies. Their descendants a few generations later created Jewish institutions in the newly formed United States. Jewish women filled the women's galleries in the first synagogues, promoted Jewish education, established benevolent societies, spearheaded relief work during the Civil War, and became leading teachers, writers, and educators in the nineteenth century.[4]

But it was the second wave of feminism, beginning in the 1960s, that provided the context for moves toward gender equality in religious participation. Women who had grown up in liberal families and received the same education as their brothers increasingly demanded equity in Jewish practice. Thanks to the "elasticity" of Judaism in the United States, "a hallmark of American culture," women's demands for equality were realized.[5] Today's women rabbis, egalitarian liturgy, and even Orthodox women's prayer groups can be seen as effects on Judaism of both American culture and feminism.

One indication of American Judaism's ability to "uniquely reformulate the trends of the dominant culture"[6] is the almost universal adoption of bat mitzvah ceremonies. The widespread acceptance of this rite of passage can be attributed partly to the influence of American culture around the globe. In Liberal branches of Judaism, the service is likely to be identical to a boy's bar mitzvah, with the girl wearing a tallit and reading from the Torah. In Orthodox congregations, the bat mitzvah ceremony may be a service for women only or a special add-on before or after a regular service in the synagogue. In 1922, the year of the first American bat mitzvah, Jews could never have imagined what the future would bring—the "destination" bat mitzvah, the rise of adult bat mitzvah—nor the amount of creative thought (and funds) that would be expended on the bat mitzvah experience.

When twelve-year-old Judith Kaplan read a few prayers in the New York brownstone of the Society for the Advancement of Judaism, she had no idea that she would eventually be seen as a pioneer nor that bat mitzvah would become a Jewish ritual known around the world. Seventy years later, in a speech reprinted here thanks to the Jewish Reconstructionist Federation, Judith Kaplan was able to discern the roots of her father's decision to celebrate her unprecedented American bat mitzvah. She understood the factors that had combined to create this important event: the suffrage movement that gave women the right to vote, her father's brand of Judaism that welcomed influences from the wider culture, and their family history that included an aunt who became a scholar of Judaism.

The first entry in this section contains Judith Kaplan Eisenstein's speech and remarkable interviews with Judith's younger sisters, Selma Kaplan Goldman and Hadassah Kaplan Musher (by phone and in person, respectively). Now in their nineties, the two women graciously share their intimate childhood memories with us. Still active and involved in community affairs and the doings of three generations of descendants, both women have been blessed with extraordinary vigor and intellectual curiosity.

The contribution by Jocelyn Cohen and her mother, Monica Pastorok Cohen, illustrates the thoughtfulness and creativity that families can bring to bat mitzvah in order to gain the most meaning from the event. In their case, the Cohens shared their joy by sending gifts to a Ukrainian orphanage, a special project of Boston's Jewish Community Relations Council.

Mothers invariably share the pride of accomplishment following their daughters' bat mitzvah ceremonies. But a mother's experience of the event often differs from that of the girl who is front and center. Ruth Nemzoff and her daughters detail those contrasts intimately and honestly. For Ruth, a resident scholar at Brandeis's Women's Studies Research Center, the preparations and ceremonies for each of her three daughters involved different anxieties. Daughters Rebecca and Sarabeth Berman remember the separate challenges that they faced.

While mothers usually are instrumental in the planning of daughters' bat mitzvah celebrations, only rarely do they participate together in the ceremony. Sara (the mother) and Hannah (the daughter) Aftergood are rare examples, having shared their bat mitzvah in Los Angeles. Sara's story shows that big bat mitzvah bashes can be vehicles for tzedaka, a foundation of Jewish life, as well as joy and celebration on a large scale.

The relative newness of bat mitzvah as a public ritual, without long historical tradition or declarations of standard procedure by the various branches of Judaism, has made (and still makes) innovation possible. Geri Garfinkel-Gershon remembers that she was the first girl in her community to wear a tallit during her bat mitzvah ceremony. While it was not easy to be a pioneer, she set the standard in her Liberal synagogue for the girls who came after.

Shulamit (Shula) Reinharz is the founding director of the Women's Studies Research Center and the Hadassah-Brandeis Institute at Brandeis University, and she is the co-editor of this collection. Her essay reveals a surprisingly common aspect of bat mitzvah: it may be even more meaningful to the family members than to the bat mitzvah girl herself. In Shula's case, many of her family members were Holocaust survivors to whom the event was of great importance, but one of the main things that she recalls is what she wore. Another memory is of the gathering of her mostly non-Jewish friends in a party that culminated in an unplanned frenzy of smashing pumpkins, which may be emblematic of America's pluralistic society, but thankfully did not become a new Thanksgiving tradition.

Brandi Fenton, a cherished daughter and friend to everyone who knew her, was a girl of many talents who took great delight in sharing her love of Judaism. The essay included here was found on Brandi's computer after her tragic death in a car accident in 2003, a year after her bat mitzvah, when she was in the eighth grade. Her family generously agreed to share her thoughts.

Judith Kaplan Eisenstein, Hadassah Kaplan Musher,
and Selma Kaplan Goldman

JUDITH KAPLAN EISENSTEIN

Thank you, all of you, on behalf of Jewish women. Let's not fool ourselves: this isn't my party. It's the celebration of women's move into the heart of Jewish life, becoming part of the lifeblood of the community, nourishing it, and being, in turn, nourished by it. And that's what is important. All the questions I've been asked over the years about that event in 1922 are really a bit irrelevant.

"How did you feel about it?"
Proud, happy, and scared. (The word *ambivalent* was not yet in vogue.)

"Just what did you do in that ceremony?"
Not too much. Just read a passage from the weekly parasha from the Chumash and said the berakhot.

"Did you know you were making history?"
Nonsense. My idea of history at the time was a series of dates: 1440, the printing press; 1492, Columbus discovers America; 1688, defeat of the Spanish Armada.

"Do you think that the fact that your father [Mordecai Kaplan, founder of the Reconstructionist movement of Judaism] had four daughters was the cause of his promotion of the bat mitzvah idea?"

Aha! There is a question that must be answered, and once and for all, put to rest. There is no doubt that having four daughters added urgency to Father's promotion of women's rights in Judaism. But the fact remains that Father himself had a precedent for his championship in the behavior of his own father. Father had an older sister, my beloved Aunt

Sophie. Back in Svenciany, she had already been a "first," namely, a first to be taught her Chumash and Rashi alongside some of Grandpa's bright male students. Teaching a girl Chumash was considered serious heresy by the upright Jews of Svenciany. Grandpa was threatened with expulsion and excommunication. But he remained undeterred. One of my cherished memories of Aunt Sophie was of finding her, during a period in her life when she was having many difficulties, sitting in her living room and reading from the Bible, checking it with the French translation. Oh, yes. Papa came by his early feminism directly from his own father.

Also, it must be remembered that in 1922 our country was in the first flush of active feminism. It was only two years after the adoption of the woman suffrage amendment, an issue that had been hotly debated just two years earlier, before the presidential election. . . . During those years, when Father was just beginning to formulate what later became known as Reconstructionism, he felt that Judaism had to draw on the best of American values—on democracy, in particular, and on its corollary, the complete equality of women. . . .

Yes, indeed, we've come a long way. And perhaps we should consider this celebration symbolic of our faith that it's never too late to change and grow! For me, personally, that was the significance of putting on the tallit [during this event], which I have never done before.[7]

HADASSAH KAPLAN MUSHER

I barely remember my sister Judy's bat mitzvah. She was twelve and I was ten. My father had just formed the Society for the Advancement of Judaism. Services were in a house with a long living room and a dais in the front. He decided the day before, and gave her a passage to read. One of my sisters said she overheard the two grandmothers talking. They couldn't understand why our father wanted to do this.

My sister Judy was an intellectual who would have long discussions with my father at the dinner table when we were growing up. She became a musicologist, and she and her husband, Ira Eisenstein, wrote a lot of music together. My father died at 102 and a half. He lived to see the creation of 103 Reconstructionist synagogues. He believed that art, history, and literature are all part of Judaism—a religio-cultural emphasis. He kept a

Mordecai and Lena Kaplan with (*left to right*) Hadassah, Judith,
Naomi, Selma, 1916 (the third adult is unidentified). Judith had the
first bat mitzvah in the United States in 1922. Photo courtesy of
the Jewish Reconstructionist Federation.

journal that ultimately amounted to twenty-three volumes. The first volume has been published recently.

SELMA KAPLAN GOLDMAN

Since I was only six years old at the time of Judith's bat mitzvah, I think we should refer first to the two people who were directly involved—Judith and my father. My father's brief remarks are found in the first volume of his diary.[8] He wrote: "Last Sabbath, a week ago, I inaugurated the ceremony of the bas mitzvah at the SAJ [Society for the Advancement of Judaism] Meeting House about which more details later. My daughter

Judith Kaplan Eisenstein in 1992, the year of her second
bat mitzvah in Flushing, New York. Photo courtesy of the
Jewish Reconstructionist Federation.

Judith was the first one to have her bas mitzvah celebrated there." But he
never got back to discussing it, at least not in this volume of the diaries.

In August 1922, his diary states that on a trip with some SAJ members,
he attended a service at a synagogue in Rome. He wrote, "I was very much
pleased to see that they had the custom of taking cognizance of a girl's becoming bas mitzvah. They called it entering 'minyan' [traditionally, ten
men required for a religious service] at the age of twelve. "⁹ He noted that
the girls accompanied their fathers to the reading stand, and when the father finished his part, the daughter said *She-hehiyanu* [prayer of thanks for
being kept alive to reach a significant moment]. The rabbi then addressed
the girl on the meaning of her entering minyan. So, although Italian girls
participated in a kind of bat mitzvah, Judith was probably the first to read
a passage from the Chumash.

I remember going to the synagogue the day of the bat mitzvah, but I didn't understand the significance. I think I believed it was Judith's birthday. I remember going up the brownstone stoop, and then you turned right, and there was a typical residential living room where my father held services. There was a platform at one end. I remember sitting there when Judith was called up to the platform to read. I didn't realize anything special was happening. As I understand now, it was the fact that she had an aliyah that caused all the fuss.

My father was always against big parties to celebrate a bat mitzvah. He insisted continuously that a bat mitzvah was not an occasion for receiving presents. By the time of my own daughter's bat mitzvah in 1956, the ceremony was held when girls reached age thirteen. A lot of people had fancy parties by that time, but nothing like the celebrations we see today. My father would not have approved of the lavish bat mitzvahs now.

Monica Pastorok Cohen
and Jocelyn Cohen

MONICA PASTOROK COHEN

As Jocelyn began preparing for her bat mitzvah, I realized that it was the first time that she was doing something that I had not done, and with which I could not help her. A year before her bat mitzvah, we had moved from another state and had to start from scratch in a new temple and a new town. Our first concern was making sure that she was comfortable with her mastery of Hebrew. One of the best gifts we gave her was private Hebrew tutoring so that she could excel. A month ahead of time, Jocelyn was fully prepared for her service.

As we began planning for the bat mitzvah itself, I was bothered increasingly by the fact that everyone with whom I spoke talked only about the party after the service. People were aghast that I had not yet hired a photographer, bought her a dress, or booked a reception. The emphasis on and anxiety about the party began to take all the joy out of the bat mitzvah. After much thought, our family decided to put the *mitzvah* back in bat mitzvah.

Jocelyn Cohen (*right*) of Lexington, Massachusetts, presents gifts from her bat mitzvah celebration to Maxine Lyons, the coordinator of the Dnepropetrovsk Kehillah project, who brought them to girls in Ukraine, 2002.

Jocelyn told me that she wanted to help someone who might not be able to afford to have a bat mitzvah. She had saved her babysitting money and wished to contribute her earnings to this project. We read about several programs and became intrigued by the Dnepropetrovsk Project, which would enable Jocelyn to help not one, but thirty-five girls in the orphanage in Dnepropetrovsk, Ukraine. Our temple's education director had visited Dnepropetrovsk and shared her pictures and stories with Jocelyn.

After a family discussion, we decided that, instead of having flower arrangements on the party tables, we would use that money to buy or make gifts for the girls in the orphanage. We bought large, inexpensive birdcages to use as centerpieces because you could see through them and open them easily. We pored through catalogs and selected items that would be fun, useful, attractive, and lightweight (for transport to the Ukraine). Jocelyn placed the items in the birdcages—small games, jewelry, dolls, hair barrettes, and colorful, warm fleece hats. We wrote a description of the Dnep Project and included it with our invitations, suggesting that anyone attending might wish to bring small donations for the orphanage.

On the day of the bat mitzvah, Jocelyn was radiant. She led the service with as much poise as if she had just finished rabbinical school. We were incredibly proud of her. After the service, we placed a birdcage of presents in the center of each dinner table. They looked beautiful. The friends and relatives who came to share our happiness brought items such as dictionaries, CDs, pens, and pencils, which they added to the birdcages.

After the bat mitzvah, we emptied all of the birdcages and presented the gifts to the Dnep Kehillah project coordinator, who personally took them to the orphanage. We took digital photographs of Jocelyn presenting the gifts to the coordinator, and she emailed them to the orphanage. Since then, Jocelyn has received several emails from the girls.

This project was a wonderful experience for our family. It succeeded in helping all of us concentrate on the mitzvah. Coincidentally, because she was so focused on preparing the gifts for the girls in Ukraine, Jocelyn felt less anxiety about the bat mitzvah.

JOCELYN COHEN

I love giving to others because I can make others happy. That makes me feel really good inside. Being a part of this project gave my bat mitzvah another meaning. I became excited, rather than really nervous, as I was before.

When my mother and I started to go through magazines, I picked out things I would like, so I hoped the kids in Dnep would like them too. We chose things that we felt would be useful, such as hats, and other things that just seemed like fun, such as little chessboards and jewelry. As it came time for my bat mitzvah, and we purchased the birdcages for the center-pieces, I began to realize how much I had, and how little these girls in Dnep had. I knew they could never do anything as extravagant as this. I understood that the gifts I was sending were going to affect their lives. I wanted to do more for them. I wanted to go and visit. Maybe someday soon, I will. After my bat mitzvah, when I saw the pictures of the girls with the presents I had sent, and their big smiles, I smiled too. I was really touched that the girls had appreciated what I had done.

Sara Aftergood

Each of my three older brothers was called to the Torah as a bar mitzvah when he turned thirteen. It was understood, however, that girls in our family did not have b'not mitzvah. I remember a few of my friends who were brave and took the plunge. But I was not among them.

The years passed. My husband and other family members and friends were Torah readers at my sons' bar mitzvah ceremonies. Throughout the ever-changing seasons, my husband and sons officiated at services and read Torah at our shul, at summer camp, and at their colleges. But I could not do likewise. I took "remedial" Hebrew so many times, I could teach it! But I have never been a natural at foreign languages.

As Hannah, our youngest child, was beginning to think of her upcoming bat mitzvah, I had an idea. I asked her if we could do it together at our Conservative synagogue. Initially, she was not thrilled about the idea, seeming to be alternately bemused and slightly irritated. But my kids know that, when I get an idea, it's hard to stop me. So, despite her hesitation and the fact that no one else she knew had done it like this, she finally went along with the idea of a mother-daughter bat mitzvah.

Many of my friends (who asked them?) felt obliged to share their thoughts that I was imposing and infringing on Hannah's special day. But she is so smart, cute, pretty, and talented that I did not feel that I would steal any of the attention that would come her way. We were committed to study, learn, and rise to the honor of bat mitzvah in tandem.

Sara and Hannah Aftergood share the spotlight at their
mother-daughter bat mitzvah, Los Angeles, 2001.

Bat mitzvah preparation was relatively effortless for Hannah, a day
school student. It was a considerably larger challenge for me. First, I had
to improve my Hebrew reading. Then, what to do about my nervous voice? I
studied with our rabbinic intern's wife, then with our cantor and the bar/
bat mitzvah tutor at the synagogue. The running joke was that I would
sing to anyone who would listen.

The day finally came. Hannah and I had written our own divrei Torah
with my husband's editorial assistance. Hannah coolly stepped up to the
bimah to lead parts of the service. She read Torah and haftorah beauti-

fully, and became a bat mitzvah with poise. I, on the other hand, made a running start, took a giant leap—and made it. Whew! My family and friends were proud of me. I was proud of myself. Without a doubt, becoming a bat mitzvah was one of the most gratifying accomplishments of my life.

Our rabbi assured the congregation that, if they wanted faith in the Jewish future, all they had to do was look at me, a very proud mama, and Hannah, in a hot-pink silk suit and with a gorgeous smiling face.

Hannah and I became b'not mitzvah on the first day of Succot 2001. Despite the World Trade Center tragedy only a few weeks earlier, we stood side by side on the only holiday on which we are commanded to rejoice. We did that with 500 guests. After services, we had a huge *freilach* (happy) lunch and Israeli dancing for everyone we know and then some. I am very inclusive about our simchas (celebrations), inviting everyone, and, much to my husband's surprise, I am usually quite relaxed. As themes, I always prefer *haimish* (homelike), Jewish, and warm.

As we had for all of our children's b'nai mitzvah, in lieu of gifts, we asked our guests to make contributions to the local food bank. I am delighted to say that our simcha raised over $20,000 for kosher food for the needy.

Ruth Nemzoff, Rebecca Berman,
and Sarabeth Berman

RUTH NEMZOFF

We were living in New Hampshire when my oldest daughter became a bat mitzvah. She was the only Jewish student in her school, and there were only four students in her Hebrew school class. I encouraged her, a bright and inquisitive child, to take the opportunity of her bat mitzvah to learn about her people's history, as well as to learn how to participate in the Sabbath service. Because the congregation was small and there were so few young people of bar and bat mitzvah age, she was allowed to assist the rabbi in leading much of the service.

While she was preparing, I was agonizing over details. I had never had any interest in entertaining or in clothes. Thus, the task of organizing a party for a hundred relatives and friends was overwhelming. The focus on details made me incredibly nervous. I had never noticed flowers or table-cloths or menus. I had to choose between options that were mysteries to me. I had to dress the three children and myself. The night before the bat mitzvah weekend, I was still wandering the stores looking for lacy socks for my youngest daughter.

In the end, I learned a lot from the experience: organizational skills, how to focus on details, and the need to divide a large task into smaller components. It was a moment of great pride to see my daughter lead the service. I was moved by her competence and her knowledge.

My second daughter, Rebecca, became a bat mitzvah nine years later. My husband had had a heart attack and bypass surgery a couple of years before the event. The morning of the bat mitzvah, he awoke with pains in his chest and shaking chills. We were concerned. Because we did not want to upset our bat mitzvah girl, we called upon the older teenage children to contact the doctor and care for him, while I, with a smile plastered on my face, took our daughter to the synagogue. I saw her anxiously scan the audience as the service began. Her expression showed that she could not understand why the rest of the family was late for her important day. With a cheery face and a terrified heart, I tried to pretend all was normal.

Just before her aliyah, my husband arrived, propped himself against me, and we held our breath as the service proceeded. In this large synagogue in Boston, two children divided the Torah portions and haftorah, and each gave a d'var Torah. I was somewhat saddened that there was not the opportunity for Rebecca to lead the whole service. But again, I felt pride in my daughter's performance and her part in the long chain of Jewish history. Of course, my memory of the day is clouded by my husband's illness, but, thankfully, he did recover.

REBECCA BERMAN

When I think about my bat mitzvah, I mostly remember what a big deal it was and how special I felt. I remember standing in front of my friends and family to deliver the d'var Torah in my white, lacy dress that had taken days to find. I remember going to lessons with the cantor, who was also my voice teacher—someone I looked up to. He had a quirky sense of humor, and we just clicked. I always left his office laughing (except when

I hadn't practiced, in which case I'd leave feeling a bit nauseous). I suppose this seems irreligious, but I also think back to the party, to the time spent with my mother agonizing over the details, and getting to be the center of attention, a bit of a rarity during those frizzy-haired, awkward junior high days.

RUTH

My third daughter, Sarabeth, attended a Jewish day school. Her bat mitzvah was on a Rosh Chodesh. A few days before the bat mitzvah, the cantor told me that he would not be able to be there. My daughter had to lead the whole service by herself. I felt betrayed and guilty that my daughter would have to bear such a huge responsibility. My heart was in my mouth the whole time. I could not enjoy the service. Of course, I was proud of her in the end, and moved by her courage and her desire to wear tefillin, but the tension during the service was great.

SARABETH BERMAN

I clumsily placed the tefillin around my arm and head. It was a Rosh Chodesh Sunday, and I was about to walk onto the bimah as the first girl at my Jewish day school in many years to wear tefillin. I had decided that, just as my father and brother wore tefillin, so too should I. Although I was steadfast in my decision, I had a certain amount of adolescent ambivalence. Did I look silly in these leather straps? Was I doing something that girls shouldn't do?

As I began to chant, I felt proud of my decision to be part of a revolutionary movement, and that I had become an adult member of the community. I also was making a statement about what was important to me. As the year continued, more and more girls began to follow in my footsteps, placing tefillin on their bodies for prayer as they became b'not mitzvah. Now, I look back on that day in 1996 as the day on which I became a truly active member of my community, exercising my beliefs as a bat mitzvah, as a Jew, and as a woman.

RUTH

My memories of my daughters' b'not mitzvah contrast with their own memories. We each lived a different experience, though at the same time and place. For me, the bat mitzvah ceremonies themselves were so mixed with other factors that the spirituality of the days eluded me. But we all are left with the pride of accomplishment, and the knowledge that we are loved and appreciated.

Geri Garfinkel-Gershon

Geri's Big Day. That's what my mom called it, and she wrote this acrostic poem that began with my name:

> Geri's Bat Mitzvah's the fifth day of May
> Excited is she her haftorah to say
> Rehearsed and recited 'til she knew it well
> It's at 9:30 AM at Temple Beth El.

That morning, I was a nervous wreck. Some weird (to me) nineteen-year cycle had tripped the cantor up, and I had learned the wrong maftir portion. With just a week of practice behind me, I had learned—but not mastered—the new portion, and I was nauseous.

My bat mitzvah dress was beautiful, bride-like: a white blouse tucked into a long white skirt with large embroidered flowers. But how was I to carry the Torah down the bimah steps in that long straight skirt? How was I going to walk in those ridiculous white shoes Mom had bought? *Oy!* So many worries.

My bat mitzvah took place in 1979 during what I have termed the Great Conservative Schism. Each congregation could decide the rules for itself—whether women could read from the Torah, have aliyot, and wear tallitot. Our rabbi was not a strong decision maker, and I took advantage of that. I said that I would lead the whole erev Shabbat service, the Torah service, and all of musaf (additional prayer service) too. And I would wear a kippah—hot-pink velvet to match the flowers in my long skirt.

But before the Torah service began, the rabbi unexpectedly called Abraham Garfinkel to the bimah. There I stood, uncertain about what was going on. Why was Grandpa Abe on the bimah? What was that white box in his hands? My heart pounded.

Grandpa Abe opened the box. He told the congregation that it contained a tallis from Israel, white to match my outfit. He helped me to recite the blessing and placed it around my shoulders. For many years, I had wondered if my grandparents regretted that I wasn't a grandson. On that day, I realized that they supported me. Even with my feminist and radical ideas, they supported my embrace of Judaism.

I was the first bat mitzvah in that congregation to wear a tallis. No one talked to girls about tallis etiquette. I had to figure it out for myself. No one told me what to do with the tallis when I went to the bathroom, or when it is traditional to wear it. No one ever told me to be careful about getting lip gloss on the corners when I kissed it. I had to figure out that I could kiss my thumbs holding up the corners, rather than stain the tzitzit.

For nearly twelve years, in USY (United Synagogue Youth), in college, and even in Israel, many people asked me why I wore a tallis. Not disrespectfully, but as if it never occurred to them that a woman should or could wear a tallis. And for many years, I felt rebellious, defensive, heretical, or out-of-place with it on. Still, I always wore it as a statement.

I still wear my bat mitzvah tallis, although occasionally I wear the one from my wedding huppah (canopy). I never wear lipstick or gloss on Shabbat, and the questions about why I wear a tallis have ceased. I recently had the opportunity to chant my Torah portion again, with the same white tallis around my shoulders. Luckily, I didn't have to worry about the maftir this time!

This old white tallis will always mean so much to me: an enduring gift from my grandparents, a symbol of my feminist rebellion, and an emblem of my lifelong commitment to Judaism.

Shulamit Reinharz

I was born in 1946 in Amsterdam, Holland, and had my bat mitzvah when I was thirteen, in 1959. My family was living in New Jersey at the time. I am the oldest grandchild of the oldest son of my grandparents. On my mother's side, I have few relatives because her parents and many others were murdered during the Holocaust. This bat mitzvah was the first in the new generation and thus was especially meaningful to my family. An elderly man in Teaneck, New Jersey, where I went to Hebrew school, trained me and gave me a recording of my haftorah. Perhaps he wasn't as old as he seemed to me!

My task for the bat mitzvah ceremony was to recite the haftorah, but for some reason, the ceremony was on a Friday night, when the Torah and haftorah are not traditionally read. My two major memories of the occasion are the dress I wore—bright blue chiffon with very puffy sleeves, a narrow waist, and a flared skirt—and the fact that many relatives attended.

On that Friday night, my father officiated as the rabbi, and my relatives filled the front rows. I don't know what memories my bat mitzvah conjured up for her, but my father's aunt, sitting in the first row, cried throughout the entire event. She filled my vision; I saw her tears constantly. Later, I realized that the ceremony was significant beyond the specificity of its being *my* bat mitzvah. I represented Jewish continuity to her, and probably to many others. I was pleased that I could do something that meant so much to others. I don't remember anything else about the ceremony.

The next day, all the relatives who had come for the occasion arrived at our house. My grandmother gave me a watch that I wore for years. My mother created a luncheon of some sort, and I was entitled to invite friends over to the house. I didn't have many Jewish friends at the time because our neighborhood was almost entirely Catholic, and my Hebrew school friends lived in another town and couldn't visit me on Shabbat. So most of the friends invited to our house for my bat mitzvah were not Jewish.

We crowded into the basement, which had been remodeled as a rec room and, to the best of my memory, simply hung out. After a while, we became restless and went outside. Some of the rougher boys found pumpkins on people's front stoops and smashed them. I remember thinking that I belonged to two worlds: the world of blue chiffon dresses and crying aunts, and the world of non-Jewish, roughhousing American teenagers. Somehow, on that day, I knew that my life would always contain both elements.

Brandi Fenton

The yellow sunlight danced through my shutters, slowly waking me up. At first, it seemed like just a normal morning, just a normal day. I was reluctant to get up; my bed felt like it had me tied down. Then I remembered! Today was my day! I jumped out of my bed and rushed to the kitchen.

Brandi Fenton holds the Torah during her bat mitzvah
ceremony in Tucson, Arizona, 2002

There, I found my family and relatives. "Today's the day!" I heard, but only faintly. I had too many thoughts running through my head. My mom had made eggs just the way I like them. The bright yellow color made them seem unreal, almost fake, like they were too good to be true. While enjoying my breakfast, I listened to my relatives telling me how proud they were of me. What a great way to start the day, huh?

All morning, I lounged about, thinking of the next hours to come. The hours passed. After getting all dressed up and ready, we piled into the car and set off for what had been a work in progress for six months. Everything had seemed carefree and relaxing—until now. Now, I felt the yellow butterflies fluttering vigorously within me.

The time had come. I stepped onto the stage. Seeing all my family and friends glowing with happiness for me made the yellow butterflies slow down a notch.

Finally, the hard part was over! The speeches, prayers, lessons I had to learn were finished. Now it was time for the fun part! They opened the doors and we immediately ran in. Everyone else who entered the room saw it as a party. I entered the room seeing it as my past laid out before me. Every single person there was shining with a yellow glow. They had their own color, just for me. . . .

I remember that night as if it were yesterday. I savored every drop of it. Ask me any question dealing with my special day, and I can tell you. Any girl would remember her bat mitzvah!

NOTES

1. Norma Baumel Joseph, "Canadian, Jewish and Female," in H. Epstein, ed., *Jewish Women 2000*, 123.

2. Ibid.

3. Penina Adelman, Ali Feldman, and Shulamit Reinharz, *The JGirl's Guide* (Woodstock, VT: Jewish Lights, 2005).

4. Jonathan Sarna, *American Judaism: A History* (New Haven, Conn.: Yale University Press, 2004).

5. Hasia Diner, *The Jews of the United States, 1654 to 2000* (Berkeley: University of California Press, 2004), 358.

6. Riv-Ellen Prell, "Jewish Women in the United States," in H. Epstein, ed., *Jewish Women 2000*, 15.

7. In March 1992, when she was eighty-two, the biblical lifespan of seventy plus twelve, Judith Kaplan Eisenstein had a second bat mitzvah celebration. In addition to her family, prominent women from politics and the arts came to Flushing, New York, to pay tribute to Judith and to the equality of women in Jewish ritual that began at her first bat mitzvah, the first in the United States. Judith, who died four years later, presented these remarks during that evening of celebration.

8. Mel Scult, ed., *Communings of the Spirit: The Journals of Mordecai M. Kaplan,* vol. 1: *1913–1934* (Detroit, Mich.: Wayne State University Press and the Reconstructionist Press, 2001), 159.

9. Ibid., 163.

GLOSSARY

Because Hebrew does not use the same alphabet as English, there are many different spellings of Hebrew words. We have listed here some of the variations used in this text (we have maintained the spellings originally used by the authors), but the listing is by no means comprehensive.

Adon Olam: A hymn sung at the end of most services.

aliyah (aliya; pl. aliyot): Lit. "ascent." This can refer either to the honor of being called to ascend the bima during a service (having an aliyah) or to the act of immigrating to Israel (making aliyah).

Aron Kodesh (Aron Hakodesh): The ark of the Torah, where the scroll is stored when not in use.

baal tefilah: A prayer leader.

bar mitzvah (pl. b'nai mitzvah): Lit. "son of the commandment." This ceremony marks the assumption of Jewish adult responsibilities for boys at age thirteen.

Baruch atah Adonai (Baruch ata Adonai): Lit. "Blessed are you, Lord." This phrase appears at the beginning of most blessings (berakhot).

Baruch Haba: A song or prayer sung in the synagogue as part of a service.

bat mitzvah (bas mitzvah; pl. b'not mitzvah): Lit. "daughter of the commandment." This term refers both to the girl who completes the Jewish coming-of-age ceremony (at age twelve in traditional branches of Judaism or at age thirteen in liberal branches) and to the ritual itself. Some authors here use an English-type plural (bat mitzvahs) instead of the Hebrew one.

Beit Din: A rabbinical court that makes judgments in areas of Jewish law. In Israel, the Beit Din also carries considerable authority outside of religious circles.

bima (bimah): The platform (usually raised) from which the Torah is read, located either in the center of the synagogue or at the front.

bracha (brocha; pl. berakhot, brachot): A blessing. Jewish practice calls for many different blessings to be said at different times of the day, when performing different daily activities, and when performing commandments.

brit (brit milah): The religious ceremony of circumcision for a baby boy at eight days of age, by which he is considered to have entered into the covenant of Judaism.

Chabad (Chabad-Lubavitch): An Orthodox Chassidic movement based in New York that sends representatives to establish Chabad centers to reinvigorate Jewish communities around the world.

Chassidism (Chasidism, Hasidism): A branch of Judaism focused on spirituality, joy, and integrating Jewish mysticism into religious practice. A person practicing this type of Judaism is known as a Hasid or Chasid.

chayil (chajil): Valor, traditionally used to describe women (*eshet chayil* is a woman of valor). Bat chayil is another name sometimes given to the coming-of-age ceremony for young women.

chazan (chazzan, chassen, hazan, hazzan): A cantor, the person who leads the singing of prayers in synagogue services.

cheder (chader): Religious school. Here, it typically refers to Jewish religious education given in addition to secular schooling. In Orthodox communities, the first full-time school that young boys attend is called by the same name.

Chumash (Humash): One of the names for the five books of Moses (called Genesis, Exodus, Leviticus, Numbers, and Deuteronomy in English, and also known in Hebrew by the first distinctive words of each book). At a typical seat in a synagogue, there are two books: a siddur and a Chumash.

dvar Torah (d'var Torah, devar Torah; pl. divrei Torah): A brief speech, often given by the bat mitzvah girl, about the content of the Torah reading of the day.

erev: Lit. "eve." In Jewish tradition, days are counted from sunset to sunset, so the eve of a holiday is the day when that holiday begins at sunset. Friday each week is erev Shabbat.

gabbai: The ritual director who helps ensure that services run smoothly. Often, one of the gabbai's major responsibilities is to ensure that the reading from the Torah is carried out correctly.

haftorah (haftarah, haftara, haphtarah): A selection from Prophets. Prophets (Nevi'im) is the second part of the Hebrew Bible (Tanach), coming after the five books of Moses (collectively called the Torah) and before the final section, Writings (Ketuvim). A selection from the haftorah is assigned to each portion of the Torah, with variations for holidays.

halacha (halakha; Adj. halachic, halakhic): Jewish religious law, as laid out in the Torah and in the later interpretations by rabbis and scholars.

halutz (masc.), halutza (fem.), halutzim (pl.): Pioneers, typically young vigorous people, who moved to pre-state Israel to work the land.

Hashem: Lit. "the name." This is one way to refer to God, and is sometimes preferred by observant Jews to more direct references.

Hasidism. *See* **Chassidism.**

Havdalah (Havdala): Lit. "separation." This refers specifically to the service that marks the end of Shabbat on Saturday night.

hazan (hazzan). *See* **chazzan.**

Kabalat (Kabbalat) Shabbat: lit. "receiving the Sabbath." Friday evening service welcoming the arrival of the Sabbath.

kashrut: Jewish dietary laws governing what may and may not be eaten by observant Jews and how to slaughter animals. Foods, kitchens, serving or eating dishes, and utensils that are in accordance with these laws are "kosher" or "kasher."

kiddush (kaddish): A blessing said over wine or grape juice at the conclusion of Shabbat services; also a ritual meal served at the synagogue following the recitation of the blessing and the end of services.

kippah (pl. kippot): The Hebrew word for a skullcap worn to fulfill the commandment to cover one's head to show fear of God (called a yarmulke in Yiddish).

Kotel: The Western Wall, a fragment of the wall that surrounded the ancient Temple in Jerusalem; a site of Jewish prayer and pilgrimage.

limud: Lit. "learning." This can refer either to the activity of studying Jewish texts or to what one has learned in doing so.

maariv: The evening prayer service, sometimes held immediately after the afternoon (mincha) service.

maftir: The last section of the Torah to be read in a particular service.

Ma Tovu: A song of praise, recited at home, frequently upon awakening, or in the synagogue.

mehitza (mechitsa, mechitza): The barrier that divides men and women in traditional synagogues. Traditional thinking suggests that this division (men in front of the mehitza, near the bima, and women behind it) preserves both women's modesty and men's concentration on the liturgy.

midrash: Lit. "to study." This refers specifically to a particular way of studying Jewish texts. The place where such study takes place is traditionally known as a beit midrash, a house of study.

mikvah (mikve): A ritual bath used for purification. Perhaps the primary use is by observant women at the end of their menstruation each month, but it is also used before marriage and to make kitchen implements kosher, among other things.

minhag (pl. minhagim): Custom, especially a specific local custom.

minyan: Ten Jewish adults, the minimum number required to perform certain religious obligations. Traditionally, only men are counted in a minyan, but more liberal congregations now also count women.

misheberach: A prayer for healing those who are ill.

mitzvah (mitsva): A commandment, also sometimes a good deed or an honor one receives (they gave her the mitzvah of carrying the Torah).

motzi (moza'ei) Shabbat: The end of Shabbat (and thus the beginning of the work week). Jewish law calls for this to be ritually marked by a specific prayer and the Havdalah service.

musaf (mussaf): An additional prayer service celebrated on Shabbat, usually in conjunction with the Saturday morning service.

naches (nachas): A Yiddish word meaning "joy." This usually specifically refers to the joy a parent feels in a child's achievement.

parasha (parsha, sidra, sedra): The weekly Torah portion.

parokhet: The curtain on the front of the Aron Kodesh that covers the Torah scrolls.

pasuk (pl. pesukim; tehillim): Verses from the book of Psalms used in Jewish worship.

rabbi: A Jewish religious leader.

rebbe: Another term for a rabbi, often referring to a more traditional leader; sometimes also specifically the leader of a Hasidic Jewish group.

rebbetsin (rebbitsen, rebbitzen): The wife of a rabbi.

Rosh Chodesh (Rosh Hodesh): A minor holiday at the beginning of a new Hebrew month, which always coincides with a new moon. It is sometimes considered a women's holiday, as women are specifically exempted from work on it in the Talmud. There are many beautiful modern rituals around it.

sefer Torah (pl. sifrei Torah): A Torah scroll, handwritten by a scribe, and read from in the synagogue.

Shabbat (Shabbes, Shabbos; pl. Shabbatot): The Sabbath, celebrated in Jewish tradition from sundown on Friday night until sundown on Saturday. Observant Jews refrain from work (as defined in religious texts) during this period.

shacharit: The morning prayer service held daily, including on Shabbat.

Shadai: Lit. "Almighty." One of the many words referring to God.

Shavuot (Shavuoth): A Jewish holiday in late May or early June on the Gregorian calendar that commemorates the day that God gave the Torah to the Israelites at Mount Sinai. This is a popular time for bat mitzvah ceremonies.

Shema (Sh'ma, Shemá): A prayer that is the central statement of the Jewish faith. The first word, *shema*, means "hear" or "listen."

shul: Synagogue.

siddur (pl. siddurim): Prayer book.

sidra (sedra). *See* parasha.

Simchat Torah: A Jewish holiday marking the beginning of a new annual cycle of reading the Torah.

Succot (Succoth): A Jewish holiday commemorating the forty years the Israelites spent wandering in the desert after leaving Egypt. During this holiday, meals are taken in a temporary dwelling called a succah.

tallit (talit, tallis, tallith; pl. tallitot): A rectangular prayer shawl with fringes (tzitzit). Although traditionally worn only by men, modern women have begun to wear them also as they have taken on reading from the Torah and other historically male religious duties.

Talmud: A central text of Judaism. It contains a record of extensive rabbinic discussions of Jewish law, texts, ethics, philosophy, and more.

Tanach (Tanaj): The Hebrew bible, consisting of the Torah, Prophets (Nevi'im), and Writings (Ketuvim).

tefilah (tefila, tefillah, tfila): A specific prayer, or the act of praying.

tefilin (tefillin): Small, black leather boxes containing Torah verses that are attached to leather straps. Observant Jews lay tefilin on their upper arms and forehead, usually during weekday morning services.

tehillim. *See* pasuk.

tikkun olam: Lit. "repairing the world." This is a goal of Jewish practice and action. Fulfilling Jewish religious commandments is one traditional way to carry out tikkun olam, while social justice work and charitable projects are others.

teshuva (teshuvah): Repentance.

Tu b'Shvat: Lit. "New Year of the Trees." A minor Jewish holiday traditionally celebrated by planting trees and by eating dried fruits and nuts. It usually falls in late January or early February on the Gregorian calendar.

tzedakah (tzedeka, tsedakah, tzedekah): Charity.

tzneeus: Modesty, a traditional value of Jewish women, which traditionally applies to both dress and behavior.

tzitzit: Ritual fringes on the corners of a prayer shawl.

yarmulke (yamalka): The Yiddish word for a skullcap worn to fulfill the commandment to cover one's head to show fear of God (kippah in Hebrew).

yom tov (pl. yom tovim): Jewish holiday.

z″l: An abbreviation for the Hebrew phrase *zikhrono* (masc.) or *zikhronah* (fem.) *livrakha*, which means "may his/her memory be a blessing." It is sometimes written after the name of someone who is deceased.

FURTHER READING

Adelman, Penina, Ali Feldman, and Shulamit Reinharz. *The JGirl's Guide: The Young Jewish Woman's Handbook for Coming of Age*. Woodstock, Vt.: Jewish Lights, 2005.

Berkman, Marsha Lee, and Elaine Marcus Starkman. *Here I Am: Contemporary Jewish Stories from Around the World*. Philadelphia, Pa.: Jewish Publication Society, 1998.

Bruder, Edith. *The Black Jews of Africa: History, Religion, Identity*. New York: Oxford University Press, 2008.

Epstein, Helen, ed. *Jewish Women 2000*. Waltham, Mass.: Hadassah-Brandeis Institute, 2001.

Jaffe-Gill, Ellen. *The Jewish Woman's Book of Wisdom: Thoughts from Prominent Jewish Women on Spirituality, Identity, Sisterhood, Family, and Faith*. New York: Kensington, 2000.

Jewish Women from Muslim Societies Speak (prepared by Susan M. Kahn and Nancy F. Vineberg). Waltham, Mass.: Hadassah-Brandeis Institute, 2003.

JOFA Journal, Bat Mitzvah issue, 9 (2010): 1–52.

Kulanu. www.kulanu.org/newsletters.

Leneman, Helen. *Bar/Bat Mitzvah Basics: A Practical Family Guide to Coming of Age Together*, 2nd ed. Woodstock, Vt.: Jewish Lights, 2007.

Oppenheimer, Mark. *Thirteen and a Day: The Bar and Bat Mitzvah across America*. New York: Farrar, Straus and Giroux, 2005.

Primack, Karen, ed. *Jews in Places You Never Thought Of*. Hoboken, N.J.: KTAV in association with Kulanu, 1998.

———. *Under One Canopy: Readings in Jewish Diversity*. Silver Spring, Md.: Kulanu, 2003.

Silliman, Jael. *Jewish Portraits, Indian Frames*. Waltham, Mass.: Brandeis University Press, 2003.

Vinick, Barbara, ed. *Esther's Legacy: Celebrating Purim around the World*. Waltham, Mass.: Hadassah-Brandeis Institute, 2002.

Weiss, Arnine Cumsky. *Becoming a Bat Mitzvah: A Treasury of Stories*. Scranton, Pa.: University of Scranton Press, 2004.